T0266590

THARPA PUBLICATIONS

CONISHEAD PRIORY
ULVERSTON
CUMBRIA
LA12 9QQ
NGDOM

PLEASE
PLACE
STAMP
HERE

" Only by creating peace within our own mind and helping others do the same can we hope to achieve peace in this world. "

VENERABLE GESHE KELSANG GYATSO RINPOCHE

www.tharpa.com

5 WAYS TO CONNECT, RECEIVE & SHARE DHARMA WISDOM

Moisten, Fold & Send

RETURN THIS CARD
Complete and return this card if you would like to receive the following...

☐ **Full-colour catalogue** of Tharpa's acclaimed range of books on Buddhism, audiobooks, CDs and Buddhist art.

☐ Tharpa's **e-newsletter** with product updates & promotions. (Include email below)

☐ Information on your nearest **Kadampa Centre**, offering meditation courses and study programmes based on these books.

Name..

Address ....

....

Postcode...Country ....

Email..

In which book did you find this card?...

Your comments on the book...

....

LIKE
TharpaPublicationsUK

Tharpa Publications UK Facebook page
Receive and share Dharma inspiration

FOLLOW
@tharpauk

Tharpa Publications UK Twitter page
Share the wisdom of modern Buddhism

REVIEW
www.tharpa.com

Share your thoughts on any Tharpa Book
Leave a review on any product page of our website

VISIT
www.tharpa.com/centres

Your Local Kadampa Meditation Centre
Find over 1200 Centres and branches worldwide

www.tharpa.com - **Tel:** +44 (0)1229 588599 - **Email:** info.uk@tharpa.com

Tharpa Publications is part of the New Kadampa Tradition – International Kadampa Buddhist Union, Reg. Charity Number [England]: 1015054

Tantric Grounds
and Paths

Suggested study or reading order for beginners of books by Venerable Geshe Kelsang Gyatso Rinpoche

How to Transform Your Life
How to Understand the Mind
Joyful Path of Good Fortune
The Mirror of Dharma with Additions
The New Heart of Wisdom
Modern Buddhism
Tantric Grounds and Paths
The New Guide to Dakini Land
Essence of Vajrayana
The Oral Instructions of Mahamudra
Great Treasury of Merit
The New Eight Steps to Happiness
Introduction to Buddhism
How to Solve Our Human Problems
Meaningful to Behold
The Bodhisattva Vow
Universal Compassion
The New Meditation Handbook
Living Meaningfully, Dying Joyfully
Ocean of Nectar
Heart Jewel
Clear Light of Bliss
Mahamudra Tantra

This book is published under the auspices of the
NKT-IKBU International Temples Project
and the profit from its sale is designated for public
benefit through this fund.
[Reg. Charity number 1015054 (England)]
Find out more:
tharpa.com/benefit-all-world-peace

VENERABLE GESHE KELSANG
GYATSO RINPOCHE

Tantric Grounds and Paths

HOW TO ENTER, PROGRESS ON,
AND COMPLETE THE
VAJRAYANA PATH

THARPA PUBLICATIONS
UK • US • CANADA
AUSTRALIA • ASIA

First published 1994 - 4 Impressions
Second edition 2016 - Impression 2 (2021)

The right of Geshe Kelsang Gyatso
to be identified as author of this work
has been asserted by him in accordance with
the Copyright, Designs, and Patents Act 1988.

Tharpa Publications UK
Conishead Priory
Ulverston, Cumbria
LA12 9QQ, UK

Tharpa Publications US
47 Sweeney Road
Glen Spey, NY 12737
USA

There are Tharpa Publications offices around the world,
and Tharpa books are published in most major languages.
See pages 340-341 for contact details.

© New Kadampa Tradition – International Kadampa
Buddhist Union 1994, 2016

Cover design: © NKT-IKBU 2020

Library of Congress Control Number: 2003100131

British Library Cataloguing in Publication Data
A catalogue record for this book is
available from the British Library.

ISBN 978-1-910368-46-6 – paperback
ISBN 978-1-910368-47-3 – ePub
ISBN 978-1-910368-48-0 – kindle

Set in Palatino by Tharpa Publications.
Printed and bound by CPI Group (UK) Ltd.

Paper supplied from well-managed forests and other controlled
sources, and certified in accordance with the rules of the
Forest Stewardship Council.

Contents

Illustrations   vi
Acknowledgements   vii

Introduction   1
The Lower Tantras   27
Highest Yoga Tantra   55
Generation Stage   87
Isolated Body   121
Isolated Speech and Isolated Mind   169
Illusory Body, Clear Light and Union   201
The Final Results   225
Dedication   241

Appendix I – The Condensed Meaning of the Text   243
Appendix II – The Preliminary Practices   261
  Liberating Prayer   263
  A Handbook for the Daily Practice of Bodhisattva
    Vows and Tantric Vows   265
  Great Liberation of the Mother   281
  Great Liberation of the Father   293
  An Explanation of the Practice   305

Glossary   313
Bibliography   329
Study Programmes of Kadampa Buddhism   335
Tharpa Offices Worldwide   340
Index   342
Further Reading   358
Finding Your Nearest Kadampa Meditation Centre   360

Illustrations

The line illustrations depict the Mahamudra lineage Gurus

Vajradhara	viii
Manjushri	8
Je Tsongkhapa	16
Togden Jampel Gyatso	26
Baso Chokyi Gyaltsen	36
Drubchen Dharmavajra	46
Gyalwa Ensapa	56
Khedrub Sangye Yeshe	64
Panchen Losang Chokyi Gyaltsen	72
Drubchen Gendun Gyaltsen	80
Drungpa Tsondru Gyaltsen	88
Konchog Gyaltsen	96
Panchen Losang Yeshe	104
Losang Trinley	112
Drubwang Losang Namgyal	122
Kachen Yeshe Gyaltsen	130
Phurchog Ngawang Jampa	138
Panchen Palden Yeshe	148
Khedrub Ngawang Dorje	158
Ngulchu Dharmabhadra	168
Yangchen Drubpay Dorje	178
Khedrub Tenzin Tsondru	188
Je Phabongkhapa Trinlay Gyatso	202
Vajradhara Trijang Rinpoche Losang Yeshe	226
Dorjechang Kelsang Gyatso Rinpoche (*included at the request of faithful disciples*)	240
Tantric commitment objects	274

Acknowledgements

Because there is great interest in the practice of Buddhist Tantra, a comprehensive guide is needed from a fully qualified Tantric Master. This need is met in this book, *Tantric Grounds and Paths*, by Venerable Geshe Kelsang Gyatso Rinpoche, who has prepared here a definitive manual for pure Tantric practice.

Tantric Grounds and Paths explains the relationship between Sutra and Tantra, and the necessity of basing Tantric practice upon Sutra. It then provides an authoritative and comprehensive guide to the four classes of Tantra in general, and to the generation stage and completion stage of Highest Yoga Tantra in particular.

The author describes directly from his own experience all the stages of the path to enlightenment. Never before in the history of Buddhist literature has such a clear, profound and comprehensive guide been published. From the depths of our hearts, we thank Venerable Geshe Kelsang Gyatso Rinpoche for his inconceivable kindness in composing this book.

We also thank all the dedicated, senior Dharma students who assisted the author with the rendering of the English and who prepared the final manuscript for publication.

Roy Tyson,
Administrative Director,
Manjushri Kadampa Meditation Centre,
May 1994.

Vajradhara

Introduction

So that living beings might attain great liberation, or full enlightenment, Buddha revealed two paths: the common path and the uncommon path. Here, 'path' refers to an internal path or spiritual realization that leads us to liberation from suffering, or permanent inner peace. The uncommon path is the Vajrayana path. Vajrayana path, Tantric path, and path of Secret Mantra are synonyms. These are explained extensively in this book. The common path is revealed by Buddha in his Sutra teachings. The stages of the common path are the twenty-one spiritual paths from the realization of relying upon the Spiritual Guide up to the realization of superior seeing. These are known as 'Lamrim', or the 'stages of the path'. Training in these common paths is the foundation for the practice of the Vajrayana path. The Vajrayana path is like a vehicle that takes us directly to our final destination, and the common paths are like the road on which that vehicle travels. Therefore, to extract the greatest essence from this precious human life by attaining full enlightenment, we need first to train in the common paths of Lamrim, and then in the uncommon Vajrayana paths.

The practices of all the common paths are included in a very condensed Lamrim text composed by Je Tsongkhapa, which is usually known as the *Prayer of the Stages of the Path*. This text is like the root text of Lamrim. It does not require a separate commentary, because if we study a complete

1

presentation of Lamrim, such as that found in the books *Joyful Path of Good Fortune* or *The New Meditation Handbook*, we will naturally understand the entire meaning of this root text.

If you want to practise the Vajrayana paths explained in this book, you should receive a Highest Yoga Tantra empowerment such as the empowerment of Heruka or Vajrayogini, and train in Lamrim, the stages of the path. You should memorize the *Prayer of the Stages of the Path* and recite it mentally or verbally every day while concentrating on its meaning. Then, whenever you want to read this book, please begin by reciting this root text. First visualize the holy beings as follows:

In the space before me is the living Buddha Shakyamuni, surrounded by all the Buddhas and Bodhisattvas, like the full moon surrounded by stars.

Then recite the prayer:

PRAYER OF THE STAGES OF THE PATH

The path begins with strong reliance
On my kind Teacher, source of all good;
O Bless me with this understanding
To follow him with great devotion.

This human life with all its freedoms,
Extremely rare, with so much meaning;
O Bless me with this understanding
All day and night to seize its essence.

My body, like a water bubble,
Decays and dies so very quickly;
After death come results of karma,
Just like the shadow of a body.

With this firm knowledge and remembrance
Bless me to be extremely cautious,
Always avoiding harmful actions
And gathering abundant virtue.

Samsara's pleasures are deceptive,
Give no contentment, only torment;
So please bless me to strive sincerely
To gain the bliss of perfect freedom.

O Bless me so that from this pure thought
Come mindfulness and greatest caution,
To keep as my essential practice
The doctrine's root, the Pratimoksha.

Just like myself all my kind mothers
Are drowning in samsara's ocean;
O So that I may soon release them,
Bless me to train in bodhichitta.

But I cannot become a Buddha
By this alone without three ethics;
So bless me with the strength to practise
The Bodhisattva's ordination.

By pacifying my distractions
And analyzing perfect meanings,
Bless me to quickly gain the union
Of special insight and quiescence.

When I become a pure container
Through common paths, bless me to enter
The essence practice of good fortune,
The supreme vehicle, Vajrayana.

The two attainments both depend on
My sacred vows and my commitments;
Bless me to understand this clearly
And keep them at the cost of my life.

By constant practice in four sessions,
The way explained by holy Teachers,
O Bless me to gain both the stages,
Which are the essence of the Tantras.

May those who guide me on the good path,
And my companions all have long lives;
Bless me to pacify completely
All obstacles, outer and inner.

May I always find perfect Teachers,
And take delight in holy Dharma,
Accomplish all grounds and paths swiftly,
And gain the state of Vajradhara.

It is often said that the path of Tantra is superior to the path of Sutra, but to understand why this is so we need to engage in a precise study of both Sutra and Tantra; otherwise our statements about the superiority of Tantra will be mere words. Moreover, if we do not study both Sutra and Tantra well, we will find it difficult to understand how to practise the union of Sutra and Tantra, and then there will be a great danger of our either rejecting the practice of Tantra or ignoring the practice of Sutra.

The teachings of Tantra, or Secret Mantra as it is sometimes called, are the rarest and most precious of Buddha's teachings. It is only by following the path of Secret Mantra that we can attain enlightenment, or Buddhahood. Why can we not attain full enlightenment just by practising the paths of Sutra? There are two main reasons. First, to attain Buddhahood we need to accomplish both the Truth Body and the Form Body of a Buddha. Although Sutra teachings present a general explanation of how these two bodies are accomplished in dependence upon the stages of the path of wisdom and method, they do not give precise explanations of the actual direct, substantial causes of these two bodies. The direct, substantial cause of the Truth Body is meaning clear light, and the direct, substantial cause of the Form Body is the illusory body. These are explained only in Secret Mantra.

The second reason why Sutra paths cannot lead us to full enlightenment is that Sutra teachings do not present methods for overcoming the very subtle obstructions to omniscience – the subtle dualistic appearances associated with the minds of white appearance, red increase and black near-attainment. These three minds become manifest when our inner winds dissolve within the central channel during sleep, during the death process or during completion stage meditation. Although these minds are subtle minds, they are nevertheless contaminated minds because their objects – the appearance of space pervaded by white light, the appearance of space pervaded by red light and the appearance of space pervaded by darkness – appear as inherently existent. These appearances of inherent existence are subtle dualistic appearances and very subtle obstructions to omniscience. Because Sutra teachings do not explain how to recognize the subtle minds of white appearance, red increase and black near-attainment, Sutra Bodhisattvas are unable even to recognize the subtle dualistic appearances associated with them, let alone abandon them. In general, dualistic appearance is the appearance to a mind of both its object and inherent existence. All the

5

minds of living beings, with the exception of the exalted awareness of meditative equipoise of Superior beings, have this appearance.

A direct realization of emptiness with a gross mind does not have the power to overcome the subtle dualistic appearances associated with the minds of white appearance, red increase and black near-attainment. The only way to abandon these subtle dualistic appearances is to realize emptiness directly with a very subtle mind of clear light. Since the methods for manifesting and using the very subtle mind of clear light are explained only in Secret Mantra, anyone who wishes to attain Buddhahood definitely needs to enter this path.

It is said that only the fourth, eleventh, and last of the thousand Buddhas of this Fortunate Aeon will teach Secret Mantra. Does this mean that the followers of the other Buddhas will not have the opportunity to attain enlightenment? For example, will no one attain enlightenment under the guidance of Buddha Maitreya? Although Buddha Maitreya will not teach Tantra, many of his followers will reach the tenth Sutra ground of a Bodhisattva by practising his Sutra teachings. Then the Buddhas of the five families throughout the ten directions will appear to them, grant them Tantric empowerments and show them how to attain meaning clear light, the fourth of the five stages of completion stage. By meditating on meaning clear light, these Bodhisattvas will eventually attain Buddhahood. Therefore, even though Buddha Maitreya will not personally reveal the path of Secret Mantra, he will nevertheless open the way for countless living beings to attain Buddhahood.

Buddha taught three 'vehicles', or means to progress towards enlightenment: the Hinayana, the Paramitayana and the Vajrayana. Of these, the Vajrayana, or Secret Mantra Vehicle is the supreme vehicle because it takes us directly to Buddhahood. If we engage in Tantric practice wholeheartedly, with a pure motivation and deep faith, we will attain full enlightenment easily and swiftly without having to endure great hardships. We should therefore consider ourself extremely fortunate to have the opportunity to study these teachings on Secret Mantra.

The gateway to the practice of Secret Mantra is receiving a Tantric empowerment from a qualified Tantric Spiritual Guide. We then need to learn precisely how to practise Secret Mantra, and how to progress through the spiritual grounds and paths by depending upon Tantric practice. If we understand this clearly and unmistakenly, and put our understanding into practice sincerely, we can attain Buddhahood in this very life.

Some people say that Buddhahood is an unattainable goal, while others say that Secret Mantra is too advanced and that it is better to concentrate on Sutra. Such ideas are quite common nowadays, but those who have received Tantric empowerments must not allow themselves to become discouraged in this way. If we give up the wish to attain Buddhahood because we think it is unattainable we will incur a root downfall of our Bodhisattva vows; and if we abandon the intention to practise Secret Mantra because we think it is too difficult we will incur a root downfall of our Tantric vows. Through studying the teachings on Tantric grounds and paths given in this book, we will understand how it is possible to attain Buddhahood by relying upon Secret Mantra, and we will develop great enthusiasm for Tantric practice. In this way, we will be protected from breaking our Bodhisattva and Tantric vows.

Manjushri

We may wonder why, if Secret Mantra is the direct path to Buddhahood, did Buddha teach the Sutra paths at all? The reason is that Sutra is the foundation for Tantra. Tantra is like an aeroplane that takes us directly to Buddhahood, but Sutra is like the runway. Without a runway an aeroplane cannot take off, and without the foundation of Sutra we cannot attain authentic experience of Secret Mantra. Therefore, those who wish to attain Buddhahood need to practise the union of Sutra and Tantra.

To become a fully enlightened being we must accomplish all the paths to Buddhahood. In general, there are two types of path: external paths and internal paths. We can understand external paths by consulting maps and so forth, but they do not help us to reach liberation. Even if we travelled in a spaceship to the other side of the universe, we would never reach liberation. The only way to reach liberation is to follow correct internal paths, which are explained only in Dharma.

Buddhas have ten special qualities not possessed by sentient beings, which are called the 'ten forces', and one of these is the force knowing all paths. Buddhas know all internal paths and where they lead to. Out of their great compassion, they teach living beings how to discriminate between correct paths and incorrect paths. If Buddhas did not teach Dharma, we would never know about the paths to liberation and, because of our familiarity with self-grasping, we would wander in samsara forever with no hope of escape. We have been following incorrect paths since beginningless time but now, through the kindness of Buddha Shakyamuni, we have the opportunity to study a complete presentation of the spiritual paths to liberation and full enlightenment.

There are two types of internal path: mundane internal paths and supramundane internal paths. Mundane internal paths lead us deeper into samsara, whereas supramundane internal paths lead us to liberation and enlightenment. There are two types of mundane path: virtuous mundane paths and non-virtuous mundane paths. Virtuous mundane paths are virtuous actions that lead to rebirth as a human being, demi-god or god, and non-virtuous mundane paths are non-virtuous actions that lead to rebirth as an animal, a hungry ghost or a hell being. Detailed explanations of mundane paths can be found in Buddha's teachings on karma and the twelve dependent-related links.

Supramundane paths are virtuous minds that lead to liberation and enlightenment. With respect to supramundane paths, path, ground, spiritual vehicle and exalted awareness are synonyms. The definition of spiritual path is an exalted awareness conjoined with non-fabricated renunciation. There are two types of spiritual path: Hinayana paths and Mahayana paths. There are five Hinayana paths: the Hinayana paths of accumulation, preparation, seeing, meditation and No More Learning. Hinayana paths lead to the small enlightenment of a Hearer or the middling enlightenment of a Solitary Conqueror. There are also five Mahayana paths: the Mahayana paths of accumulation, preparation, seeing, meditation and No More Learning. Mahayana paths lead to the complete enlightenment of a Buddha.

The definition of spiritual ground is a clear realization that acts as the foundation of many good qualities. Like spiritual paths, spiritual grounds are of two types: Hinayana grounds and Mahayana grounds. There are eight Hinayana grounds, all of which are included in the five Hinayana paths; and there are ten Mahayana grounds, all of which are included in the five Mahayana paths. Just as the earth is the basis for the growth of plants, trees, crops and so forth, so the Hinayana grounds are the basis for the development of Hinayana good qualities, and the Mahayana grounds are the basis for the development of Mahayana good qualities.

The definition of spiritual vehicle is an exalted awareness that leads to one's final spiritual destination. There are two types of spiritual vehicle: the Hinayana, or Lesser Vehicle, and the Mahayana, or Great Vehicle. The Mahayana is subdivided into the Paramitayana, or Perfection Vehicle, and the Vajrayana, or Vajra Vehicle. Of the five paths, the first four are known as 'progressing paths', or 'progressing vehicles', because they take us to our final spiritual destination; and the fifth path, the Path of No More Learning, is known as the 'Resultant Path', or the 'Effect Vehicle'.

The definition of exalted awareness is a spiritual realization that knows perfectly the nature of its principal object. All spiritual paths are exalted awarenesses. Exalted awareness differs from wisdom in that wisdom necessarily realizes its object through its own power, whereas exalted awareness may realize its object through the power of another mind. Bodhichitta, for example, is an exalted awareness but not a wisdom. Bodhichitta knows the nature of its principal object, enlightenment, but it does so through the power of its attendant mental factor wisdom rather than through its own power. By the same token, other mental factors associated with bodhichitta, such as concentration, intention and feeling, are also exalted awarenesses but not wisdoms.

Thus, bodhichitta is at once a path, a ground, a spiritual vehicle and an exalted awareness. From the point of view of its leading to enlightenment, it is a path; from the point of view of its being the foundation of the many good qualities of the Mahayana, it is a ground; from the point of view of its being the means to progress towards enlightenment, it is a vehicle; and from the point of view of its knowledge and its way of understanding its object, it is an exalted awareness.

Because living beings have varying inclinations and mental capacities, Buddha Shakyamuni taught three vehicles: the Hinayana, the Paramitayana and the Vajrayana. To suit those of limited aspiration who are mainly concerned with their own release from suffering, Buddha taught the Hinayana. Hinayanists are very aware of the faults of attachment and regard attachment as their main object to be abandoned. For this reason, the Hinayana is sometimes known as the 'Separation from Attachment Vehicle'. To abandon attachment temporarily, Hinayanists renounce their families, homes and so forth, retire to an isolated place, and meditate on unattractiveness; and to abandon attachment completely they meditate on emptiness.

For those who are attracted to the vast path, Buddha expounded the Paramitayana, in which he taught the six perfections and the ten Bodhisattva grounds. The main objects to be abandoned by Bodhisattvas are the obstructions to omniscience. Bodhisattvas are not afraid of attachment, because they know how to transform it into the spiritual path. Just as farmers use impure substances such as manure to fertilize their soil, so Superior Bodhisattvas use delusions such as attachment as aids to attaining Buddhahood, having rendered them harmless through the strength of their wisdom and compassion.

For those who are attracted to profound Dharma, Buddha taught the third vehicle, the Vajrayana. The Vajrayana, or Secret Mantra Vehicle, is sometimes called the 'Attachment

Vehicle' because, instead of trying to abandon attachment immediately, practitioners of this vehicle use attachment as an aid to generating spontaneous great bliss, with which they then meditate on emptiness. Furthermore, when they finally attain enlightenment, even though they have no desirous attachment they nevertheless display the aspect of having attachment by appearing as Tantric Buddhas in the aspect of Father and Mother in sexual embrace.

Although we can transform attachment into the spiritual path by practising Secret Mantra, we need great skill to be able to do this because normally, when attachment develops strongly, it automatically disturbs our peaceful mind. The main reason why most Buddhas will not expound Secret Mantra is that there is a danger that unqualified practitioners will use it for the sake of worldly pleasure; and qualified practitioners among disciples are very rare. Buddha Shakyamuni, however, is an exception. Through the power of his previous prayers and special determination, his disciples have special karma to practise Secret Mantra.

There is a prophecy that when the Dharma of Buddha Shakyamuni is about to end, the practice of Secret Mantra will briefly flourish very widely in this world, as a candle flame flickers brightly just before it finally burns out. It appears that nowadays there are many books about Tantra, many Teachers teaching Tantra and many students trying to practise Tantra. However, not all these books and teachings are pure and authentic. Therefore, it is becoming increasingly important to discriminate between authentic Tantric teachings and those that have been mixed with non-Buddhist teachings. We are extremely fortunate to have met the completely pure Tantric teachings that have been passed down from Buddha Shakyamuni through Je Tsongkhapa and many realized Teachers of the new Kadampa Tradition. Je Tsongkhapa, who was an emanation of the Wisdom Buddha Manjushri, clarified many aspects of Tantric practice that had frequently been misunderstood in the past. In particular, he showed how it is possible, and indeed essential, to practise the union of Sutra and Tantra. Before Je Tsongkhapa appeared, many people thought that Secret Mantra and Vinaya moral discipline were contradictory, and that one person could not practise both; but Je Tsongkhapa showed how, rather than being contradictory with the Vinaya, the practice of Secret Mantra is the supremely skilful means for keeping the Vinaya discipline purely. I feel extremely fortunate to be able to pass on the pure Tantric teachings of Je Tsongkhapa, and the reader too should feel fortunate to have the opportunity to study them.

THE GOOD QUALITIES OF SECRET MANTRA

We can understand the nature, functions and good qualities of Secret Mantra by considering the various names that Buddha gave to it: Secret Vehicle, Mantra Vehicle, Effect Vehicle, Vajra Vehicle, Method Vehicle and Tantric Vehicle. These will now be explained.

SECRET VEHICLE

Because Tantra is the very essence of Buddha's teachings, it is like a rare and precious treasure. People generally keep their most valuable possessions hidden, showing them only to their closest relatives and friends. If we owned a priceless diamond, for example, we would be very unwise to display it on our mantelpiece for anyone to see, for this would only attract thieves. In the same way, it is unwise to reveal Tantric teachings to those without empowerments or without deep faith in Buddhadharma, for this invites many obstacles. Therefore, we should practise Tantra discreetly.

Secret Mantra is unique to Buddhism. Although there are certain non-Buddhist teachings that superficially resemble Secret Mantra, in reality they are completely different. Furthermore, Secret Mantra is exclusively a Mahayana practice and, of Mahayanists, only those with great faith, merit and wisdom can practise it. Although Secret Mantra is extremely precious and profound, it is not suitable for those who lack these qualities. Vajradhara compared Secret Mantra to the milk of a snow lion. If this milk is stored in a golden vessel it remains sweet and invigorating, but if it is put into a vessel made of an inferior substance it immediately turns sour. In the same way, if a person with little faith studies Tantric teachings and tries to practise them, without relying upon a qualified Vajrayana Spiritual Guide, he or she is likely to develop harmful misunderstandings.

MANTRA VEHICLE

'Mantra' means 'mind protection'. Through the power of practising Secret Mantra, our mind is protected from ordinary appearances and ordinary conceptions. According to Tantra, ordinary appearances and ordinary conceptions are the root of samsara and the foundation of all suffering. Ordinary appearance is any appearance that is due to an impure mind, and ordinary conception is any mind that conceives something due to ordinary appearance. Because phenomena appear to us as ordinary, and we conceive them as ordinary, we create contaminated karma and wander in

Je Tsongkhapa

samsara. Ordinary conceptions are obstructions to liberation and ordinary appearances are obstructions to omniscience.

When we cling to being an ordinary person, thinking 'I am Peter', 'I am Sarah', etc., we are developing ordinary conceptions. Because we cling to an ordinary identity, if someone attacks us we feel fear, or if we run out of money we become anxious. If instead of clinging to an ordinary identity we were to overcome ordinary conceptions by developing the divine pride of being Heruka or Vajrayogini, we would not develop fear, anxiety or any other negative state of mind. How can anyone harm Heruka? How can Vajrayogini run out of money?

Why do we develop the ordinary thought of being Peter, Sarah, etc.? Ordinary conceptions depend upon ordinary appearances. We think of ourself as an ordinary person in dependence upon ordinary aggregates appearing to our mind. Because a gross, impure body and gross, impure states of mind appear to us, we develop the thought 'I', and conceive ourself to be an ordinary being. Through acting under the influence of such ordinary conceptions, we create contaminated karma and thereby sow the seeds for the appearance of an ordinary body, mind and world to arise again in the future. If we then assent to these ordinary appearances and relate to ourself and our world in an ordinary way, we will simply perpetuate this cycle of ordinary experience. To break this cycle, we need to overcome ordinary appearances by visualizing ourself as a Deity and overcome ordinary conceptions by generating divine pride of being the Deity. Most Tantric paths are methods for overcoming ordinary appearances and conceptions.

Ordinary conceptions are not necessarily delusions because they are not necessarily wrong awarenesses, but they are

17

obstructions to liberation. For Tantric practitioners, the main objects to be abandoned are not the delusions, but ordinary appearances and ordinary conceptions, because, when these manifest strongly, Tantric practice does not work. Qualified Tantric practitioners are not afraid of delusions. Indeed, in some Tantras, Buddha gives Tantric practitioners permission to develop desirous attachment, and in other Tantras he gives them permission to develop anger and jealousy. However, there is a debate about whether or not Buddha gives permission to develop ignorance. Some scholars argue that he does not, because there can never be any benefit from developing ignorance. They say that whereas attachment can be used to generate bliss, and anger can be transformed into a force for benefiting others, ignorance can never be put to a good use. Other scholars say that by giving permission to develop anger and attachment, Buddha implicitly gives permission to develop ignorance, which is the root of all delusions. It should be noted, however, that although Tantric practitioners do not regard delusions as their principal objects to be abandoned, they nevertheless do have the intention to abandon them eventually. In fact, when practitioners reduce or abandon ordinary appearances and ordinary conceptions, they automatically reduce or abandon their delusions.

EFFECT VEHICLE

Here, 'effect' refers to the four ultimate effects of spiritual practice: the pure environment of a Buddha, the pure body of a Buddha, the pure enjoyments of a Buddha and the pure deeds of a Buddha. These are also known as the 'four complete purities'. Secret Mantra is called the 'Effect Vehicle' because practitioners bring these four complete purities into the spiritual path. For example, if we are practising Vajrayogini Tantra, we bring the pure environment of a Buddha into the spiritual path by visualizing our surroundings as Vajrayogini's mandala; we bring the pure body of a Buddha into the path by visualizing our body as Vajrayogini's body; we bring the pure enjoyments of a Buddha into the path by imagining that our food, drink and so forth are nectar, and offering it to ourself generated as Vajrayogini; and we bring the pure deeds of a Buddha into the path by helping living beings while maintaining the divine pride of being Vajrayogini. These practices are the quick method for attaining the four complete purities.

VAJRA VEHICLE

The principal connotation of the word 'vajra' is 'indivisible' or 'indestructible'. Secret Mantra is called the 'Vajra Vehicle' because it contains yogas of indivisible method and wisdom, which are meditations that principally accumulate merit and wisdom simultaneously. According to Sutra, there is no single concentration that principally creates the cause of the Form Body and the Truth Body simultaneously, but according to Secret Mantra there are such concentrations. For example, when we meditate on generation stage of Highest Yoga Tantra, in one single concentration one part of that mind meditates on the Deity's body while another part meditates on its emptiness. Meditating on the Deity's body is a cause for attaining the Form Body, and meditating on emptiness is a cause for attaining the Truth Body. When we attain meaning clear light, the fourth of the five stages of completion stage, we meditate on the union of bliss and emptiness, which is the actual indivisible method and wisdom. This single concentration serves to complete both the collection of merit and the collection of wisdom simultaneously, and thus acts as the main cause of both the Form Body and the Truth Body. For these reasons, Vajrayana is the supreme vehicle that is superior to Sutrayana.

METHOD VEHICLE

Although Sutra teaches the stages of the method path, these methods are not as profound, as skilful, or as swift as those explained in Tantra. The actual swift and direct methods for attaining Buddhahood, such as isolated body, isolated speech, isolated mind, illusory body and clear light, are taught only in Secret Mantra. However, all the key practices of Sutra are also explained in Tantra. Bodhichitta, for example, is taught in both Sutra and Tantra. Although the nature of bodhichitta is the same in both Sutra and Tantra, the way we meditate on bodhichitta in Tantra is more profound. In Tantra we meditate on bodhichitta in conjunction with bringing the future result into the path. We begin every Tantric meditation session by generating bodhichitta in the usual way, but then, with the motivation of becoming a Buddha for the sake of all living beings, we imagine that we immediately become a Buddha and perform enlightened deeds. In this way, our meditation on self-generation becomes a powerful method for enhancing our bodhichitta and for accomplishing the aim of bodhichitta. When qualified Tantric practitioners generate bodhichitta, they know exactly what full enlightenment is – the union of meaning clear light and illusory body – and they know exactly what the actual paths to full enlightenment are – isolated body, isolated speech, isolated mind and so on. As a result, their bodhichitta wish to attain enlightenment is very qualified. Therefore, the way of practising bodhichitta according to Tantra is superior to the way of practising according to Sutra. There are many other special Tantric techniques for improving and strengthening bodhichitta.

TANTRIC VEHICLE

There are four types of Tantra: base Tantras, path Tantras, effect Tantras and textual Tantras. Our ordinary body, speech and mind are called the 'base Tantra' because they are the basis to be purified by Tantric practice; the yogas of the four classes of Tantra such as the yogas with signs and the yoga without signs of Action Tantra, and the yogas of generation stage and completion stage of Highest Yoga Tantra, are path Tantras; the three bodies of a Buddha attained by means of path Tantras are effect Tantras; and any scripture that reveals these three types of Tantra is a textual Tantra. By purifying base Tantras by means of path Tantras we eventually attain the effect Tantras. This is accomplished by relying upon textual Tantras.

In *Great Exposition of the Stages of Secret Mantra* Je Tsongkhapa mentions seven special benefits of practising Secret Mantra:

(1) We receive the blessings of the Buddhas and Bodhisattvas more swiftly.
(2) We come under the care and guidance of our personal Deity, or Yidam.
(3) We will be able to remember the Buddhas at the time of death, during the intermediate state and in future lives.

(4) We quickly complete the collections of merit and wisdom.

(5) We will become free from all obstacles.

(6) We will accomplish both the common attainments – the pacifying, increasing, controlling and wrathful attainments, and the eight great attainments – and the uncommon attainment of the Union of No More Learning, or Buddhahood.

(7) Our everyday bodily and verbal actions become causes to accumulate a great stock of merit.

THE FOUR CLASSES OF TANTRA

Because from the point of view of wisdom, merit and mental capacity, there are many different levels of practitioners of Secret Mantra, Buddha taught four classes of Tantra: Action Tantra, Performance Tantra, Yoga Tantra and Highest Yoga Tantra. One way to distinguish these four classes of Tantra is by the methods they reveal for transforming sensual pleasure into the spiritual path. Beings of the desire realm are very attached to sensual pleasures such as beautiful forms, pleasant sounds, fragrant smells, delicious tastes and smooth or stimulating tactile objects. When we enjoy these five objects of desire, we experience a degree of bliss, but unfortunately this bliss usually gives rise to attachment and so acts as a cause for samsaric rebirth. Thus the bliss ordinary beings experience from encountering attractive sense objects indirectly causes them to experience suffering. With his infinite skill, Buddha taught special methods for transforming worldly pleasure into the spiritual path, so that instead of leading to future suffering it becomes a cause of the ultimate bliss of Buddhahood. By relying upon these methods, we can take advantage of our natural fondness for sensual pleasure and, rather than having to abandon the five objects of desire, use them to stimulate our spiritual practice.

As the great Mahasiddha Saraha said, most people in this world regard sexual bliss as very important and put a great deal of energy into obtaining it, but no one understands how to experience this bliss in a meaningful way and prevent it from increasing their delusions. Buddha taught several methods for transforming sexual pleasure into the spiritual path, some of which are suited to those with superior mental faculties and some to those with lesser faculties.

Each of the four classes of Tantra contains its own special techniques for transforming sensual bliss. For example, when practitioners of Action Tantra generate themselves as a male Action Tantra Deity such as Manjushri or Avalokiteshvara, they visualize a beautiful Goddess in front of them and, by gazing at the Goddess, they generate bliss, which they then use to meditate on emptiness. To enhance their experience of bliss, clear appearance and divine pride they also engage in many ritual practices such as mudras and ritual bathing. Practitioners of Performance Tantra, in addition to visualizing an attractive Goddess in front of them, visualize her smiling at them enticingly, and in this way generate bliss, which they use to meditate on emptiness. They also engage in ritual practices, but in Performance Tantra, meditation and external actions are given equal emphasis. Practitioners of Yoga Tantra imagine that they are holding hands with the Goddess, and use the bliss that they generate to meditate on emptiness. When they engage in rituals, they emphasize internal practices over external practices. Practitioners of Highest Yoga Tantra imagine that they are in sexual embrace with the Goddess, and then transform the bliss that they

23

generate into the spiritual path by meditating on emptiness. Before we can transform the bliss of embracing into the spiritual path, we need to be able to transform the bliss of holding hands, and before we can do this we need to be able to transform the bliss that arises from just looking at a male or female Deity. Therefore, anyone who wishes to practise transforming bliss into the path according to Highest Yoga Tantra must first practise transforming bliss into the path according to the three lower Tantras.

By training in transforming the bliss of looking at a visualized Goddess, seeing her smile, holding hands with her and embracing her, eventually we will gain the ability to transform the bliss of actual sexual intercourse into the path. Without training in meditation, however, it is impossible to transform sexual activity into the spiritual path. Misunderstanding Tantra, some people with no experience of meditation indulge in sexual misconduct and claim to be great Tantric practitioners. Such people are destroying the Buddhadharma and creating the cause to be reborn in hell.

We need to judge our own capacity and practise accordingly. First, within divine pride of the Deity, we should try to transform the bliss of looking at a visualized male or female Deity and then, when we have some experience of this, try to transform the bliss of looking at an actual man or woman. From this practical point of view we are then a practitioner of Action Tantra. Next we imagine that the Deity is smiling at us, and use the bliss that arises to meditate on emptiness. When we can do this, we can try to transform the bliss of looking at our partner smiling at us. Eventually, with strong divine pride of a Highest Yoga Tantra Deity such as Heruka or Vajrayogini, we can visualize ourself in sexual embrace with our consort. Whether we are a man or a woman, if we are generating ourself as Heruka we visualize ourself embracing Vajrayogini, and if we are generating ourself as Vajrayogini we visualize ourself embracing Heruka. When we can transform the bliss of embracing a visualized consort, we can try to transform the bliss of actual sexual intercourse into the quick path to Buddhahood.

Our motivation for doing this practice must be compassion and bodhichitta; and, when we develop an experience of bliss through any of the methods mentioned above, we should try immediately to mix that bliss with emptiness and remain single-pointedly on the unification of bliss and emptiness. This is the way to train in transforming sensual pleasures into the spiritual path that is the very essence practice of Vajrayana. Success in this practice depends upon the strength of our understanding of emptiness and experience of bliss.

The purpose of transforming bliss into the path will be explained more fully in the section on Highest Yoga Tantra. The essence of Highest Yoga Tantra practice is the union of bliss and emptiness. If we are skilled in transforming bliss into the path, we will be able to transform our enjoyment of all five objects of desire into powerful causes of Buddhahood.

It is important not to neglect the lower Tantras. Je Tsongkhapa said that a person who has not studied the lower Tantras cannot claim that Highest Yoga Tantra is supreme. The lower Tantras are a preparation for Highest Yoga Tantra. Only by understanding the three lower Tantras can we fully appreciate the profundity of Highest Yoga Tantra.

Togden Jampel Gyatso

The Lower Tantras

ACTION TANTRA

Buddha reveals the stages of the path of Action Tantra in various scriptures, notably *General Secret Tantra*, *Excellent Establishment Tantra*, *Tantra Requested by Subahu* and *Concentration Continuum Tantra*. These four are the root Tantras of Action Tantra. In *General Secret Tantra*, Buddha explains three thousand eight hundred types of mandala of Action Tantra. In *Excellent Establishment Tantra*, he explains how to meditate on the wrathful Deity Susiddhi. In *Tantra Requested by Subahu*, he explains how to do Action Tantra close retreats and how to accomplish pacifying, increasing, controlling and wrathful actions. In *Concentration Continuum Tantra*, he explains the four concentrations of Action Tantra. In addition to these four root Tantras, there are many branch Tantras and Tantric commentaries.

In *Great Exposition of the Stages of Secret Mantra*, Je Tsongkhapa presents the stages of the path of Action Tantra in four parts: empowerments, vows and commitments, close retreats, and common and uncommon attainments. Although the practices of Action Tantra are very extensive, Je Tsongkhapa includes them all in these four divisions, thereby making them easy to understand. Since Je Tsongkhapa's presentation is so clear and practical, I will base my commentary principally on his outlines.

Action Tantra will now be explained in six parts:

1 Receiving empowerments, the method for ripening our mental continuum
2 Observing the vows and commitments
3 Engaging in close retreat, the method for attaining realizations
4 How to accomplish the common and uncommon attainments once we have experience of the four concentrations
5 How to progress through the grounds and paths in dependence upon Action Tantra
6 The families of Action Tantra Deities

RECEIVING EMPOWERMENTS, THE METHOD FOR RIPENING OUR MENTAL CONTINUUM

To practise Action Tantra, we need to receive an empowerment. Action Tantra empowerments are much simpler than Highest Yoga Tantra empowerments, and consist mainly of a water empowerment and a crown empowerment. In these empowerments, the Vajrayana Spiritual Guide bestows special blessings upon the disciples' mind and body using holy water from the vase, and a crown, to ripen their seeds of the stages of the path of Action Tantra.

OBSERVING THE VOWS AND COMMITMENTS

Since there is no empowerment of the Vajrayana Spiritual Guide in Action Tantra, there is no basis for bestowing Tantric vows. However, the Bodhisattva vows are granted. There are also certain commitments, which vary from empowerment to empowerment depending upon the family of the Deity.

ENGAGING IN CLOSE RETREAT, THE METHOD FOR ATTAINING REALIZATIONS

A close retreat is a method for drawing closer to our Yidam, or personal Deity, both in the sense of bringing our mind closer to an external Deity whom we visualize in front of us, and in the sense of ourself becoming more like the Deity through training in self-generation. The final result of close retreat is that we become a Deity. A Deity or Yidam is a Tantric enlightened being. There are four types of Deity: Deities of Action Tantra, such as Muni Trisamaya Guhyaraja, Avalokiteshvara, White Tara, Green Tara and Amitayus; Deities of Performance Tantra, such as the one hundred and seventeen Deities of the mandala of Buddha Munivairochana; Deities of Yoga Tantra, such as Sarvavid and the other ninety-six Deities; and Deities of Highest Yoga Tantra, such as the sixty-two Deities of Heruka's mandala, the thirty-seven Deities of Vajrayogini's body mandala and the thirty-two Deities of Guhyasamaja's mandala.

To receive the attainments of our personal Deity, we need to practise four concentrations:

1 Concentration of the four-limbed recitation
2 Concentration of abiding in fire
3 Concentration of abiding in sound
4 Concentration of bestowing liberation at the end of sound

CONCENTRATION OF THE FOUR-LIMBED RECITATION

This has four parts:

1 Accomplishing the self base
2 Accomplishing the other base
3 Accomplishing the mind base
4 Accomplishing the sound base

ACCOMPLISHING THE SELF-BASE

In Action Tantra, 'self base' means meditation on self-generation. In *Tantra Requested by Subahu* and *Concentration Continuum Tantra* Buddha explains how to practise self-generation by meditating sequentially on six Deities: the Deity of emptiness, the Deity of sound, the Deity of letters, the Deity of form, the Deity of the mudra and the Deity of signs. Just as in Highest Yoga Tantra we meditate on bringing the three bodies into the path before engaging in the actual meditation on self-generation, so in Action Tantra we meditate on these six Deities before engaging in the actual meditation on self-generation. These six Deities will now be explained in terms of generating ourself as the Deity Avalokiteshvara.

THE DEITY OF EMPTINESS

After going for refuge, generating bodhichitta and so forth, we begin by remembering that we are empty of inherent existence, and that Avalokiteshvara is also empty. We think:

I am not my body and not my mind, but besides my body and mind there is no I. I am therefore empty of inherent existence.

By contemplating reasons such as this, we try to overcome the appearance of our normal I and perceive only emptiness. We then apply the same reasoning to Avalokiteshvara and conclude that Avalokiteshvara is also empty of inherent existence. Since all emptinesses are the same nature, our emptiness and Avalokiteshvara's emptiness are not different; therefore on an ultimate level we are equal and indistinguishable.

If there are two glasses on a table, the nature of the space inside the two glasses is not different. Thus, if the glasses are broken we cannot distinguish the space of one glass from the space of the other. From an ultimate point of view, we and Avalokiteshvara are like the space of two glasses. When we begin to meditate on emptiness, we feel that our ultimate nature and Avalokiteshvara's ultimate nature are different but, when we succeed in overcoming the conventional appearances of ourself and Avalokiteshvara, it is like breaking the glasses; we discover that our ultimate nature and Avalokiteshvara's ultimate nature are exactly the same – mere lack of inherent existence. We meditate on the indistinguishability of the emptiness of ourself and the emptiness of Avalokiteshvara, thinking:

I and Avalokiteshvara have now become the same, like water poured into water.

Observing this undifferentiated absence of inherent existence, we identify it as the Truth Body and develop divine pride of being the Truth Body. All that appears to us is emptiness. This emptiness, which is the inseparability of our ultimate nature and Avalokiteshvara's ultimate nature, is now the basis of imputation of our I.

We may think that we are our body or our mind, but our body and mind are the basis for imputing our I, not the I itself. Thus, whenever our body or mind appear to us, we think 'I'. In a similar way, when we are meditating on the Deity of emptiness, emptiness itself becomes the basis for imputing our I. Observing emptiness, we develop the thought 'I'. It is important to understand that we do not need a physical body to develop a sense of I. Gods of the formless realm, for example, have no physical body, but they do have a sense of I.

Whereas imputing I onto an ordinary body or mind causes us to develop self-grasping ignorance and thereby to remain in samsara, imputing I onto emptiness causes us to be released from samsara. It is very important for Secret Mantra practitioners to learn to develop the thought of I using emptiness as the basis of imputation. If possible, we should bring to mind actual emptiness, mere absence of inherent existence and, observing this emptiness, develop the thought 'I'. If we do not understand emptiness, we should simply imagine a vacuity and, observing this, think 'I'. However, if our meditation is to act as an actual antidote to self-grasping, we need to recognize lack of inherent existence and impute I onto this. An I imputed onto the emptiness, or ultimate nature, of ourself and our Yidam is the Deity of emptiness, or the ultimate Deity.

THE DEITY OF SOUND

After meditating on the Deity of emptiness for a while, we imagine that from the state of emptiness comes the sound of Avalokiteshvara's mantra, OM MANI PÄME HUM, like the sound of distant thunder rumbling in an empty sky. We do not visualize the letters in written form, but simply hear the sound of the mantra with our mind. The sound does not come from anywhere in particular but pervades the whole of space. Recognizing the sound of the mantra as our mind appearing in the aspect of sound, we impute I onto it. This I imputed onto the sound of the mantra is the Deity of sound. According to the Madhyamika-Prasangika system, an imputed object and its basis of imputation are contradictory, which means that the basis of imputation of the I is necessarily not the I. Just as at present our five contaminated aggregates are the basis for imputing our I but are not our I, so the sound of the mantra is the basis for imputing the Deity of sound but is not that Deity.

THE DEITY OF LETTERS

After meditating on our mind in the aspect of the sound of the mantra for a while, we imagine that our mind transforms into a white translucent moon mandala. The sound of the mantra gathers above the moon and takes on the physical shape of the letters OM MANI PÄME HUM, standing clockwise around the circumference of the moon mandala. We think that these letters and the moon mandala are in essence our own mind and on this basis develop the thought 'I'. This I imputed onto the letters of the mantra is the Deity of letters.

THE DEITY OF FORM

After meditating on the Deity of letters for a while, we imagine that the letters on the moon mandala radiate light throughout the ten directions. At the tip of each ray of light is Avalokiteshvara. The rays reach the crown of each and every living being, blessing them and purifying all their negative karma of body, speech and mind. The six realms of samsara are purified and transformed into Avalokiteshvara's Pure Land, and all living beings are transformed into Avalokiteshvara. Then the purified environment and beings melt into white light and dissolve into the mantra rosary and moon mandala, which then transform into the body of Avalokiteshvara. We can visualize Avalokiteshvara as having one face and two arms, one face and four arms, or eleven faces and a thousand arms. Observing the physical form of Avalokiteshvara we develop the thought 'I'. This I imputed onto the physical form of Avalokiteshvara is the Deity of form.

THE DEITY OF THE MUDRA

Having generated ourself as Avalokiteshvara, we now need to bless the five principal places of Avalokiteshvara's body with a special mudra. To do this we place our palms together in the mudra of prostration but leave the finger tips slightly apart, like the petals of a lotus flower starting to open, and tuck our thumbs inside to symbolize a precious jewel hidden within the lotus. This is called the 'commitment mudra of the Lotus family'. With our hands in this mudra, we then touch our heart, the point between our eyebrows, our throat, our right shoulder and our left shoulder, while reciting the mantra OM PÄMA UBHAWAYE SOHA. As we touch our heart we visualize Akshobya, as we touch the point between our eyebrows we visualize Vairochana, as we touch our throat we visualize Amitabha, as we touch our right shoulder we visualize Ratnasambhava, and as we touch our left shoulder we visualize Amoghasiddhi. Although the Deities are marked on our body, this is not a body mandala because the substantial cause of the five Deities is our mind rather than parts of our body. These Deities are the Deities of the mudra. We develop the conviction that these five Deities are in essence our own mind and meditate on this.

THE DEITY OF SIGNS

Here, 'signs' refers to the uncommon signs, or character-istics, of Avalokiteshvara's body. To meditate on the Deity of signs, we examine Avalokiteshvara's body from head to foot to improve the clarity of our visualization. This improves both our clear appearance and divine pride of being Avalokiteshvara. An I imputed onto the body of Avalokiteshvara after engaging in analytical meditation on the uncommon signs of Avalokiteshvara is the Deity of signs.

The purpose of meditating on the Deity of emptiness is to attain the mind of the Deity. The purpose of meditating on the Deity of sound and the Deity of letters is to attain the speech of the Deity. The purpose of meditating on the Deity of form, the Deity of the mudra and the Deity of signs is to attain the body of the Deity. Meditating on the yogas of the six Deities in this order helps us to overcome ordinary appearances and conceptions and to develop clear appearance and strong divine pride of being the Deity. If we do not practise these Deities sequentially, but try immediately to generate ourself as a Tantric Deity, we will find it almost impossible to overcome ordinary appearances and conceptions.

To generate ourself as an Action Tantra Deity other than Avalokiteshvara, we meditate on the same sequence of six Deities, but with a few minor modifications. For example, if we wish to generate ourself as Manjushri, when we meditate

Baso Chokyi Gyaltsen

on the Deity of sound we imagine that the whole of space is filled with Manjushri's mantra OM AH RA PA TSA NA DHI instead of OM MANI PÄME HUM, and when we meditate on the Deity of form and the Deity of signs we visualize ourself as Manjushri with an orange-coloured body, one face and two arms, holding a sword and a text. The way to meditate on the Deity of the mudra is also different. Instead of touching the five places of our body with the commitment mudra of the Lotus family, we visualize at our crown a letter OM, at our throat a letter AH and at our heart a letter HUM, and recognize these letters as having the nature of Vairochana, Amitabha and Akshobya respectively. We then invite the wisdom beings to enter into us while reciting DZA HUM BAM HO and performing the appropriate hand mudras as explained in the book *The New Guide to Dakini Land*.

ACCOMPLISHING THE OTHER BASE

'Other base' refers to the Deity generated in front. If our practice is Avalokiteshvara, we visualize Avalokiteshvara and his retinue in front of us. These are the commitment beings. We invite the actual Deities, the wisdom beings, to dissolve into the commitment beings, and then make prostrations, offerings, confession, requests to receive attainments, and torma offerings. If we have time we can visualize a mantra rosary at the heart of the in-front-generated Deity and recite the mantra. These practices are known as 'accomplishing the other base'.

ACCOMPLISHING THE MIND BASE

To accomplish the mind base, after meditating on the Deity of signs we visualize our mind in the aspect of a tiny white moon disc lying horizontally at our heart. This moon is called the 'mind base' because it is an aspect of our root mind. With strong conviction that the moon is our mind, we try to perceive it as clearly as possible. We then gather our inner winds inside and dissolve them into the moon. There are nine 'doors' through which winds enter or leave our body: the nostrils, the mouth, the crown of the head, the point between the eyebrows, the two eyes, the two ears, the navel, the sex organ and the anus. In addition to these nine doors, the winds can also enter our body through any of the pores in our skin. One reason why it is advisable to wash frequently is that, if we do not, our pores become blocked and our health may suffer as a result.

Just as a turtle withdraws its head and limbs into its body and remains motionless even when it is disturbed, so we imagine that our inner winds withdraw into our body through the nine doors and the pores of the skin, and dissolve into the moon disc at our heart. We focus single-pointedly on this for a short time while holding our breath. With one part of our mind we remember that our winds have dissolved into the moon, and with another part we meditate on the uncommon signs of the Deity so as to improve both clear appearance and divine pride. When we have a relatively clear mental image of the body of the Deity, we meditate on this single-pointedly. This is the actual meditation on self-generation.

Because gross conceptual thoughts observing external objects can function only if the winds are flowing outwards, by gathering the winds into our heart we reduce distracting conceptions and naturally develop stable concentration. Without the interference of ordinary appearances and conceptions we find it much easier to concentrate on the body of the Deity, perceive it clearly, and develop stable divine pride.

Generally, Dharma practitioners regard the attainment of tranquil abiding as important, and for practitioners of Action Tantra this attainment is of special importance. The meditation on the breath described above is similar to the vase breathing described in Highest Yoga Tantra, but its purpose is different. The main purpose of vase breathing is to bring the winds into the central channel, whereas the main purpose of meditating on the mind base is to facilitate the attainment of tranquil abiding.

ACCOMPLISHING THE SOUND BASE

The sound base is mantra recitation. The time to practise the sound base is after meditating on the mind base, when our concentration is beginning to weaken and we feel the need to relax. If we have generated ourself as Avalokiteshvara, we visualize that on the centre of the moon disc at our heart stands a white letter HRIH, the seed of Avalokiteshvara, with the mantra OM MANI PÄME HUM standing clockwise around it. The letters are made of white light and are in essence Avalokiteshvara's wisdom. Tantric scriptures repeatedly stress the importance of regarding the mantra and the Deity as inseparable. Since the body, speech and mind of a Buddha are the same nature, it is quite possible for a Buddha's mind to manifest as the sound or written letters of a mantra.

There are two types of mantra recitation: gross recitation and subtle recitation. Reciting mantras out loud or under our breath is gross recitation. To practise subtle recitation we imagine that the letters of the mantra visualized at our heart are making the sound OM MANI PÄME HUM, and simply listen to that sound.

There are five main purposes of practising gross and subtle recitation:

(1) To receive the blessings of the Deity.
(2) To draw closer to the Deity.
(3) To request the attainments of the Deity.
(4) To accomplish pacifying, increasing, controlling, and wrathful actions.
(5) To purify negative karma and accumulate merit.

Pacifying actions include dispelling our negativities, eliminating obstacles and pacifying interferences from evil spirits. Increasing actions include increasing our lifespan, merit, realizations, and good qualities of listening, contemplating and meditating. Controlling actions include controlling evil spirits and maras by peaceful methods. Wrathful actions include controlling them by wrathful methods when necessary. Whenever we engage in wrathful actions, it is essential that our motivation is one of pure compassion.

We can fulfil all our wishes by reciting mantras purely. For people who have relied sincerely upon their Deity in previous lives, and who have engaged in close retreats and so forth, reciting mantras acts to ripen the harvest already sown in those lives and so, for them, results can appear very quickly. Other people who have not practised the Deity in previous lives, or who have had negative thoughts against the Deity in the past, need to recite mantras for a long time before they accomplish pacifying, increasing, controlling and wrathful actions.

Another important factor in determining how soon we attain results from mantra recitation is the power of our faith and concentration. If our faith is weak, and we are unable to overcome distractions, we may not attain results even after many years of reciting the mantra. However, we should not conclude from this that the mantra and the Deity have no power, but should make a determined effort to improve our faith and overcome distractions. In general, just saying mantras is beneficial because the very sound has been blessed by Buddhas, but to accomplish all the attainments described in Tantric texts we need to recite them purely, with unwavering faith and strong concentration.

We have now completed the explanation of the first concentration, the concentration of the four-limbed recitation. In general, all Action Tantra concentrations can be included within two categories: concentrations with recitation and concentrations without recitation. Meditation on the six Deities of the self base, and meditation on the other base and the mind base are the foundation for mantra recitation; and the sound base is the mantra recitation itself. For this reason, the four limbs of the first concentration are called 'concentrations with recitation', while the remaining three concentrations are called 'concentrations without recitation'.

CONCENTRATION OF ABIDING IN FIRE

To practise the concentration of abiding in fire, we begin by remembering emptiness and allowing our mind to mix with it. We then imagine that the union of our mind and emptiness appears in the aspect of a tiny flame burning steadily on a moon disc at our heart. While focusing on the flame single-pointedly, and remembering that the flame is in essence our mind mixed with emptiness, we imagine that from within the flame there comes the sound of the mantra OM MANI PÄME HUM. We do not recite the mantra, either verbally or mentally, but simply feel that we are listening to the sound of the mantra within the flame. Taking the flame and the sound of the mantra as our object of placement meditation, we concentrate on them single-pointedly, having overcome distractions, mental sinking and mental excitement.

The purpose of concentrating on the flame and mantra is to attain tranquil abiding more quickly, and to accomplish a non-conceptual wisdom inseparable from emptiness. In Action Tantra, after we have attained stable concentration on the moon disc and Deity body of the mind base, we change our object of concentration to the flame and mantra of the concentration of abiding in fire. Since these are more subtle than the object of the mind base, it is easier to attain tranquil abiding if we take them as our object of meditation. However, we must first attain a degree of stability on the mind base if our meditation on abiding in fire is to be powerful.

Another purpose of the concentration of abiding in fire is to cause a special inner heat to develop and increase, and through this to accomplish a non-conceptual bliss. Through engaging in this meditation repeatedly, we will receive certain signs. We will develop a special physical and mental suppleness, we will not experience hunger or thirst even if we do not eat or drink for a long time, and, when we do eat or drink, we will produce less urine and excrement. Moreover, our special inner heat and inner bliss will increase, and external and internal interferences will have no power to harm us. We should continue to meditate on abiding in fire until we receive these signs.

CONCENTRATION OF ABIDING IN SOUND

When we have attained stability in the concentration of abiding in fire, we can practise the concentration of abiding in sound. To do this, we meditate on the flame and mantra in exactly the same way but, when our concentration is firm, we stop the appearance of the flame and concentrate exclusively on the sound of the mantra. We meditate on this until, through the force of familiarity, we feel that we hear the mantra directly with our mental awareness, as we would hear sounds with our mental awareness in a dream. When some practitioners reach this stage, they hear all six letters of the mantra, OM MANI PÄME HUM, simultaneously.

To attain tranquil abiding, Action Tantra practitioners meditate on each of the concentrations from the Deity of emptiness up to abiding in sound. The practices of the mind base, the concentration of abiding in fire, and the concentration of abiding in sound are all principally methods for improving our concentration. The concentration of abiding in sound has a special power to induce physical and mental suppleness and it leads directly to the attainment of tranquil abiding. This concentration has three good qualities: its nature is bliss, its object appears very clearly and it is free from distracting conceptuality. The last two qualities are related, because the fewer distracting conceptual thoughts we have, the more clearly we will perceive the object.

In *Lamp for the Path to Enlightenment* Atisha says that to attain tranquil abiding we must remain with one object, but according to the system of Action Tantra we change the object of meditation several times. There is no contradiction here, because Atisha's advice is intended for those who do not possess stable concentration. To attain stable concentration, at the beginning it is necessary to remain with one object because, if we keep changing the object, our concentration will never improve. However, when our concentration has become very firm, it is advisable to switch objects and to continue our training in tranquil abiding using a more subtle object. Thus, an Action Tantra practitioner meditates principally on the mind base until he or she reaches the third or fourth mental abiding. Then he switches to the more subtle object of the concentration of abiding in fire, and, when he receives signs of success in this concentration, he switches to the concentration of abiding in sound. To gain some familiarity with all the stages of Action Tantra, sometimes we can meditate briefly on all the concentrations from the Deity of emptiness up to the concentration of abiding in sound, but, if we are sincerely interested in attaining tranquil abiding, we should principally meditate on the mind base until we attain very stable concentration on this.

CONCENTRATION OF BESTOWING LIBERATION AT THE END OF SOUND

To practise the concentration of bestowing liberation at the end of sound, we meditate briefly on each of the concentrations from the Deity of emptiness up to abiding in sound. As we progress from the mind base through the concentration of abiding in fire to the concentration of abiding in sound, the object of meditation becomes progressively more subtle. After concentrating on the sound of the mantra for a while, we then stop the appearance of the sound, remember the emptiness that is lack of inherent existence, and meditate on this with a blissful mind.

Even if we understand emptiness correctly, if we fail to eliminate conventional appearances in meditation we will never realize emptiness directly, and so our meditation will not have the power to destroy delusions or the obstructions to omniscience. The main function of the fourth concentration is to overcome dualistic appearance and mix our mind more fully with emptiness. To accomplish this, the meditator employs both analytical and placement meditation on emptiness. Initially, he will have to alternate between these two types of meditation, but, when he attains a suppleness induced by wisdom, he gains the ability to analyze emptiness while remaining single-pointedly absorbed in emptiness. With this special wisdom, which is called 'superior seeing observing emptiness', the practitioner can go on to experience a non-conceptual bliss inseparable from emptiness.

The fourth concentration causes us to attain the Truth Body of a Buddha. The word 'liberation' in the name of this concentration refers to great liberation, or non-abiding nirvana, which is the Truth Body of a Buddha that is the ultimate nature of a Buddha's mind. The first three concentrations, from the Deity of emptiness up to the concentration of abiding in sound, principally cause us to attain the Form Body of a Buddha. According to the system of Action Tantra these four concentrations are sufficient causes of the two bodies of a Buddha.

The four concentrations are included within three yogas: the yoga of the great seal of body, the yoga of the speech of mantra and the yoga of the mind of the Truth Body. The first yoga comprises the meditations on the six Deities of the self base, as well as the other base, the mind base and the sound

Drubchen Dharmavajra

base, and principally causes the attainment of the body of a Buddha. The second yoga comprises the concentrations of abiding in fire and abiding in sound, and principally causes the attainment of the speech of a Buddha. The third yoga is the concentration of bestowing liberation at the end of sound, and principally causes the attainment of the mind of a Buddha. All practices of Action Tantra are included within these three yogas.

The yogas of body and speech are sometimes called 'yogas with signs' and the yoga of mind is called the 'yoga without signs'. Here, 'signs' refers to conventional objects. The yogas from the Deity of emptiness up to the concentration of abiding in sound focus principally on a conventional object, while the concentration of bestowing liberation at the end of sound focuses only on emptiness. All the paths of Action Tantra are either yogas with signs or yogas without signs.

HOW TO ACCOMPLISH THE COMMON AND UNCOMMON ATTAINMENTS ONCE WE HAVE EXPERIENCE OF THE FOUR CONCENTRATIONS

Through attaining deep experience of the four concentrations, we can accomplish the common and uncommon attainments. Common attainments include pacifying, increasing, controlling and wrathful actions, and are accomplished through the practice of both the yoga of self-generation as the Deity of the mind base, and the gross and subtle mantra recitation of the sound base. Through stable concentration on abiding in fire and abiding in sound, we will accomplish the eight great attainments:

1 The attainment of pills
2 The attainment of eye lotion

3 The attainment of seeing beneath the ground
4 The attainment of the sword
5 The attainment of flying
6 The attainment of invisibility
7 The attainment of longevity
8 The attainment of youth

When we accomplish the attainment of pills, we have the power to bless pills through the force of our concentration and mantra recitation. These pills can cure disease and increase the lifespan and good fortune of whoever tastes them. When we accomplish the attainment of eye lotion, we can bless medicinal substances through the force of concentration and recitation, so that whoever applies them to their eyes can see for a great distance and even through mountains. The attainment of seeing beneath the ground enables us to see hidden treasures. The attainment of the sword enables us to subdue our enemies and avert wars without bloodshed simply by holding aloft a ritual sword. The attainment of flying enables us to fly in the sky. The attainment of invisibility enables us to become invisible with the aid of a special substance. The attainment of longevity enables us to live for many aeons through the power of our concentration. The attainment of youth enables us to remain youthful and healthy, free from the sufferings of ageing and sickness.

Uncommon attainments are accomplished through completing both the yogas with signs and the yoga without signs. The supreme uncommon attainment is Buddhahood.

HOW TO PROGRESS THROUGH THE GROUNDS AND PATHS IN DEPENDENCE UPON ACTION TANTRA

We enter the path of accumulation of Action Tantra when we develop a spontaneous wish to attain enlightenment for the sake of all living beings by relying upon the paths of Action Tantra, and have also attained some experience of the yogas with signs. When we attain the realization of the concentration of bestowing liberation at the end of sound, we advance to the path of preparation. When, through continually meditating on the concentration of bestowing liberation at the end of sound, we attain a non-conceptual bliss inseparable from emptiness, we advance to the path of seeing. At the same time, we reach the first Bodhisattva ground and abandon intellectually-formed delusions. When our realization of emptiness acquires the power to abandon innate delusions, we advance to the path of meditation. On the path of meditation, we continue to meditate on both the yogas with signs, which are the method practices, and the yoga without signs, which is the wisdom practice, and through these meditations abandon first the innate delusions and then the obstructions to omniscience. When we have abandoned the most subtle obstructions to omniscience, we attain the Form Body and the Truth Body of a Buddha, and at the same time advance to the Path of No More Learning.

THE FAMILIES OF ACTION TANTRA DEITIES

There are three families of Action Tantra Deities: the Tathagata family, the Lotus family and the Vajra family. The Deities of the Tathagata family are manifestations of the vajra body of all the Buddhas. They are also known as the 'Vairochana family'. The principal Deities of the Tathagata family are Buddha Muni Trisamaya Guhyaraja, Buddha Muni Vajrasana, and Vajrasattva. The Lord of the Tathagata family is Manjushri, and the Mother of the family is Mairichi. Mairichi is a female Buddha whose name literally means 'Endowed with Rays of Light'. It is said that when the sun rises in the morning, Mairichi appears in the rays of sunlight. In Tibet it is customary for travellers to pay their respects to Mairichi at sunrise and recite her mantra, OM MAIRICHI MAM SOHA. If travellers say this mantra with faith, Mairichi blesses and protects them, removing dangers and obstacles on their journey and ensuring that their trip is successful. In the past, travellers faced dangers from wild animals and brigands, but these days they face the danger of car accidents and so forth. Contemplating the dangers faced by travellers, we should develop compassion and pray to Mairichi to protect them throughout their journey, and to help them return home safely and happily.

Other Deities of the Tathagata family of Action Tantra include Ushnishasitatarpati, Ushnishavijaya, Ushnishavimala, Ushnishachakravarti, Ushnishalalita, and the wrathful Deities Krodavijayakalpaguhyam, Chundidevi and Vasudhara.

The Deities of the Lotus family are manifestations of the vajra speech of all the Buddhas. They are also known as the 'Amitabha family'. The principal Deity of the Lotus family is Amitayus, the Lord of the family is Avalokiteshvara, and the Mothers are White Tara and Green Tara. Other Deities in this family include wrathful Hayagriva and Shri Mahadevi.

The Deities of the Vajra family are manifestations of the vajra mind of all the Buddhas. They are also known as the 'Akshobya family'. The principal Deity of the Vajra family is Buddha Unmoving, the Lords of the family are Vajravidarana and Vajrapani, and the Mother is Vajrajitanalapramohaninamadharani. Other Deities in the family include wrathful Kundalini and Vajradundi.

In the names of the three families, 'Tathagata' is a general name for Buddhas, 'Lotus' signifies the speech of Buddha, and 'Vajra' signifies the mind of Buddha. The Tathagata family is sometimes referred to as the 'higher family', the Lotus family as the 'middling family' and the Vajra family as the 'lower family'. However, this does not mean that the Deities of the Tathagata family are superior to the Deities of the other two families; it simply means that if we receive an empowerment into a Deity of the Tathagata family, we are automatically empowered to practise any Deity of the Lotus family or the Vajra family, and if we receive an empowerment into a Deity of the Lotus family, we are automatically empowered to practise any Deity of the Vajra family.

The explanation of Action Tantra presented here is based on Kachen Yeshe Gyaltsen's work called *Clear Meaning of Action Tantra*, Khedrubje's *Presentation of General Tantra* and Je Tsongkhapa's *Great Exposition of the Stages of Secret Mantra*.

PERFORMANCE TANTRA

It is said that only three scriptures of Performance Tantra have been translated into Tibetan: *Vairochanabhisambodhitantra*, which has twenty-six chapters, *Subsequent Tantra*, which has seven chapters, and *Vajrapani Empowerment Tantra*, which has twelve chapters. In addition to these, there are several commentaries to Performance Tantra written by Tibetan scholars.

As with Action Tantra, Performance Tantra is also divided into three families. Bhagawan Vairochana Abhisambodhi belongs to the Tathagata family, Hayagriva to the Lotus family and Vajrapani to the Vajra family.

Vairochanabhisambodhitantra explains the stages of Performance Tantra in great detail. According to this Tantra, Buddha Shakyamuni first attained enlightenment in Akanishta Pure Land in the form of an Enjoyment Body called Munivairochana. The sadhana of Munivairochana is explained in *Vairochanabhisambodhitantra*. We visualize Munivairochana as yellow in colour, sitting cross-legged on a white lotus. He has one face and two hands in the mudra of meditative equipoise. The mandala of Munivairochana has two floors and three sections: the inner mandala, the outer mandala and the outermost mandala. Munivairochana himself resides in the inner mandala together with thirty Deities. In addition to these there are forty-nine Deities in the outer mandala, and thirty-seven Deities in the outermost mandala, making one hundred and seventeen Deities in all.

To practise Performance Tantra, we first need to receive an empowerment of Performance Tantra. This is similar to an Action Tantra empowerment except that there is also an empowerment of four vases: the vase that purifies lower rebirth, the vase of all goodness, the vase that dispels obstructions, and the vase of love. The water of the first vase purifies taking rebirth in the lower realms, the water of the second purifies samsaric rebirth in general, the water of the third enables us to complete the collections of merit and wisdom, and the water of the fourth sows the seed of a Buddha's body.

The practices of Performance Tantra are very similar to those of Action Tantra and include the four concentrations and the yogas with signs and the yoga without signs.

YOGA TANTRA

The root Tantra of Yoga Tantra is *Condensation of Thatness Tantra*. Vajradhara taught an autocommentary to this called *Vajra Peak Explanatory Tantra*. In addition to these Tantras, there are many branch Tantras of Yoga Tantra.

The principal Deity of Yoga Tantra is Sarvavid, which literally means 'All-knowing One'. He is white in colour and very peaceful, with four faces and two hands in the mudra of meditative equipoise holding an eight-spoked wheel. He wears precious garments and sits in the vajra posture.

Yoga Tantra can be practised only by those who have received a Yoga Tantra empowerment, which is very similar to a Highest Yoga Tantra empowerment. As with Highest Yoga Tantra empowerments, Yoga Tantra empowerments include empowerments of the five Buddha families and the empowerment of the Vajrayana Spiritual Guide. Because the empowerments of the five Buddha families are granted, the disciples take on the commitments of the five Buddha families, and because the Vajrayana Spiritual Guide empowerment is granted, the disciples also take Tantric vows.

The practices of Yoga Tantra are explained in terms of basis, path and fruit. The basis is the objects to be purified, namely our ordinary body, speech and mind. The path consists of the four 'seals', or mudras, that purify the basis: the great seal of body, the seal of the speech of Dharma, the seal of the mind of commitment, and the seal of enlightened actions. These four seals lead to four fruits or final effects: the body of a Buddha, the speech of a Buddha, the mind of a Buddha, and the enlightened actions of a Buddha.

The great seal of body resembles generation stage of Highest Yoga Tantra and is accomplished when the practitioner develops perfect clear appearance of himself or herself generated as the Deity. When, having attained this realization, the practitioner can recite the mantra perfectly, he attains the seal of the speech of Dharma. The seal of the mind of commitment is a realization of the union of appearance and emptiness that is attained by meditating on emptiness while observing the body of the self-generation, and recognizing the Deity as a manifestation of emptiness. Having attained the seal of the mind of commitment, once the practitioner is able to overcome all ordinary appearances of his body, speech and mind, perceive all his bodily, verbal and mental actions as the actions of the Deity, and benefit others through these actions, he or she has attained the seal of enlightened actions.

The first, second and fourth seals are yogas with signs because their principal objects of meditation are conventional phenomena. The third seal is a yoga without signs because its principal object of meditation is emptiness. The third seal is called the 'seal of the mind of commitment' because it is a commitment of Yoga Tantra to practise the union of appearance and emptiness. The first, second and fourth seals are method practices, and the third seal is a wisdom practice. Through practising the union of method and wisdom, the practitioner attains a direct realization of emptiness and then progresses through the Bodhisattva grounds as explained in the other systems, until he or she finally attains Buddhahood.

Highest Yoga Tantra

Buddha Vajradhara revealed many different Tantras of Highest Yoga Tantra, but they are all included within two categories: Father Tantras and Mother Tantras. A Father Tantra principally reveals methods for attaining the illusory body, and a Mother Tantra principally reveals methods for attaining clear light. Examples of Father Tantras are Guhyasamaja Tantra and Yamantaka Tantra, and examples of Mother Tantras are Heruka Tantra and Hevajra Tantra. Some scholars assert that Father Tantras reveal methods for attaining male Deities and Mother Tantras methods for attaining female Deities, but this is incorrect. Heruka Tantra, for example, reveals methods for attaining a male Deity, but it is a Mother Tantra.

Highest Yoga Tantra is explained in four parts:

1 The five paths and the thirteen grounds of Highest Yoga Tantra
2 The Tantric vows and commitments
3 Generation stage
4 Completion stage

THE FIVE PATHS AND THE THIRTEEN GROUNDS OF HIGHEST YOGA TANTRA

There are five paths of Highest Yoga Tantra:

Gyalwa Ensapa

1 The path of accumulation of Highest Yoga Tantra
2 The path of preparation of Highest Yoga Tantra
3 The path of seeing of Highest Yoga Tantra
4 The path of meditation of Highest Yoga Tantra
5 The Path of No More Learning of Highest Yoga
   Tantra

To attain the path of accumulation of Highest Yoga Tantra
we must enter the path of Highest Yoga Tantra. Usually
it is said that a Highest Yoga Tantra empowerment is
the gateway to Highest Yoga Tantra, but receiving such
an empowerment merely qualifies us to engage in the
practice of Highest Yoga Tantra; it does not necessarily mean
that we have entered the path of Highest Yoga Tantra. To
enter the path of Highest Yoga Tantra, we must develop
Highest Yoga Tantra bodhichitta. This is done by developing
a spontaneous wish to attain the Union of No More Learning
for the sake of all living beings, on the basis of having
received a Highest Yoga Tantra empowerment. The Union
of No More Learning is the enlightenment of Highest Yoga
Tantra. When we generate a spontaneous wish to attain the
enlightenment of any vehicle, we have entered the path of
that vehicle. For example, when we develop a spontaneous
wish to attain a Hearer's enlightenment, we have entered the
path of the Hearers' Vehicle; when we develop a spontaneous
wish to attain a Solitary Conqueror's enlightenment, we
have entered the path of the Solitary Conquerors' Vehicle;
and when we develop a spontaneous wish to attain great
enlightenment, we have entered the path of the Great Vehicle.

Sutra Bodhisattvas have a bodhichitta that is a wish to
attain great enlightenment, or Buddhahood, but they do not
have a bodhichitta that is a wish to attain the Union of No

More Learning. The Union of No More Learning is explained only in Highest Yoga Tantra, and so only Bodhisattvas who practise this Tantra can develop a bodhichitta that is a wish to attain the Union of No More Learning. To understand the Union of No More Learning, we need to understand the union that needs learning; to understand this, we need to understand clear light and illusory body; to understand these, we need to understand isolated mind and isolated speech; and to understand these, we need to understand generation stage.

In Highest Yoga Tantra we can generate bodhichitta by bringing the future result into the present path. We do this by generating ourself as a Highest Yoga Tantra Deity, with the motivation of wishing to attain the Union of No More Learning for the sake of all living beings. Simply generating ourself as a Highest Yoga Tantra Deity without a special motivation is not bodhichitta, but doing so with the motivation just described is a powerful method for enhancing our bodhichitta that brings us much closer to the desired result. From this we can see that, from the point of view of how it is generated, Tantric bodhichitta is more profound than Sutra bodhichitta.

We enter the path of accumulation of Highest Yoga Tantra when we generate spontaneous Highest Yoga Tantra bodhichitta, and we remain on this path until we attain the realization of our inner winds entering, abiding and dissolving within the central channel through the force of completion stage meditation. In general, all the realizations of a person on generation stage, such as his or her realizations of renunciation, bodhichitta, emptiness, clear appearance and divine pride, are paths of accumulation of Highest Yoga Tantra.

When we attain completion stage realizations through dissolving our winds within the central channel, we advance to the path of preparation. We remain on this path until we attain a direct realization of emptiness with the mind of spontaneous great bliss, that is, until we attain the realization of meaning clear light, at which point we advance to the path of seeing and become a Superior being of Highest Yoga Tantra. There are five stages of completion stage: isolated speech, isolated mind, illusory body, clear light and union. All the realizations from the initial attainment of completion stage realizations up to just before meaning clear light are paths of preparation of Highest Yoga Tantra; all the realizations from the initial attainment of meaning clear light up to just before the attainment of the union of meaning clear light and illusory body are paths of seeing of Highest Yoga Tantra; all the realizations from the initial attainment of the union of meaning clear light and illusory body up to just before the attainment of Buddhahood are paths of meditation of Highest Yoga Tantra; and all the realizations of a Buddha are Paths of No More Learning of Highest Yoga Tantra.

There are thirteen grounds of Highest Yoga Tantra:

1 Very Joyful
2 Stainless
3 Luminous
4 Radiant
5 Difficult to Overcome
6 Approaching
7 Gone Afar
8 Immovable
9 Good Intelligence

10 Cloud of Dharma
11 Without Examples
12 Possessing Exalted Awareness
13 Holding the Vajra

The names of the first ten grounds are the same as the names of the ten Bodhisattva grounds explained in Sutra but they have different meanings. According to Highest Yoga Tantra, a Bodhisattva attains the first ground, Very Joyful, when he or she attains meaning clear light by realizing emptiness directly with the mind of spontaneous great bliss. When he rises from this meditative equipoise on emptiness, his meaning clear light becomes temporarily unmanifest and he attains the pure illusory body. At the same time he abandons all the delusion-obstructions. The simultaneous existence within one person's continuum of the pure illusory body and the abandonment of delusion-obstructions is called the 'union of abandonment', or the 'ordinary union'. After engaging in the practices of subsequent attainment during the meditation break, the Bodhisattva again manifests meaning clear light, either by means of meditation or by means of an action mudra. When in dependence upon either of these two methods he or she manifests meaning clear light again, the Bodhisattva attains the union of meaning clear light and pure illusory body, which is called the 'union of realization', or the 'principal union'. At this point he advances to the second ground, Stainless, and begins the path of meditation. The ordinary union is part of the path of seeing and part of the first ground, and the principal union prior to abandoning big-big obstructions to omniscience is part of the path of meditation and the second ground. In the book *Clear Light of Bliss* it says that when a Yogi emerges from the state of meaning clear light, at that moment he or she attains the pure illusory body and the path of meditation of Secret Mantra. The meaning here is that the Yogi attains the pure illusory body immediately upon rising from meaning clear light, and then goes on to attain the path of meditation.

With the attainment of the principal union, the Bodhisattva begins to abandon the obstructions to omniscience, such as dualistic appearances and ordinary appearances. There are nine levels of obstructions to omniscience, which are distinguished in terms of subtlety. They are: big-big, middling-big, small-big, big-middling, middling-middling, small-middling, big-small, middling-small and small-small. Just as when we wash very dirty clothes, the first wash removes the grossest dirt and later washes progressively remove more and more subtle stains, so we remove the grossest levels of obstructions to omniscience first and then progressively remove more and more subtle levels.

On the second ground, the Bodhisattva strives to abandon big-big obstructions to omniscience, and when he has done so he advances to the third ground. The fourth ground is attained when the middling-big obstructions have been abandoned, the fifth when the small-big obstructions have been abandoned, the sixth when the big-middling obstructions have been abandoned, the seventh when the middling-middling obstructions have been abandoned, the eighth when the small-middling obstructions have been abandoned, the ninth when the big-small obstructions have been abandoned, and the tenth when the middling-small obstructions have been abandoned. The eleventh and twelfth grounds are divisions of the tenth ground. The initial attainment of the tenth ground is called 'Cloud of Dharma'.

When this becomes very powerful for eliminating the small-small obstructions to omniscience, it transforms into Without Examples, and when it becomes powerful enough to function as the direct antidote to the small-small obstructions to omniscience, it transforms into Possessing Exalted Awareness. The ground of Possessing Exalted Awareness is an uninterrupted path. It is also known as the 'wisdom of the final continuum' and the 'vajra-like concentration of the path of meditation'. This is the last mind of a sentient being. The very next moment, the Bodhisattva attains the thirteenth ground, Holding the Vajra, which is the Union of No More Learning.

According to Sutra, the last part of the first ground belongs to the path of meditation, but according to Highest Yoga Tantra the first ground is necessarily a path of seeing. Unlike the path of seeing of Sutra, which abandons only intellectually-formed self-grasping, the path of seeing of Highest Yoga Tantra also abandons innate self-grasping.

These thirteen grounds are all grounds of Superior Mahayanists. If we include the ground of ordinary Bodhisattvas, there are fourteen grounds of Highest Yoga Tantra. The ground of ordinary Bodhisattvas comprises the paths of accumulation and preparation, and is usually called the 'ground of imaginary engagement' because on these two paths the Bodhisattva realizes emptiness by means of a generic image.

The way to progress through and complete the fourteen grounds of Highest Yoga Tantra is gradually to practise and complete the practices of the two stages – generation stage and completion stage. These days many people talk about Tantra, but there are few who teach the two stages. There are even teachers who never mention the two stages and yet claim to be teaching something even higher than Highest Yoga Tantra! I wonder what sort of Buddhahood these so-called Tantric Masters attain? It must be a very deluded kind of Buddhahood! Rather than following these 'modern Buddhas', we would do much better to emulate the great Yogis of the past, such as the eighty-four Mahasiddhas, and especially the highly renowned Nagarjuna.

There are predictions that, as times become more impure, people will become increasingly attracted to false Dharma and begin to show contempt for pure Dharma. False Dharma will flourish widely and it will become more and more difficult to meet pure Dharma. Since these predictions seem to be coming true, we are extremely fortunate to have met the pure and authentic teachings of Je Tsongkhapa. Je Tsongkhapa did not display miracle powers and clairvoyance, but instead taught the paths of Sutra and Tantra with unparalleled clarity and set an immaculate example for us to follow. It is rare to meet Buddhadharma, but it is even rarer to meet the Dharma of Je Tsongkhapa. To have met this perfect Dharma in such impure times is almost unbelievable good fortune!

THE TANTRIC VOWS AND COMMITMENTS

When we take a Highest Yoga Tantra empowerment, we take the vows of Highest Yoga Tantra as well as a number of commitments. It is very important to keep these commitments purely. If we keep our Tantric vows and commitments purely, and on this basis practise the generation and completion stages, we can attain Buddhahood in this life; but if we break our vows and commitments we create immense obstacles to our spiritual development. Keeping commitments is the best

Khedrub Sangye Yeshe

means to attain success in our generation and completion stage practices; it is the very life of Tantric practice.

There are two types of commitment: the commitments of the individual five Buddha families, and the commitments of the five Buddha families in common.

THE COMMITMENTS OF THE INDIVIDUAL
FIVE BUDDHA FAMILIES

There are nineteen commitments of the individual five Buddha families: the six commitments of the family of Buddha Vairochana, the four commitments of the family of Buddha Akshobya, the four commitments of the family of Buddha Ratnasambhava, the three commitments of the family of Buddha Amitabha and the two commitments of the family of Buddha Amoghasiddhi. The main purpose of the *Six Session Yoga*, which all Highest Yoga Tantra practitioners recite six times every day, is to remind us of these nineteen commitments of the five Buddha families, and to help us to keep them purely. The nineteen commitments will now be explained in detail.

THE SIX COMMITMENTS OF THE FAMILY OF
BUDDHA VAIROCHANA

1 To go for refuge to Buddha
2 To go for refuge to Dharma
3 To go for refuge to Sangha
4 To refrain from non-virtue
5 To practise virtue
6 To benefit others

A detailed explanation of the practice of going for refuge to the Three Jewels, and the practice of the three moral disciplines – the moral discipline of refraining from non-virtue, the moral discipline of gathering virtuous Dharmas and the moral discipline of benefiting other living beings – can be found in the book *Joyful Path of Good Fortune* and other Lamrim texts.

THE FOUR COMMITMENTS OF THE FAMILY OF BUDDHA AKSHOBYA

1 To keep a vajra to remind us to emphasize the development of great bliss through meditation on the central channel
2 To keep a bell to remind us to emphasize meditation on emptiness
3 To generate ourself as the Deity while realizing all things that we normally see do not exist
4 To rely sincerely upon our Spiritual Guide who leads us to the practice of the pure moral discipline of the Pratimoksha, Bodhisattva and Tantric vows

To keep a vajra to remind us to emphasize the development of great bliss through meditation on the central channel. There are two types of vajra: the outer vajra and the inner vajra. The outer vajra is a metal ritual object and the inner vajra is the mind of spontaneous great bliss. The inner vajra is also called the 'definitive vajra', or 'secret vajra'. To remind us that the development of the inner vajra of great bliss is our main practice, we have to keep an outer vajra, or at least a picture of one.

To keep a bell to remind us to emphasize meditation on emptiness. There are two types of bell: the outer bell and the inner bell. The outer bell is a metal ritual object and the inner bell is the wisdom directly realizing emptiness. To remind us of the meaning of emptiness, we have to keep an outer bell, or a picture of one. Through continually practising great bliss and emptiness, eventually we will attain the union of great bliss and emptiness, which is the very essence of Secret Mantra.

Keeping an outer vajra and bell also has many other great meanings. The vajra, for example, symbolizes the attainment of the five omniscient wisdoms and the five Buddha families. The five upper prongs of the vajra symbolize the attainment of the five omniscient wisdoms, and the five lower prongs symbolize the attainment of the five Buddha families. The bell symbolizes the practitioner's personal Deity and mandala. The rosary of vajras at the base of the bell symbolizes the protection circle; the rings above and below these symbolize the circle of the eight great charnel grounds (either outside or inside the protection circle); the space between the vajras and the lotus petals above them symbolizes the main mandala; the five prongs at the very top symbolize the assembly of the five wheels of Deities of Heruka's mandala; the face below these is the face of the Great Mother Perfection of Wisdom, who is the nature of Vajrayogini; and the eight letters symbolize the eight female Bodhisattvas, and the eight lotus petals the eight male Bodhisattvas, in the retinue of the Great Mother. Those who are practitioners of Deities other than Heruka or Vajrayogini can apply this explanation to their Deity and mandala in a similar way.

In conclusion, the significance of the vajra and bell is that, by accomplishing our personal Deity and the Deity's mandala, we will attain the five omniscient wisdoms and the five Buddha families. Realizing that the vajra and bell represent our personal Deity and mandala, we should always regard them as objects of the Field for Accumulating Merit and make offerings to them.

To generate ourself as the Deity while realizing all things that we normally see do not exist. The most effective way to overcome ordinary appearances and ordinary conceptions, which are the root of samsara, is to meditate on self-generation; therefore, we need to become very familiar with this practice. To help us to do this, Vajradhara gave us a commitment to generate ourself as our Deity, or Yidam, six times every day. Ideally we should maintain divine pride and clear appearance of being the Deity twenty-four hours a day but, if we cannot, we should at least try to restore our divine pride and clear appearance by meditating briefly on self-generation once every four hours. Even if we do not have the time to meditate in detail on the body of the Deity, we should at least remember it by thinking, 'I am Heruka', or, 'I am Vajrayogini'. If we maintain divine pride of being the Deity, all our daily actions, even those that are seemingly non-virtuous, will become methods for attaining enlightenment and benefiting others. Therefore, we should think, 'To benefit all living beings, I must attain the holy body of my Yidam and a holy mind that is inseparable from great bliss and emptiness.' Then, with this motivation, we should generate ourself in the aspect of our Deity, hold the vajra, and play the bell.

To rely sincerely upon our Spiritual Guide who leads us to the practice of the pure moral discipline of the

Pratimoksha, Bodhisattva and Tantric vows. Since all the attainments of Secret Mantra depend upon our receiving the blessings of our Vajrayana Spiritual Guide, relying sincerely upon him or her is the most important practice for Secret Mantra practitioners. Therefore, we have a commitment to remember our Spiritual Guide at least six times every day so as to increase our faith in him or her.

THE FOUR COMMITMENTS OF THE FAMILY OF BUDDHA RATNASAMBHAVA

1 To give material help
2 To give Dharma
3 To give fearlessness
4 To give love

To give material help. The actual commitment here is to develop the thought to give material things six times every day, and then, when we are out of meditation, to give as much as we are able. Even if we are poor, we can give a little food to birds and animals or practise the kusali tsog offering.

To give Dharma. Here the commitment is to remember six times every day that it is our duty to help others through giving Dharma. Even if we cannot give formal Dharma teachings, we should take every opportunity to help others by giving them spiritual advice in skilful ways. We can also give Dharma by dedicating our spiritual practice to others, imagining that we are surrounded by all living beings and reciting prayers and mantras on their behalf; or we can give Dharma by practising the yoga of purifying migrators, in which we send out light rays to all living beings, purifying them of all their obstructions.

To give fearlessness. We give fearlessness by protecting others from fear and danger. If we cannot do anything directly to protect others, at least we should make prayers and dedicate our merit so that others may become free from fear and danger.

To give love. To fulfil this commitment, we should try to develop the thought, 'How wonderful it would be if all living beings could be happy. May they be happy. I will help them to become happy.' We should begin by developing such thoughts about our family and friends, and then gradually increase the scope of our love until it embraces all living beings. In short, we should try to cherish others and maintain affectionate love for all living beings.

THE THREE COMMITMENTS OF THE FAMILY OF BUDDHA AMITABHA

1. To rely upon the teachings of Sutra
2. To rely upon the teachings of the two lower classes of Tantra
3. To rely upon the teachings of the two higher classes of Tantra

To fulfil these commitments, we need to listen to, contemplate and meditate on the instructions of the three vehicles of Sutra – the Hearers' Vehicle, the Solitary Conquerors' Vehicle and the Perfection Vehicle – and on the instructions of Action Tantra and Performance Tantra (the two lower classes of

Tantra), and Yoga Tantra and Highest Yoga Tantra (the two higher classes of Tantra). The simplest way to rely upon the instructions of the three vehicles of Sutra is to study, contemplate and meditate on Lamrim, because Lamrim includes all these instructions. Buddha gave the instructions of the Hearers' and Solitary Conquerors' Vehicles in the *Sutra on the Four Noble Truths*. These instructions are all included in the teachings of the intermediate scope of Lamrim. As for the instructions of the Perfection Vehicle, these were given by Buddha in the *Perfection of Wisdom Sutras* and are all included in the teachings of the great scope of Lamrim. The simplest way to rely upon the teachings of the four classes of Tantra is to follow Atisha's advice to the translator Rinchen Sangpo, which is explained in the book *The New Guide to Dakini Land*.

The three commitments of Buddha Amitabha teach us that we must take all Buddha's teachings as personal advice and put them into practice. We should remember this six times every day.

THE TWO COMMITMENTS OF THE FAMILY OF BUDDHA AMOGHASIDDHI

1 To make offerings to our Spiritual Guide
2 To strive to maintain purely all the vows we have taken

To make offerings to our Spiritual Guide. This commitment is to make outer, inner, secret and thatness offerings to our Spiritual Guide.

To strive to maintain purely all the vows we have taken. We fulfil this commitment by reminding ourself that we need to

Panchen Losang Chokyi Gyaltsen

keep to the best of our ability all the vows and commitments we have taken.

THE COMMITMENTS OF THE FIVE BUDDHA
FAMILIES IN COMMON

We keep these commitments by abandoning the fourteen root downfalls and other downfalls of the Secret Mantra vows.

THE FOURTEEN ROOT DOWNFALLS OF THE
SECRET MANTRA VOWS

The fourteen root downfalls are:

1 Abusing or scorning our Spiritual Guide
2 Showing contempt for the precepts
3 Criticizing our vajra brothers and sisters
4 Abandoning love for any being
5 Giving up aspiring or engaging bodhichitta
6 Scorning the Dharma of Sutra or Tantra
7 Revealing secrets to an unsuitable person
8 Abusing our body
9 Abandoning emptiness
10 Relying upon malevolent friends
11 Not recollecting the view of emptiness
12 Destroying others' faith
13 Not maintaining commitment objects
14 Scorning women

Abusing or scorning our Spiritual Guide. In this context our Spiritual Guide is anyone from whom we have received both the empowerment of our personal Yidam and the commentary to that practice. If we decide not to rely upon our Spiritual Guide any more, we incur a root Tantric downfall. Developing non-faith or anger towards our Spiritual Guide are very heavy negative actions and block Tantric realizations but, unless we make a definite decision to abandon him or her, they do not constitute a root downfall.

Showing contempt for the precepts. We incur this downfall by showing contempt for any Pratimoksha, Bodhisattva, or Tantric vows we have taken by thinking, 'I do not need to observe this vow.' For example, if, after having taken Tantric vows, we hold the view that it does not matter if we break our Pratimoksha or Bodhisattva vows, we incur a root downfall.

Criticizing our vajra brothers and sisters. All those who have received a Tantric empowerment from the same Spiritual Guide are vajra brothers and sisters, irrespective of whether or not they received empowerments at the same time. If we criticize our vajra brothers or sisters with a bad motivation, we incur a root downfall. However, since the object of this downfall must be a person who has Tantric vows in his or her continuum, if a vajra brother or sister has broken their Tantric vows and we criticize him or her, we do not incur an actual root downfall.

Abandoning love for any being. We incur this downfall by wishing for someone to experience suffering or by strongly deciding never to help someone.

Giving up aspiring or engaging bodhichitta. This downfall is the same as the last root downfall of the Bodhisattva vows. Since bodhichitta is the foundation of all Tantric practice, if we abandon bodhichitta we incur a root Tantric downfall.

Scorning the Dharma of Sutra or Tantra. If we criticize any teaching of Buddha, claiming that it is not the word of Buddha, and if someone else hears our criticism, we incur a root Tantric downfall. This downfall teaches us that Tantric practitioners must respect Sutra teachings because Sutra practices are the foundation for all Tantric realizations.

Revealing secrets to an unsuitable person. We incur this downfall by knowingly teaching Secret Mantra to those who have not received a Tantric empowerment. The function of an empowerment is to ripen the disciple's mind for Tantric practice. Unless our minds are ripened by an empowerment, we cannot attain Tantric realizations, no matter how long we meditate. If we teach Secret Mantra to people without an empowerment, they may be tempted to meditate on it and, when they fail to attain results, conclude that Secret Mantra does not work. For this reason, Vajradhara made a rule against teaching Tantra to people without empowerments.

Abusing our body. To practise Secret Mantra we need a strong and healthy body because, if our bodily strength decreases, our drops will also decrease, and then it will be difficult for us to generate spontaneous great bliss. For this reason, if we deliberately cause the strength of our body to decrease by engaging in ascetic practices motivated by the thought that the body is impure, we incur a root downfall. Instead of regarding our body as impure, we should generate ourself in a Deity body. We also incur this downfall if we decide to commit suicide.

Abandoning emptiness. Success in generation and completion stage practices depends upon an understanding of emptiness. If we do not yet understand the Prasangika view of emptiness, we should at least study and meditate on the Chittamatra view. If we completely stop trying to develop or improve our understanding of emptiness, we incur a root downfall.

Relying upon malevolent friends. We incur this downfall by allowing ourself to come under the influence of people who criticize the Three Jewels or our Spiritual Guide, who harm Buddhadharma, or who interfere with the spiritual practice of many living beings. Mentally we should develop love and compassion for such people, but we should not become too close to them physically or verbally. We also incur this downfall if we have the power to help such people through pure wrathful actions but do not attempt to do so.

Not recollecting the view of emptiness. If we have some understanding of the view of emptiness as taught in the Chittamatra or Prasangika schools and we remain for a day without recollecting emptiness, with the motivation to neglect Vajradhara's speech, we incur a root downfall. Vajradhara made it a commitment to remember emptiness because the practice of emptiness is most important for all Tantric realizations.

Destroying others' faith. If we cause someone's faith in Secret Mantra to degenerate by telling him that the practice of Secret Mantra is very dangerous and advising him to remain with Sutra practices, we incur a root downfall.

Not maintaining commitment objects. One way to incur this downfall is to refuse to accept the various commitment substances passed round during an empowerment or the substances offered in a tsog offering puja, thinking that these substances are unclean. Another way is not to keep a vajra and bell, thinking that these objects are meaningless. Yogis or Yoginis who have attained the realization of isolated mind also incur this downfall if they refuse to accept an action mudra without good reason.

Scorning women. If a male practitioner criticizes women, saying, 'Women are bad', he incurs a root downfall. Among women, there are many emanations of Vajrayogini, and by criticizing women in general we criticize these emanations and thereby block our development of bliss. Female practitioners incur a similar root downfall if they criticize men.

Abandoning these root downfalls is called the 'root commitment'. Besides these, there are three types of branch commitment:

1 The commitments of abandonment
2 The commitments of reliance
3 The additional commitments of abandonment

THE COMMITMENTS OF ABANDONMENT

The general commitment of abandonment is to try to abandon any faults we possess. We cannot abandon all faults immediately, but at least we should have the aspiration to do so. If we lose this aspiration, we break the commitment of abandonment. Specifically, the commitments of abandonment are to abandon negative actions, especially killing, stealing, sexual misconduct, lying and taking intoxicants.

Atisha said that the Bodhisattva vows and Tantric vows are more powerful if they are taken on the basis of the Pratimoksha vows. Although it is not absolutely necessary for lay people to take the five precepts of the Pratimoksha vows before receiving Tantric vows, if they are serious about attaining Tantric realizations they will definitely try to keep these five precepts. The five precepts are: to abandon killing, to abandon stealing, to abandon sexual misconduct, to abandon lying and to abandon taking intoxicants. If we take these five precepts with the motivation of renunciation, they are Pratimoksha vows. Lay Tantric practitioners should possess these vows. The reason for the fifth vow is that drinking alcohol, smoking cigarettes, taking drugs, etc., cause our mindfulness, concentration, and mental and physical suppleness to degenerate, and thereby create serious obstacles to our gaining realizations of either Sutra or Tantra.

THE COMMITMENTS OF RELIANCE

The commitments of reliance are to rely sincerely upon our Spiritual Guide, to be respectful towards our vajra brothers and sisters, and to observe the ten virtuous actions. To keep these commitments, we need to rely upon our Spiritual Guide with faith and respect; maintain respect for our Dharma friends, regarding male friends as Heroes and female friends as Heroines; and practise the ten virtuous actions, especially trying to gain experience of Lamrim and the two stages of Secret Mantra.

THE ADDITIONAL COMMITMENTS OF ABANDONMENT

The additional commitments of abandonment are to abandon the causes of turning away from the Mahayana, to avoid scorning gods and to avoid stepping over sacred objects. To keep these commitments, we should abandon actions and attitudes that cause our Mahayana practice to deteriorate, such as hatred, wishing to attain liberation for ourself alone, thinking that Buddhahood is too great a goal for us to attain, or falling under the influence of people who dislike the Mahayana. We must also avoid showing contempt for gods, demi-gods, nagas and spirits; and avoid stepping over statues or pictures of Buddhas, Bodhisattvas and our Spiritual Guide, or over Dharma books, ritual implements such as vajras and bells, and flowers, food, water and so forth that have been offered to the Three Jewels.

THE GROSS DOWNFALLS OF THE
SECRET MANTRA VOWS

Gross downfalls are lighter than root downfalls but heavier than branch downfalls. There are eleven gross downfalls:

1 Relying upon an unqualified mudra
2 Engaging in union without the three recognitions

Drubchen Gendun Gyaltsen

3 Showing secret substances to an unsuitable person
4 Fighting or arguing during a tsog offering ceremony
5 Giving false answers to questions asked out of faith
6 Staying seven days in the home of someone who rejects the Vajrayana
7 Pretending to be a Yogi while remaining imperfect
8 Revealing holy Dharma to those with no faith
9 Engaging in mandala actions without completing a close retreat
10 Needlessly transgressing the Pratimoksha or Bodhisattva precepts
11 Acting in contradiction to the *Fifty Verses on the Spiritual Guide*

Relying upon an unqualified mudra. For qualified practitioners, relying upon an action mudra or consort is the best method for generating and increasing great bliss. An action mudra must have certain qualifications. At the very least, he or she must have received a Tantric empowerment, keep the Tantric commitments and understand the meaning of the two stages of Secret Mantra. If we rely upon an unqualified consort solely out of desirous attachment, we incur a gross downfall.

Engaging in union without the three recognitions. When we engage in union with a consort, we must maintain three recognitions throughout: to recognize our body as the body of a Deity, to recognize our speech as mantra and to recognize our mind as the Truth Body. If we engage in union without these recognitions we incur a gross downfall.

Showing secret substances to an unsuitable person. We incur this downfall if, without a good reason, we show our Tantric ritual objects such as our vajra and bell, mandala, Tantric scriptures, mala, statue or picture of our Yidam, hand implements of the Deity, damaru, khatanga, or skullcup to those without empowerments or to those who have received empowerments but who have no faith. However, if our motivation for displaying these objects is to encourage others to develop faith in Secret Mantra we do not incur a downfall.

Fighting or arguing during a tsog offering ceremony. During a tsog offering ceremony we need to maintain divine pride and pure view, seeing the assembly as Heroes and Heroines. If we lose pure view, develop anger and start arguing or fighting we incur a gross downfall.

Giving false answers to questions asked out of faith. If someone out of faith asks us a sincere question about Dharma, and out of miserliness we refuse to give a correct answer, we incur a gross downfall.

Staying seven days in the home of someone who rejects the Vajrayana. We incur this downfall if, without a good reason, we stay for more than seven days in the home of a person who is critical of the Vajrayana.

Pretending to be a Yogi while remaining imperfect. We incur this downfall if we claim to be a great Tantric Yogi or Yogini just because we know how to perform Tantric rituals.

Revealing holy Dharma to those with no faith. We incur this downfall if we teach Secret Mantra to those who have received an empowerment but who have no faith in Secret Mantra.

Engaging in mandala actions without completing a close retreat. If we perform a self-initiation, grant initiation to others, or perform a fire puja and so forth, without having completed the appropriate retreats, we incur a gross downfall.

Needlessly transgressing the Pratimoksha or Bodhisattva precepts. If we think that since we are now Tantric practitioners we can ignore our Pratimoksha or Bodhisattva vows, we incur a gross downfall.

Acting in contradiction to the *Fifty Verses on the Spiritual Guide*. The *Fifty Verses on the Spiritual Guide* explain how we should rely upon our Spiritual Guide by means of action. If we neglect these instructions, we incur a gross downfall.

THE UNCOMMON COMMITMENTS OF MOTHER TANTRA

There are eight uncommon commitments of Mother Tantra:

1 To perform all physical actions first with our left, to make offerings to our Spiritual Guide and never to abuse him
2 To abandon union with those unqualified
3 While in union, not to be separated from the view of emptiness

4 Never to lose appreciation for the path of attachment

5 Never to forsake the two kinds of mudra

6 To strive mainly for the external and internal methods

7 Never to release seminal fluid; to rely upon pure behaviour

8 To abandon repulsion when tasting bodhichitta

To perform all physical actions first with our left, to make offerings to our Spiritual Guide and never to abuse him. In Secret Mantra, the left symbolizes the wisdom of clear light, the main practice of Mother Tantra. Whenever we engage in physical actions, if possible we should begin from the left. For example, when we take hold of something we should do so first with our left hand, and then switch to the right hand if necessary. Similarly, when we arrange offerings on the shrine we should begin from the left hand side of the object to which the offerings will be made. The purpose of this commitment is to remind us to accomplish the wisdom of clear light.

To abandon union with those unqualified. When the time comes for us to rely upon an action mudra, we must rely upon a consort who does the same generation and completion stage practices as we do, and who has a good nature and loving-kindness. If we do this, we will attain great results from union with a consort, just like Mahasiddha Ghantapa in the true story told in the book *The New Guide to Dakini Land*. On the other hand, if we rely upon an unqualified consort solely out of attachment, we will experience great obstacles to our daily practice.

While in union, not to be separated from the view of emptiness. By maintaining the view of emptiness while in union with a consort, we will experience the bliss of union in a meaningful way, we will prevent it from causing our delusions to increase, and our act of union will be a cause for our developing and increasing the realizations of Tantra.

Never to lose appreciation for the path of attachment. Secret Mantra is sometimes known as the 'path of attachment' because it is the method for transforming attachment into a cause for generating spontaneous great bliss. Because the beings of this world have very strong attachment, we definitely need to practise Secret Mantra, and so, having found such a wonderful practice, we must never lose our appreciation for it.

Never to forsake the two kinds of mudra. The two kinds of mudra are action mudras and wisdom mudras. When we are qualified, we should accept an action mudra. Until then we should rely upon a visualized wisdom mudra to help us to develop great bliss.

To strive mainly for the external and internal methods. The external method for developing spontaneous great bliss is to rely upon a wisdom mudra or action mudra, and the internal method is to meditate on our channels, drops and winds.

Never to release seminal fluid; to rely upon pure behaviour. Although we should try to develop great bliss in dependence upon external or internal methods, we should try not to release red or white drops. Releasing our drops interferes with our development of great bliss.

To abandon repulsion when tasting bodhichitta. If we do lose our drops, we should regard them as the secret substance from the union of the Father and Mother Deities and mentally imagine that we taste them and receive the secret empowerment. When doing so, we should abandon any feelings of repulsion.

It is possible that there are some Tantric commitments that we cannot keep at the moment. This does not matter. The most important thing is to know all these commitments and never to abandon the intention to keep them purely in the future. By keeping this intention, we keep our commitments. It is especially important to keep the precious mind of bodhichitta and the correct view of emptiness in our mind day and night by practising Lamrim. If we can do this, there will be no basis for our incurring downfalls of our Sutra vows. If, in addition, we can keep clear appearance and divine pride by practising generation stage, there will be no basis for our incurring downfalls of our Tantric vows. From this we can see that the practices of Lamrim and Tantra are of equal importance.

Generation Stage

Generation stage is explained in five parts:

1 Definition and etymology of generation stage
2 Divisions of generation stage
3 How to practise actual generation stage meditation
4 The measurement of having completed generation stage
5 How to advance from generation stage to completion stage

DEFINITION AND ETYMOLOGY
OF GENERATION STAGE

The definition of generation stage is a realization of a creative yoga prior to attaining the actual completion stage, which is attained through the practice of bringing any of the three bodies into the path. It is called a 'creative yoga' because its object is created, or generated, by correct imagination. Generation stages are so called because they are stages of the path and their objects are generated by correct imagination. Generation stage, fabricated yoga and yoga of the first stage are synonyms.

Generation stage is a yoga of divine body. A yoga is a path to liberation or enlightenment. A yoga of divine body is a yoga that has the aspect of either the Form Body or the Truth

Drungpa Tsondru Gyaltsen

Body of a Buddha. If a yoga of divine body possesses the following four attributes it is classed as generation stage: (1) it is not developed through the winds entering, abiding and dissolving within the central channel through the force of meditation; (2) it functions to ripen the realizations of completion stage; (3) it is similar in aspect to any of the three bodies of death, intermediate state, or rebirth; and (4) its main object is an imagined Deity body.

The first attribute excludes meditation on self-generation and on bringing the three bodies into the path performed after attaining completion stage realizations. The second and third attributes exclude the yogas of Action Tantra and Performance Tantra. Although these Tantras include yogas of divine body, these yogas do not serve to ripen the realizations of completion stage, nor are they similar in aspect to any of the three bodies of death, intermediate state, or rebirth. The fourth attribute indicates that the Deity body of generation stage is not an actual Deity body but simply an imagined or mentally generated one. For example, when generation stage practitioners generate themselves as Vajrayogini, the object of their meditation is not the actual body of Vajrayogini but an imagined Deity body. Just as a potter is not a pot, but the production of a pot depends upon him, so although the imagined Deity body of generation stage is not the actual Deity body, nevertheless the development of an actual Deity body depends upon it. Thus, through the force of our meditating on an imagined Deity body, eventually our continuously residing body, or very subtle wind, will become an actual Deity body. From this we can see that generation stage meditation is indispensable for the attainment of Buddhahood.

It is very important to understand precisely what is the observed object, appearing object and conceived object of generation stage meditation. Let us take the example of a Vajrayogini practitioner called John. Normally when he thinks, 'I am John', he does not think that his body is John or that his mind is John; rather, he observes either his body or mind and simply thinks, 'I am John.' Therefore, his mind thinking 'I am John' is not a wrong awareness but a valid cognizer. In a similar way, when he meditates on the generation stage of Vajrayogini, he first generates himself as Vajrayogini in accordance with the sadhana and, when he reaches the actual generation stage meditation, he observes the imagined body or mind of Vajrayogini that he has generated and simply thinks, 'I am Vajrayogini.' At that time, he has changed his basis for imputing I. He does not think that John is Vajrayogini, or that the imagined body or mind of Vajrayogini that he generated is Vajrayogini; rather, he simply observes the body or mind of Vajrayogini that he generated and thinks, 'I am Vajrayogini.' Therefore, his mind thinking 'I am Vajrayogini' is not a wrong awareness but a valid cognizer.

From this, we can understand that the observed object, appearing object and conceived object of generation stage meditation is an imagined Deity body that is generated by pure concentration. The imagined Deity body is a form that is a phenomena source, which means that it is a form that appears clearly only to the mental awareness. Other forms such as tables and chairs are form sources because they appear clearly to the eye awareness. Phenomena sources are the sources from which mental awarenesses develop, and form sources are the sources from which sense awarenesses develop.

Before Je Tsongkhapa appeared in Tibet, many Tantric practitioners experienced great confusion about generation stage meditation. Some even believed that it had no correct object and was therefore a wrong awareness, and they concluded that meditation on generation stage was pointless. Je Tsongkhapa however explained very clearly the purpose of generation stage, and explained precisely what are the objects of generation stage meditation. Through his kindness, we now know how to enter into, progress through and complete generation stage; and so we have great confidence that we can attain the realization of generation stage, and thereby the Union of No More Learning, or Buddhahood, in this life.

As Nagarjuna explained, attaining enlightenment, or Buddhahood, is simply a matter of progressing step by step through the common paths, then the paths of generation stage and then the paths of completion stage, from which we can proceed directly to our final destination of Buddhahood. The paths of generation stage are extremely beneficial because they lead to the paths of completion stage, and the paths of completion stage lead directly to Buddhahood. By practising the paths of generation stage, we will be cared for by our personal Deity throughout this and all our future lives. We will receive powerful blessings from our personal Deity and, as a result, receive all the attainments. Moreover, meditation on generation stage is an extremely effective method for overcoming ordinary appearances and ordinary conceptions, and is a powerful purification practice that purifies our environment, enjoyments, body, speech and mind. There is no doubt that a pure practitioner of generation stage will be reborn in the Pure Land of his or her Deity if he or she so wishes.

If we practise meditation on an imagined Deity body continually, we will gradually perceive that Deity body more and more clearly. The generic image will become more and more transparent until it finally disappears altogether and we attain a yogic direct perceiver of the imagined Deity body. If we then improve this yogic direct perceiver by means of completion stage practices, eventually we will obtain the actual divine body, the illusory body.

It is not only in Tantra that a mentally generated object transforms into a real object. Even in Sutra it is said that if we meditate on a mentally generated object for long enough with strong concentration, eventually it will appear clearly to a direct perceiver. Dharmakirti said that even if we concentrate on an incorrect object, eventually through the force of familiarity it will appear clearly to our mind. If we are strongly attached to someone, we see his or her body as very attractive. His eyes, his hair, his figure and so forth all appear directly to our eye awareness as beautiful, but where does this beauty come from? After all, not everyone sees him as beautiful. The beauty we perceive has been generated by our mind. How? Because we have focused our mind exclusively on his attractive qualities, finally his body appears directly to our sense awareness as attractive, and we conceive him as attractive. If we later quarrel with that person, he or she will start to appear as unattractive to us. Why? Simply because our attitude towards him has changed. Chandrakirti said that the mind generates everything. If our mind generates Buddhahood, we will attain Buddhahood, and if it generates a hell, we will be in hell.

The world and the beings who inhabit it all depend upon the mind. When we look around, we naturally feel that everything we see exists from its own side, but, if we check more carefully, we will see that in reality everything depends upon the mind for its existence. For example, the house we live in began in an architect's mind. If no one had conceived of this house, it would never have been built. The mind makes a plan and the body carries out the plan. Without first forming an idea of what we want to make in our minds, we can never physically make anything. If external phenomena such as houses depend upon the mind, it goes without saying that internal phenomena such as the three bodies of a Buddha also depend upon the mind.

The most important practices of generation stage are the three bringings: bringing death into the path to the Truth Body, bringing the intermediate state into the path to the Enjoyment Body, and bringing rebirth into the path to the Emanation Body. These can be practised both at the level of generation stage and at the level of completion stage.

The definition of bringing death into the path to the Truth Body is a yoga, similar in aspect to the experience of death, that has the divine pride of being the Truth Body. To meditate on this, we gather all appearances of the world (the container), and all living beings and other conventional objects (the contents) into emptiness by following the instructions in the sadhana. We imagine that all these phenomena melt into light and dissolve into emptiness, while at the same time imagining that we experience progressively all the signs of death. We think that this emptiness is the Truth Body and impute I onto it, thinking, 'I am the Truth Body.'

The definition of bringing the intermediate state into the path to the Enjoyment Body is a yoga, similar in aspect to the experience of the intermediate state, or bardo, that is attained after bringing death into the path to the Truth Body, and that has the divine pride of being the Enjoyment Body. To meditate on this, we imagine that, from the sphere of the bliss and emptiness of the Truth Body, our mind arises in the form of the seed-letter of the Deity, or some other representation of the Deity. Observing this, and experiencing it as similar in aspect to the intermediate state, we generate divine pride thinking, 'I am the Enjoyment Body.'

The definition of bringing rebirth into the path to the Emanation Body is a yoga, similar in aspect to the experience of rebirth, that is attained after bringing the intermediate state into the path to the Enjoyment Body, and that has the divine pride of being the Emanation Body. To meditate on this, while in the aspect of the seed-letter, or some other symbolic form, we imagine that a new, pure world and inhabitants develop. We then imagine that we are reborn in this world in the form of our Yidam and, observing this, generate divine pride thinking, 'I am the Emanation Body.'

If we understand how to practise the three bringings in conjunction with one Deity, we can then apply this understanding to other Deities. There now follows an explanation of how to practise the three bringings in conjunction with Vajrayogini.

BRINGING DEATH INTO THE PATH
TO THE TRUTH BODY

This practice has three main functions: it purifies ordinary death, it causes the realization of clear light to ripen, and it increases our collection of wisdom. In this meditation we cultivate experiences similar to those that we experience when we die by imagining that we perceive the signs that occur during the death process, from the mirage-like appearance to the appearance of clear light.

We begin by practising the preliminaries, including Guru yoga, according to the sadhana. Then, having requested our

Guru to bless our mind and imagined that he has entered our heart, we develop three recognitions: (1) the nature of our Guru's mind is the union of great bliss and emptiness; (2) our Guru's mind has mixed inseparably with our own mind, transforming it into the union of great bliss and emptiness; and (3) our mind of great bliss is in the aspect of a red letter BAM at our heart. We meditate on this for a while.

Then the letter BAM begins to increase in size, gradually melting our body into blissful red light, just as warm water melts ice when it is poured onto it. The letter BAM expands until it has absorbed our whole body. Continuing to expand, it gradually absorbs our room, our house, our town, our country, our continent, our world and finally the whole universe, including all the living beings who inhabit it. Everything is absorbed and transformed into an infinitely large letter BAM that pervades the whole of space, and which is the nature of our mind of great bliss and emptiness. We perceive nothing but this letter BAM and we meditate on this single-pointedly for a while. We think, 'I have purified all living beings, together with their environments.'

After a while, the letter BAM begins to contract, gradually gathering inwards from the edges of infinite space and leaving behind only emptiness. It becomes smaller and smaller until there remains only a minute letter BAM. Then this minute letter BAM gradually dissolves, from the bottom up to the horizontal line at the head of the BAM. As mentioned before, throughout this meditation we imagine that we undergo experiences similar to those experienced by a dying person. At this point we imagine that we perceive the mirage-like appearance that arises due to the dissolution of the earth element. The head of the BAM then dissolves into the crescent moon, and we imagine that we

Konchog Gyaltsen

perceive the smoke-like appearance that arises due to the dissolution of the water element. The crescent moon then dissolves into the drop, and we imagine that we perceive the sparkling-fireflies-like appearance that arises due to the dissolution of the fire element. The drop then dissolves into the nada, and we imagine that we perceive the candle-flame-like appearance that arises due to the dissolution of the wind element.

These four appearances are the inner signs of the dissolution of the winds that support our four bodily elements. When we die, these four winds gradually absorb, and because of this we experience these four signs. Normally when the fourth sign of the death process, the candle-flame-like appearance, is perceived, all gross memory, gross inner winds and gross appearances cease, and the external breathing stops.

At this point in the meditation, all that remains is the nada. After a while we imagine that we experience the fifth sign, the mind of white appearance. With each successive dissolution, the mind becomes increasingly subtle. When the lower curve of the nada dissolves upwards into the middle curve, we imagine that we experience the mind of red increase, and when the middle curve dissolves into the upper curve, we imagine that we experience the mind of black near-attainment. Finally the upper curve dissolves into emptiness and we imagine that we experience the most subtle mind, the mind of clear light.

At this stage we should have four recognitions: (1) we imagine that our mind of clear light has actually manifested and that it is experiencing great bliss; (2) only emptiness appears to our mind; (3) we identify this emptiness as lack of inherent existence; and (4) we imagine that we have attained the Truth Body of a Buddha and think, 'I am the Truth Body.' We then meditate on the mind of clear light while trying to maintain constantly these four recognitions.

Without being distracted from the main meditation, from time to time we should use one part of our mind to check that none of these recognitions is missing. If we find that we have lost one or more of them, we should apply skilful effort to re-establish them. If we meditate in this way every day, even with weak concentration, we will increase our collection of wisdom.

When through completion stage meditation we are able to cause our inner winds to enter, abide and dissolve within our central channel at the heart chakra, we experience the isolated mind of example clear light. Once we have attained this realization, our death will no longer be an uncontrolled, samsaric process, but we will be able to control the process of dying by transforming the clear light of death into the mind of ultimate example clear light. This is the quick path to Buddhahood. When we rise from this clear light, instead of entering the ordinary intermediate state with an intermediate state body, we will attain the illusory body. From this subtle body, instead of having to take an ordinary rebirth, we will emanate a gross divine body similar to the Emanation Body of a Buddha.

In summary, the attainment of ultimate example clear light depends upon training in meditation on bringing death into the path to the Truth Body. To meditate on bringing death into the path to the Truth Body, we must first prevent all ordinary appearances by perceiving every-thing as empty. We should identify this emptiness as lack of inherent existence, and imagine that our mind merges with this emptiness. Then, with a feeling that our mind is completely one with emptiness, we should try to develop the divine pride of being the Truth Body. If we are successful in this meditation, our meditations on generating ourself as a Deity will also be successful.

Once a practitioner told Longdol Lama that, even though he tried hard to generate himself as a Deity, he was still conscious of his ordinary body, his friends, his house and all the things he usually did. He asked what he should do to correct this. Longdol Lama replied that he could solve the problem by training in the meditation on bringing death into the path to the Truth Body. If we imagine that everything dissolves into emptiness, we can overcome ordinary appearances, and this will make it easy for us to generate new, pure appearances.

BRINGING THE INTERMEDIATE STATE INTO THE PATH TO THE ENJOYMENT BODY

Immediately after an experience of clear light has ceased and the mind has become slightly grosser, a subtle body manifests. For an ordinary being, a dream body arises when the clear light of sleep ceases, and a bardo body arises when the clear light of death ceases. For a Tantric practitioner, the impure illusory body arises from the mind of ultimate example clear light, and the pure illusory body arises from the mind of meaning clear light. For a Buddha, the Enjoyment Body arises from the clear light of the Truth Body.

When we meditate on bringing death into the path to the Truth Body, we develop divine pride thinking, 'I am the Truth Body.' While maintaining this divine pride, one part of our mind should think:

If I remain only as the Truth Body I cannot benefit living beings because they are unable to see me. Therefore, I must arise in a Form Body, a Buddha's Enjoyment Body.

With this thought, we imagine that from the clear light of emptiness our mind instantly transforms into an Enjoyment Body in the aspect of a red letter BAM. We generate divine pride thinking, 'I am the Enjoyment Body', and meditate briefly on this feeling. At this stage it is more important to meditate on the feeling of being the Enjoyment Body of a Buddha than it is to dwell on the aspect of the letter BAM. The nature of our mind is great bliss and its aspect is a red letter BAM. The letter BAM has three parts: the BA, the drop and the nada. These symbolize the body, speech and mind of the bardo being, and the body, speech and mind of the Enjoyment Body. This indicates that meditation on bringing the intermediate state into the path purifies the intermediate state and causes the ripening of the illusory body, which eventually transforms into the Enjoyment Body of a Buddha.

BRINGING REBIRTH INTO THE PATH
TO THE EMANATION BODY

For ordinary beings the waking state arises from the dream body, and after death their next rebirth arises from the bardo body. Similarly, for Tantric practitioners the gross divine body arises from the illusory body, and for a Buddha the Emanation Body arises from the Enjoyment Body. When we meditate on bringing rebirth into the path to the Emanation Body, we imagine a similar process. While we are in the form of the red letter BAM standing in space, which we identify as being the Enjoyment Body, one part of our mind thinks:

If I remain only in this form, I will not be able to benefit ordinary beings because they are unable to see a Buddha's Enjoyment Body. Therefore, I must be born in an Emanation Body so that even ordinary beings can see me.

With this motivation, we look for a place in which to take rebirth. Looking down through the space beneath us, we see two red EH letters, one above the other, appearing from the state of emptiness. These transform into a phenomena source, which is shaped like a double tetrahedron standing with its fine tip pointing downwards and its broad neck facing upwards. There is an outer tetrahedron, which is white, and an inner one, which is red. They are both made of light and so they interpenetrate without obstruction. Looked at from above, the top of the double tetrahedron resembles a six-pointed star with one point of the inner tetrahedron pointing towards the front and one point of the outer tetrahedron pointing towards the back. The triangular segments at the front and the back are empty, but in each of the four remaining segments there is a pink joy swirl spinning counter-clockwise.

Inside the phenomena source there appears a white letter AH, which transforms into a white moon disc. Standing around the edge of the moon disc are the letters of the three-OM mantra: OM OM OM SARWA BUDDHA DAKINIYE VAJRA WARNANIYE VAJRA BEROTZANIYE HUM HUM HUM PHAT PHAT PHAT SOHA. The letters are red and are arrayed counter-clockwise, starting from the front. The centre of the moon disc is empty. Our mind, the red letter BAM, observes these developments from above.

The outer phenomena source symbolizes the rebirth environment, the inner phenomena source the mother's womb, the white moon disc the white bodhichitta of Father Heruka, and the red mantra rosary the red bodhichitta of Mother Vajrayogini. Because the mantra rosary is reflected in the moon, the moon is tinged with red. The moon and mantra rosary together symbolize the union of the germ cells of the father and mother at the moment of conception.

Just before a bardo being takes rebirth, it sees its future parents engaged in intercourse. Similarly we, in the aspect of the red letter BAM, observe below us the union of Father Heruka and Mother Vajrayogini in the symbolic forms of the moon and mantra rosary, and we generate a strong motivation to take rebirth there. With this motivation we, the letter BAM, descend and alight upon the centre of the moon disc inside the phenomena source. This is similar to a bardo being taking rebirth in the womb of its future mother.

Then from the letter BAM and the mantra rosary, rays of light radiate throughout space. On the tip of each ray is a Deity of Heruka's mandala. These Heroes and Heroines bestow blessings and empowerments upon all beings throughout the universe. They purify all samsaric beings and those who have entered solitary nirvana, as well as their environments, and transform them into pure beings in Vajrayogini's Pure Land. Then the transformed beings, their worlds, the phenomena source and the moon disc all melt into light and dissolve into our mind, the letter BAM. This and the mantra rosary then instantly transform into the supporting mandala and the supported Deities of Vajrayogini. We become Vajrayogini with a pure body, speech and mind, abiding in the Pure Land of Vajrayogini and experiencing pure enjoyments. We think, 'Now I am born in Dakini Land as Buddha Vajrayogini's Emanation Body.' We hold this recognition firmly and meditate on it for a while.

Je Tsongkhapa said that if we do not bring the three bodies into the path, we are not practising generation stage, even if we meditate on a mandala with a hundred Deities; but, if we meditate on the three bringings, we are practising generation stage, even if we visualize only one Deity. The purpose of the three bringings is to overcome ordinary death, intermediate state and rebirth, and to attain the three bodies of a Buddha – the Truth Body, Enjoyment Body and Emanation Body. Once we have laid the foundation of the experience of the three bringings, it will not be difficult for us to gain experience of the other practices of generation stage and completion stage.

The yogas of the three bringings in the continuum of a person who has not attained completion stage realizations are generation stages, and the yogas of the three bringings in the continuum of a person who has attained completion stage realizations are completion stages. The generation stage yogas of bringing the three bodies into the path are causes to ripen the three bodies of the path of completion stage. The way to meditate on the three bringings of generation stage and the way to meditate on the three bringings of completion stage are similar from the point of view of their aspects, but they are quite different from the point of view of their power and function. Whereas the three bringings of generation stage purify ordinary death, intermediate state and rebirth indirectly, the three bringings of completion stage purify them directly.

Some people who have received empowerments feel that meditation on the three bringings is too advanced for them and decide to postpone it until they have attained stable experience of renunciation and bodhichitta. This is a big mistake because those with Highest Yoga Tantra empowerments have a commitment to practise bringing the three bodies into

Panchen Losang Yeshe

the path, and incur a downfall if they neglect this practice. Even if we do not have genuine renunciation or bodhichitta, we should still train in the three bringings so as to place powerful potentials on our mind. To begin with, we should generate an artificial motivation of bodhichitta before we meditate on the three bringings. Then our meditation helps us to develop not only generation stage realizations, but also spontaneous bodhichitta. If we sow these two seeds at the same time, in the future we will harvest both results together, attaining spontaneous bodhichitta and generation stage realizations simultaneously.

There was once a Hinayanist who meditated on the generation and completion stages of Hevajra and attained only the fruit of Stream Enterer, the first of the four fruits of Hinayana training. The reason he attained such a small result from such powerful practices was that his motivation was very limited. The result we receive from Tantric practice depends upon our motivation. If we practise Tantra motivated by worldly concerns, we will accomplish nothing. Without bodhichitta motivation, Tantric practice will never yield complete realizations of generation stage and completion stage.

How does meditation on bringing death into the path to the Truth Body performed before attaining completion stage realizations possess the four attributes of a generation stage yoga? It possesses the first attribute because it is not developed through the winds entering, abiding and dissolving within the central channel through the force of meditation, and it possesses the second attribute because it functions to ripen the completion stage realization of mixing death with the Truth Body. It possesses the third attribute because it is similar in aspect to the death process. When we die, all the appearances of this life gather and gradually dissolve into the clear light of death. As the various levels of minds and winds dissolve, we experience the eight signs from the mirage-like appearance up to the clear light. When we meditate on bringing death into the path to the Truth Body, we imagine a similar process of absorption, visualizing the eight signs one by one. Finally, generation stage meditation on bringing death into the path to the Truth Body possesses the fourth attribute because its main object is an imagined or mentally generated Truth Body. Having dissolved all conventional appearances, we imagine that we have attained the Truth Body and, using this imagined Truth Body as the basis for imputing I, we generate the thought, 'I'. Even though an imagined Truth Body is not an actual Truth Body and is merely generated by our mind of concentration, nevertheless it exists and functions as the basis of the actual Truth Body. By improving this mentally generated Truth Body, we will eventually attain the actual Truth Body – an omniscient mind mixed inseparably with emptiness.

The object of the generation stage practice of bringing the intermediate state into the path to the Enjoyment Body is an imagined Enjoyment Body in the aspect of a seed-letter or some other symbolic form. Although this is not the actual Enjoyment Body, it is the basis of the Enjoyment Body. Similarly, the object of the generation stage practice of bringing rebirth into the path to the Emanation Body is an imagined Emanation Body in the aspect of our personal Deity, and, although this is not the actual Emanation Body, it is the basis of the Emanation Body.

Why is the generation stage meditation on an imagined Deity body a valid cognizer and not a wrong awareness? To help us to understand this, we can consider the following example. If we look at a snow-covered mountain from a distance, in certain types of light it appears to be blue in colour. Because this appearance of a blue snow mountain develops as a result of causes of error, the mind that apprehends a blue snow mountain is a wrong awareness. However, if we visualize a blue snow mountain, eventually, through the power of our concentration, a blue snow mountain will appear directly to our mental consciousness. In this case, the appearance of a blue snow mountain will have developed from the correct cause of pure concentration, and so the mind that apprehends that blue snow mountain will be a valid cognizer. The blue snow mountain apprehended by this mind will be a form that is a phenomena source.

The imagined Deity body that is the object of generation stage meditation is similar to the blue snow mountain generated through the force of concentration, and is a form that is a phenomena source. By meditating repeatedly on ourself generated as a Deity, the appearance of our ordinary body will cease and the appearance of the Deity body will become clearer and clearer. Eventually, through the force of generation stage meditation, we will directly perceive ourself in the form of the Deity. This Deity body is a mentally generated body and a form that is a phenomena source. The mentally generated Deity body of generation stage acts as the basis for attaining the illusory body of completion stage, which is an actual divine body that can be seen even by the eye awarenesses of those who possess an illusory body. Through improving the illusory body, we can eventually transform it into the Form Body of a Buddha.

DIVISIONS OF GENERATION STAGE

From the point of view of the subtlety of the object, there are two types of generation stage:

1 Gross generation stage
2 Subtle generation stage

According to the system of Vajrayogini, the objects of gross generation stage are the imagined Vajrayogini body and mandala, which is known as the 'outer mandala'; and the objects of subtle generation stage are the thirty-seven body mandala Deities, who are known as the 'inner mandala'. The outer mandala is very large and therefore a gross object, whereas the inner mandala is very small and therefore a subtle object. To begin with, we should emphasize meditation on gross generation stage until we attain stability in this meditation, and then we should switch to subtle generation stage. It is very useful from the beginning to include a brief meditation on the body mandala, but we should understand that it is impossible to develop deep experience of subtle generation stage until we have some experience of gross generation stage.

Generation stage can also be divided into three: generation stage observing an imagined Truth Body, generation stage observing an imagined Enjoyment Body and generation stage observing an imagined Emanation Body.

HOW TO PRACTISE ACTUAL GENERATION STAGE MEDITATION

Again, the way to practise actual generation stage meditation will be explained on the basis of Vajrayogini, but these instructions can easily be applied to other Deities. The actual generation stage meditation has two parts:

1 Training in gross generation stage meditation
2 Training in subtle generation stage meditation

TRAINING IN GROSS GENERATION STAGE MEDITATION

This has two parts:

1 Training in divine pride
2 Training in clear appearance

TRAINING IN DIVINE PRIDE

Divine pride is a special way of regarding ourself in which we imagine that we are a Tantric Deity and that our environment is his or her Pure Land. Although it is called 'pride', divine pride is not a delusion. It is utterly different from deluded pride. Deluded pride causes only rebirth in samsara, whereas generating the divine pride of being Vajrayogini leads only to liberation from samsara. We begin actual generation stage meditation by cultivating divine pride and then, based on this, developing clear appearance. The principal objects to be abandoned during generation stage meditation are ordinary conceptions and ordinary appearances. Divine pride overcomes ordinary conceptions and clear appearance overcomes ordinary appearances.

At the beginning, ordinary conceptions are more harmful than ordinary appearances. How this is so is illustrated by the following analogy. Suppose a magician conjures up an illusion of a tiger in front of an audience. The tiger appears to both the audience and the magician but, whereas the audience believe there actually to be a tiger in front of them and consequently become afraid, the magician does not believe that the tiger actually exists and so remains calm. The problem for the audience is not so much that a tiger appears to them, as their conception that the tiger actually exists. It is this conception rather than the mere appearance of the tiger that causes them to experience fear. If, like the magician, they had no conception that the tiger existed, then, even though they still had an appearance of a tiger, they would not be afraid. In the same way, even though things appear to us as ordinary, if we do not conceptually grasp them as ordinary this will not be so harmful. Similarly, it is less damaging to our spiritual development to see our Spiritual Guide as ordinary, and yet hold him or her to be in essence a Buddha, than it is to see our Spiritual Guide as ordinary and to believe that he or she is ordinary. The conviction that our Spiritual Guide is a Buddha, even though he or she may appear to us as an ordinary person, helps our spiritual practices to progress rapidly.

As already explained, we reduce ordinary conceptions by developing divine pride. For this reason, we need to emphasize the development of divine pride at the very outset of our training in generation stage. If we continue to perceive our ordinary body and mind, this will obstruct our development of divine pride. Therefore, when we meditate on divine pride, we must ensure that we lose all awareness of our ordinary body and mind by imagining that we have accomplished Vajrayogini's pure body and mind instead. To subdue our ordinary conceptions and improve our divine pride, we can contemplate the following three reasons:

(1) I am no longer an ordinary being because my ordinary body, mind and environment have been purified through the practice of bringing the three bodies into the path. During this practice I actually died and took rebirth as Vajrayogini in her Pure Land.

(2) Later, when I absorbed the wisdom beings, I dissolved all Buddhas in the form of Vajrayogini into myself. Therefore, I am one with Vajrayogini, and my nature is the same as that of all Buddhas.

(3) The ordinary deluded pride that I have had until now results only in suffering and continued rebirth in samsara, but divine pride will lead me to liberation and Vajrayogini's Pure Land. Therefore, I will never give up this pure pride of being Vajrayogini.

Contemplating these three reasons, or any other helpful reasons, is analytical meditation. When, as a result of this reasoning, divine pride arises in our mind, we try to hold it with single-pointed concentration in placement meditation. We then need continually to strengthen our divine pride through repeated meditation.

It is very important not to mistake the basis upon which we generate divine pride. For example, if a practitioner called John tries to develop divine pride of being Vajrayogini on the basis of his ordinary body and mind, he is completely mistaken. John's body and mind are contaminated aggregates and may be a valid basis for imputing John, but they cannot be a basis for imputing Vajrayogini. The appearances of John's body and mind are ordinary appearances, and assenting to these appearances as true is ordinary conception, which is contrary to divine pride.

Losang Trinlay

When we generate the divine pride of being Vajrayogini in her Pure Land, we must first prevent our normal conception and appearance of ourself, as well as of our environment, body and mind. We need to dispel these from our mind completely. Having eliminated ordinary appearances, we should then use our imagination to try to perceive Vajrayogini's environment and body, and look upon these as our own environment and body. These are the bases upon which we generate divine pride by firmly deciding 'I am Vajrayogini surrounded by my pure environment and pure enjoyments.'

TRAINING IN CLEAR APPEARANCE

There are two ways to train in clear appearance:

1 Training in clear appearance on the general aspect
2 Training in clear appearance on specific aspects

TRAINING IN CLEAR APPEARANCE ON THE GENERAL ASPECT

If we have already gained some skill in meditation, we can immediately begin training in clear appearance on the general aspect, that is on ourself and the complete mandala of Vajrayogini viewed as a whole; but, if we find this too difficult, we can begin by training in clear appearance on specific aspects until we gain more familiarity, and then proceed to train in clear appearance on the general aspect.

To meditate on clear appearance on the general aspect, we begin by doing analytical meditation to attain a generic image of the entire mandala. We check from the fire circle, vajra fence, charnel grounds and phenomena source up to the lotus, sun and ourself, Vajrayogini, and then back again. We continue in this way until we have a rough image of ourself, Vajrayogini, together with the entire mandala and all the beings within it. We then try to hold this image with single-pointed concentration in placement meditation. Gradually, through repeated meditation, we improve our clear appearance of ourself as Vajrayogini in her mandala.

When we have a rough image of ourself as Vajrayogini in her mandala, we have found the object of actual generation stage meditation; and we have also reached the first of the nine mental abidings, placing the mind. Through daily practice, and sometimes in short or longer retreat, we should improve this concentration until we reach the fourth mental abiding, close placement. At this point, if we enter a strict retreat with the aim of attaining tranquil abiding on generation stage, it is possible for us to accomplish this within six months. After attaining tranquil abiding on generation stage, it will not be long before we attain outer Dakini Land. More detailed explanations on the method for attaining tranquil abiding are given in the books *Joyful Path of Good Fortune* and *Meaningful to Behold*.

TRAINING IN CLEAR APPEARANCE
ON SPECIFIC ASPECTS

The 'specific aspects' are specific objects within the mandala. For example, we can focus first on the central eye of Vajrayogini until we perceive it clearly. Without forgetting this, we then focus on the other two eyes, and then on the face, neck, torso, arms, legs and so forth, until we have a mental image of the entire body. Gradually we can include the phenomena source, eight charnel grounds and protection circle. Contemplating each aspect in this way will help us finally to gain clear appearance of the entire supporting and supported mandala. Once we have accomplished this, we train in concentration as before. In this way, through training in analytical and placement meditation we should improve our clear appearance until we complete the realizations of both gross and subtle generation stages.

TRAINING IN SUBTLE GENERATION
STAGE MEDITATION

The protection circle, charnel grounds, phenomena source and self-generation all have gross and subtle features. The vajra ground, fence, tent, canopy, surrounding fires, charnel grounds, phenomena source, lotus, sun, Kalarati and Bhairawa, and our body in the aspect of Vajrayogini are the gross features. They are the objects of gross generation stage meditation. Their constituent parts, such as the tiny vajras within the vajra fence, are the subtle features. A meditation using these subtle features as the object is called 'subtle generation stage meditation'.

Through constant training in meditation to improve clear appearance of the gross objects, eventually we will perceive directly with our mental consciousness the entire mandala from the fire circle to the self-generation as clearly as we now see things with our eyes. When we gain this experience in meditation, we have attained the complete realization of gross generation stage meditation, and should then switch to training in subtle generation stage meditation.

The supreme object of subtle generation stage meditation is Vajrayogini's body mandala. We should meditate repeatedly on this inner mandala until we can see the thirty-seven Dakinis of the body mandala directly with our mental consciousness as clearly as we now see things with our eyes. When we gain this realization, we have completed subtle generation stage. If, at the same time, our winds gather and dissolve within the central channel at the heart channel wheel, we will have attained completion stage realizations. From this we can see that skilful meditation on the body mandala of Vajrayogini is a real wishfulfilling jewel that satisfies the wishes of pure practitioners.

If we find it difficult to believe that an ordinary being can directly perceive himself or herself as a Deity and his or her environment as a Buddha's Pure Land, we should consider the following. Even though our present body and mind are not our I, nevertheless, due to strong familiarity with self-grasping, we directly and vividly see our I as one with this body and mind. Because of this, whenever our body is unwell we say, 'I am unwell', and whenever our mind is unhappy we say, 'I am unhappy.' If through familiarity with self-grasping ignorance we can come to identify with a contaminated body and mind, then certainly through correct imagination and pure concentration we can come to identify with the pure body and mind of Vajrayogini. Then, through familiarizing ourself with generation stage meditation, eventually we will definitely directly perceive ourself as Vajrayogini. This has been the experience of many Tantric meditators.

There is an account of a Yamantaka practitioner who through his clear appearance of being Yamantaka saw himself as the real Deity in every detail, including the horns on his head. He felt as if he could even touch the horns, and whenever he wanted to go through a door he would bend down to allow room for his horns to pass through! Although he was not actually Yamantaka, his clear appearance of himself as the Deity Yamantaka was not a mistaken appearance. If something is a mistaken appearance it necessarily arises from ignorance, but if a Tantric practitioner sees himself or herself as a real Yamantaka or Vajrayogini, this clear appearance arises from his or her pure concentration and not from ignorance. Such experiences are evident only to the practitioner himself; other people will continue to see him as an ordinary person.

People with no experience of Tantric meditation may find it difficult to believe that it is possible to change our identity from an ordinary person into a Deity, but, by developing a correct understanding of how persons lack true existence and are mere imputations, we will realize that it is definitely possible. This will help us to experience deep realizations of Tantra and enable us to gain an understanding of the two truths according to Highest Yoga Tantra – meaning clear light and illusory body – which is essential for the practice of completion stage.

The most important thing when training in generation stage meditation is to develop familiarity with divine pride and clear appearance by practising them continually. Finally we should reach the point where our generation stage meditation possesses three characteristics:

(1) It is a concentration experiencing bliss.
(2) It perceives clearly and conceives strongly oneself as the Deity and one's environment as the mandala Pure Land.
(3) It realizes that oneself, the Deity, and one's environment and surroundings, the mandala, are

just manifestations of emptiness that do not exist
from their own side.

A single concentration that possesses these three
characteristics is a fully qualified generation stage meditation.

If we have familiarity with this meditation, when we
engage in the activities of subsequent attainment we will
be able to view all phenomena as mere manifestations of
emptiness and our mind of bliss. Through this experience,
we will be able to view ourself and all other beings as the
Deity, all environments as the Pure Land of the Deity and
all enjoyments as completely pure enjoyments. Through
training in this view with strong faith and conviction, we
will be able to avoid experiencing any impure or unpleasant
objects, and experience only pure environments, enjoyments,
bodies and minds. We will then be able to help others to
experience the same happiness by leading them into the
practice of Highest Yoga Tantra.

Since both purity and impurity depend completely upon
the mind that perceives them, if there is no impure mind
there are no impure objects. Therefore, we can purify
all objects, or all phenomena, simply by purifying the
subject, our mind. Generation stage meditation purifies our
mind by eliminating ordinary appearances and ordinary
conceptions. In this way, our mind becomes completely pure
and we experience everything as pure and pleasant, just as
enlightened beings experience things.

THE MEASUREMENT OF HAVING COMPLETED
GENERATION STAGE

There are four levels of generation stage practitioners:

1 Beginners
2 Practitioners in whom some wisdom has descended
3 Practitioners with some power over wisdom
4 Practitioners with complete power over wisdom

Beginners are generation stage practitioners who meditate principally on gross generation stage and can visualize the individual parts of the mandala and Deity clearly, but not the mandala in its entirety. Practitioners in whom some wisdom has descended are able to visualize the entire mandala very clearly and so are closer than beginners to the wisdom being. Practitioners with some power over wisdom are able to visualize the entire object of meditation of subtle generation stage clearly and are now very close to the wisdom being. Some practitioners at this level are able to bring their winds into the central channel through the force of meditating on subtle generation stage, and thereby directly enter completion stage. Complete power over wisdom is attained when we have perfect mastery of both gross and subtle generation stage.

When we are able to remain concentrated on the entire object of gross generation stage without mental sinking or mental excitement for four hours, we have attained firmness in gross generation stage; and when we can remain on this object for as long as we like, for months or even for years, we have completed gross generation stage. When we are able to remain concentrated on the entire object of subtle generation stage without mental sinking or mental excitement for four hours, we have attained firmness in subtle generation stage; and when we can remain on this object for as long as we like, we have completed subtle generation stage.

HOW TO ADVANCE FROM GENERATION STAGE TO COMPLETION STAGE

We advance from generation stage to completion stage when we attain spontaneous great bliss by means of causing the winds to enter, abide and dissolve within the central channel through the force of meditation. From this moment all our meditations of bringing the three bodies into the path are completion stages. It is as if we have used a boat to cross to the other side of a river, and can now leave the boat behind us.

Isolated Body

COMPLETION STAGE

This is explained in four parts:

1. Definition and etymology of completion stage
2. Divisions of completion stage
3. How to progress from the lower stages to the higher stages
4. The final results of completion stage

DEFINITION AND ETYMOLOGY OF COMPLETION STAGE

The definition of completion stage is a yoga of learning developed in dependence upon the winds entering, abiding and dissolving within the central channel through the force of meditation. Here, 'yoga of learning' excludes the realizations of a Buddha, which are Paths of No More Learning. When we fall asleep or die, our winds naturally enter, abide and dissolve within the central channel and subtle levels of mind become manifest, but we are unable to use or even to recognize these subtle minds because our mindfulness stops functioning at this time. If we are able to centralize our winds through the force of meditation, we can learn to retain mindfulness even when our mind is in a subtle state, and use our subtle mind to

Drubwang Losang Namgyal

meditate. Meditation performed with a subtle mind is much more powerful than meditation performed with a gross mind. The subtle mind is naturally concentrated because, when the winds dissolve within the central channel, they no longer support distracting conceptions.

Another reason why meditating with a subtle mind is so powerful is that a subtle mind mixes with its object very easily. At present, even if we understand emptiness intellectually, our meditation on emptiness has little power to transform our mind because our mind does not mix with emptiness. Such meditation does not have enough power to overcome our self-grasping. The more completely our mind mixes with emptiness, the weaker our appearance of true existence becomes and the more our self-grasping is reduced. To begin with, we develop an intellectual understanding of emptiness, but we should not be satisfied with this. We need to meditate on emptiness again and again, bringing our mind and emptiness closer and closer together until finally they mix indistinguishably. Only a mind mixed with emptiness in this way can destroy self-grasping and all other faults.

From the point of view of the object of meditation, the emptiness explained in Sutra and the emptiness explained in Tantra are exactly the same. The emptiness that Tantric Yogis meditate on is precisely the emptiness taught by Nagarjuna in *Fundamental Wisdom* and by Chandrakirti in *Guide to the Middle Way*. What makes a Tantric Yogi's meditation on emptiness special is not a difference in the object but a difference in the subject – the mind that meditates on emptiness. Whereas a Sutra Yogi realizes emptiness with a gross mind, a Tantric Yogi realizes emptiness with the very subtle mind of spontaneous great bliss. Meditating on emptiness with a gross mind is like a young child trying to fell

123

a tree with an axe, but meditating on emptiness with the very subtle mind of spontaneous great bliss is like a strong adult felling a tree. In the commentaries to Vajrayana Mahamudra, such as the book *Clear Light of Bliss*, the explanation of the object, emptiness, is exactly the same as the explanations given in Sutra; but the explanation of the way to develop the mind of spontaneous great bliss that meditates on emptiness is unique to Highest Yoga Tantra.

Completion stage, non-fabricated yoga and yoga of the second stage are synonyms. Completion stage is called a 'non-fabricated yoga' because the principal objects of completion stage meditation are not generated by mind. The principal objects of completion stage meditation are the channels, drops and winds. Since these already exist within our body, there is no need to generate them through the power of our imagination. Completion stage is called the 'yoga of the second stage' to indicate that we first need to gain the realization of the first stage – generation stage – before we can gain realizations of completion stage. The yogas of completion stage are called 'completion stage' because they are stages that lead to the completion of all aspects of objects of knowledge in the nature of spontaneous bliss. When we attain the clear light of bliss that realizes emptiness directly, from the point of view of our experience, all appearances of objects of knowledge, except the appearance of emptiness, dissolve into emptiness, and our mind of great bliss becomes inseparable from emptiness. For us, all aspects of objects of knowledge are completed in the nature of our meditation of spontaneous bliss. This bliss, which is inseparable from emptiness, is definitive Heruka. The Heruka who has shape, colour and so forth is interpretative Heruka.

When we die, all the appearances of this life gradually gather inwards and dissolve into the clear light of death. All our normal appearances cease and we perceive only clear light. When gross minds arise again, our next life will have started and we will perceive only the appearances of that life. Our present appearances depend upon the gross minds of this life, and the appearances of our next life depend upon the gross minds of our next life. Similarly, when we fall asleep, all the daytime appearances cease because the waking minds upon which they depend cease. We then experience new appearances of the dream state, which are dependent upon dream minds. Contemplating death and dreaming helps us to understand both the Chittamatra assertion that all appearances are the nature of mind and the Prasangika view that all phenomena are imputed by mind. Milarepa said:

You should be familiar with this life, the intermediate state and the next life mixed as one.

This means that we should become familiar with all our appearances of this life, the life of the bardo and the next life as the nature of our mind of great bliss. This becomes possible when we attain the experience of definitive Heruka.

DIVISIONS OF COMPLETION STAGE

In his root text entitled *Five Stages of Completion Stage*, Nagarjuna enumerates five stages of completion stage: isolated speech, isolated mind, illusory body, clear light and union. The illusory body listed here is the impure illusory body; pure illusory body is part of the fifth stage. The clear light of the fourth stage is meaning clear light; ultimate example clear light is part of isolated mind.

In *Lamp of Condensed Deeds*, Aryadeva says that if we add isolated body of completion stage to this list, there are six stages of completion stage: isolated body of completion stage, isolated speech, isolated mind, illusory body, clear light and union. These six stages will now be extensively explained.

ISOLATED BODY OF COMPLETION STAGE

This is explained in three parts:

1 Definition and etymology of isolated body of completion stage
2 Divisions of isolated body of completion stage
3 How to practise isolated body of completion stage

DEFINITION AND ETYMOLOGY OF ISOLATED BODY OF COMPLETION STAGE

The definition of isolated body of completion stage is a yoga of completion stage prior to isolated speech whose main function is to overcome ordinary appearance of body and other phenomena. An example is a mind of bliss of completion stage prior to loosening the knots of the central channel at the heart, that views body and other phenomena as manifestations of bliss and emptiness, or in the aspect of Deities. Isolated body of generation stage also views bodies and other phenomena as manifestations of bliss and emptiness, or in the aspect of Deities, but it is different from isolated body of completion stage because the bliss is different. The bliss of generation stage is a bliss that arises from the melting of the drops in channels other than the central channel through the force of generation stage meditation, whereas the bliss of completion stage is a bliss that arises from the melting of the drops inside the central channel through the force of completion stage meditation.

Isolated body is so called because its function is to overcome ordinary appearance and ordinary conception of body. Here, 'body' refers not only to our aggregate of form but to all five aggregates, the four elements, the six sources, the five objects and the five basic wisdoms. Isolated body functions to overcome ordinary appearance and conception of all these twenty-five objects.

DIVISIONS OF ISOLATED BODY
OF COMPLETION STAGE

There are two types of isolated body of completion stage:

1 Isolated body of completion stage that is meditative equipoise
2 Isolated body of completion stage that is subsequent attainment

The first is a meditation on emptiness with the bliss of completion stage, and the second is a view of body and other phenomena as manifestations of bliss and emptiness, or in the aspect of Deities.

HOW TO PRACTISE ISOLATED BODY
OF COMPLETION STAGE

This has two parts:

1 How to practise isolated body of completion stage during the meditation session
2 How to practise isolated body of completion stage during the meditation break

HOW TO PRACTISE ISOLATED BODY OF COMPLETION STAGE DURING THE MEDITATION SESSION

This has two parts:

1 A preliminary explanation
2 The actual explanation

A PRELIMINARY EXPLANATION

To practise isolated body of completion stage during the meditation session, we need to train both in the bliss of completion stage and in emptiness. To begin with, we should train in these two separately, and then we should train in the union of bliss and emptiness. We train in the bliss of completion stage by engaging in the meditations on the central channel, drop and wind explained below. At first we simply imagine that we experience bliss, but through constant familiarity with this experience, and through improving our meditation, eventually we will attain the actual bliss of completion stage.

In general, there are many different types of bliss. For example, ordinary beings sometimes experience some artificial bliss when they engage in sexual activity, and qualified meditators experience a special bliss of suppleness during deep meditation due to their pure concentration, especially when they attain tranquil abiding and accomplish the concentration of the absorption of cessation. Moreover when Dharma practitioners, through training in higher moral discipline, higher concentration and higher wisdom, attain permanent inner peace by abandoning self-grasping, they experience a profound bliss of inner peace day and night, in life after life. These types of bliss are mentioned in Buddha's Sutra teachings. The bliss of completion stage, however, is quite different from all of these, and is vastly superior. The bliss of completion stage is a bliss that possesses two special characteristics: (1) its nature is a bliss arisen from the melting of the drops inside the central channel, and (2) its function is to overcome dualistic appearance. No other form of bliss possesses these two characteristics.

A bliss possessing these two characteristics can be experienced only by human beings who are engaged in Highest Yoga Tantra practice, and by Buddhas. Even high Bodhisattvas abiding in Pure Lands have no opportunity to experience it because, even though they have very high realizations, their bodies lack the necessary physical conditions for generating bliss possessing the two characteristics. What are these conditions? They are the three elements of flesh, skin and blood that come from the mother; and the three elements of bone, marrow and sperm that come from the father. These six elements are essential for accomplishing this bliss, which is the quick path to Buddhahood. It was because humans possessed these conditions that Buddha explained Tantric teachings to us in the first place. Therefore, from this point of view, we are more fortunate than high Bodhisattvas abiding in Pure Lands who are experiencing great enjoyments. It is said that these Bodhisattvas pray to be born in the human world so that they can meet a qualified Vajrayana Spiritual Guide and practise the quick path to enlightenment. In *Song of the Spring Queen*, Je Tsongkhapa says that without experiencing this bliss there is no possibility of attaining liberation in this life. It goes without saying, therefore, that without this bliss there is no possibility of attaining full enlightenment in this life.

Kachen Yeshe Gyaltsen

If we develop and maintain this bliss through the practice of completion stage meditation, we can transform our attachment into a special method for completing the quick path to enlightenment. Before we attain this bliss, our attachment causes us to be reborn in samsara, but, once we have this bliss, our attachment causes us to be released from samsara. Moreover, once we attain this bliss we will be able to stop our samsaric rebirths very quickly. The cause of samsara is our mind of self-grasping. According to the teachings of Highest Yoga Tantra, self-grasping depends upon its mounted wind, which flows through the right and left channels. Without this wind, it cannot develop. By gaining the bliss of completion stage, we can gradually reduce the inner winds of the right and left channels until finally they cease completely. When they cease, our self-grasping ceases, and we experience liberation from samsara.

From this we can see that in Sutra alone there is no liberation, not to mention full enlightenment. The Highest Yoga Tantra teachings are Buddha's ultimate intention, and the Sutra teachings are like the basic foundation. Although there are many explanations of how to attain liberation or nirvana in the Sutra teachings, if we check precisely it is very difficult to understand from Sutra teachings how nirvana can be attained. 'Nirvana' means 'the state beyond sorrow', and its nature is emptiness. If we have never heard Tantric teachings and someone asks us precisely how we attain such a nirvana, we cannot give a perfect answer. As Je Tsongkhapa said, the final answer can be found only in the Tantric teachings.

The bliss that arises from the melting of drops inside channels other than the central channel has no special qualities. When ordinary beings engage in sexual intercourse, for example, this causes their downward-voiding wind to move upwards, and this in turn causes their ordinary tummo or inner heat to increase in their right and left channels, principally in the left. As a result the red drops of the woman and the white drops of the man melt and flow through the left channel. This flowing of the drops causes them to experience some bliss, but it is very short-lived and the drops are soon released. Having had this brief experience of bliss, they are not left with any good results, except maybe a baby!

By contrast, when a qualified Tantric practitioner practises the completion stage meditations that are explained below, he or she will cause his inner winds to gather, abide and dissolve within the central channel. This will cause the downward-voiding wind located just below the navel to move upwards. Normally this wind functions to release the drops, but because it is now rising within the central channel, the inner heat located at the navel will increase inside the central channel, thereby causing the drops to melt and flow also inside the central channel. For the practitioner of a male Deity, the white drop begins to flow down from the crown and, when it reaches the throat, the practitioner experiences a very special bliss possessing the two qualities. As the drop flows down to the heart, the bliss becomes stronger and more qualified; as it flows down to the navel, the bliss becomes even stronger and more qualified; and finally, as it flows down to the tip of the sex organ, the practitioner experiences spontaneous great bliss. Because the downward-voiding wind is reversed, the drop is not released at this point but flows up again through the central channel, causing the practitioner to experience even greater bliss. For such a practitioner, the drops are never released and so they flow up and down the central channel for a very long time, giving rise to unceasing bliss. The practitioner can cause such bliss to manifest at any time simply by penetrating the central channel with concentration.

The stronger this bliss becomes, the more subtle our mind becomes. Gradually our mind becomes very peaceful, all conceptual distractions disappear, and we experience very special suppleness. This mind is infinitely superior to the experience of tranquil abiding explained in Sutra teachings. Moreover, as our mind becomes more subtle, our dualistic appearance is reduced, and eventually our mind becomes the very subtle mind of the clear light of bliss. This is a very high realization. When the clear light of bliss concentrates on emptiness, it mixes with emptiness very easily because dualistic appearance is greatly reduced. Finally it realizes emptiness directly, and whereas previously it felt as if our bliss and emptiness were two things, now they have become one nature. This mind is the union of bliss and emptiness, or meaning clear light.

As already mentioned, the first moment of the realization of the union of great bliss and emptiness is the path of seeing of Highest Yoga Tantra. However, even though it is only the path of seeing, it has the power to eliminate both the intellectually-formed delusions and innate delusions together. In the second moment, when the practitioner rises from this concentration of the union of bliss and emptiness, he or she has abandoned all the delusions and has attained liberation. At the same time, he or she has attained the pure illusory body. From that moment, the practitioner's body is a vajra body, and so he or she will not have to experience ageing, sickness, or death.

Previously, when the practitioner was ordinary, he or she was using a body taken from others – from his or her parents.

We normally say, 'My body, my body', as if our gross body belongs to us, yet this is not our actual body but one that we have taken from others. When a Tantric practitioner attains a vajra body, however, he has manifested his own body, and when he perceives this vajra body he thinks 'I'. Such a practitioner has now become a deathless person.

We have had our very subtle body, very subtle speech and very subtle mind since beginningless time. These are the continuously residing body, the continuously residing speech and the continuously residing mind, and they are our actual Buddha nature. The Buddha nature explained in Sutra is not actual Buddha nature because it is a gross object that will cease; actual Buddha nature is explained only in Highest Yoga Tantra. Normally, for ordinary beings, the only times their very subtle body, speech and mind become manifest are during deep sleep and death. However, even though they are not normally manifest, our very subtle body is the seed of a Buddha's body, our very subtle speech is the seed of a Buddha's speech and our very subtle mind is the seed of a Buddha's mind.

The very subtle body is the very subtle wind upon which the very subtle mind is mounted. This very subtle body and very subtle mind are always together. Since they are the same nature, and are never separated, they are called the 'indestructible wind' and the 'indestructible mind'. The union of the indestructible wind and mind is normally located inside the indestructible drop, inside the central channel at the heart.

Our very subtle mind manifests only when all our inner winds dissolve within our central channel. When this happens, we gradually experience eight signs as we pass through the different levels of dissolution. Finally, with the last level of dissolution, the very subtle mind of clear light becomes manifest. At the same time, the very subtle body also becomes manifest. During death, the inner winds dissolve naturally and fully within the central channel and the very subtle mind and very subtle body naturally become manifest, but we cannot recognize them. However, by practising the meditation on completion stage explained below, we can cause our very subtle mind and body to become manifest during meditation. Until we attain the realization of illusory body, our very subtle body will not maintain a definite shape or colour. When we attain the union of bliss and emptiness, our very subtle mind transforms into meaning clear light, and, when we rise from that meditation, our very subtle body transforms into the vajra body, or pure illusory body, which does have definite shape, colour and so forth. For example, if we are a Vajrayogini practitioner, whenever we do self-generation as Vajrayogini with a red-coloured body, one face, two arms and so on, we are building the basic foundation for the illusory body. In the future, when our very subtle body transforms into the illusory body, it will look like real Vajrayogini. Previously it was merely an imagined body, but at this time it will become real. This is a very good reason for now practising generation stage very sincerely.

When we attain the pure illusory body, we will no longer think of our gross body as our body. The basis for imputing our I will have completely changed, and we will now impute I in dependence upon our subtle body. When we have reached this attainment, we will have become deathless because our body and mind will never separate. Death is the separation of body and mind, but the body and mind of those who have attained the illusory body never separate because they are indestructible. Finally, our pure illusory body will transform into Buddha's Form Body and our union of bliss and emptiness will transform into Buddha's Truth Body; and we will experience the union of Buddha's Form Body and Truth Body, the Union of No More Learning.

In the section on the benefits of bodhichitta in *Guide to the Bodhisattva's Way of Life*, Shantideva says:

> Just like the supreme elixir that transmutes into gold,
> Bodhichitta can transform this impure body we have taken
> Into the priceless jewel of a Buddha's form.
> Therefore, firmly maintain bodhichitta.

Here, 'elixir' refers to a special substance that can transform iron into gold, like that used by great Masters such as Nagarjuna. This verse says that bodhichitta is a special method that, like a supreme elixir, has the power to transform our impure body into a Buddha's Form Body. How can it do this? According to Sutra, a practitioner cannot attain enlightenment in one life but must practise for many lives until finally he or she is born into Akanishta Pure Land with a pure body. It is only with this pure body that he or she can attain Buddhahood. There is no method in either Sutra or Tantra for transforming our present impure body into a Buddha's body. This impure body must eventually die; it must be left behind. Even the holy Buddha Shakyamuni himself left behind the gross body that came from his mother when he passed away. Thus, if we ask how bodhichitta can transform this impure body into a Buddha's body, there is no correct answer within Sutra teachings. This is because, according to Sutra teachings, the gross body is the real body; the Sutras never mention the vajra body, or the subtle body.

By following the Tantric view, however, we can answer this question as follows. The body referred to by Shantideva is not the gross body, but our own body, our continuously residing body, which is the very subtle wind upon which our very subtle mind is mounted. At present this is an impure body because it is obscured by delusions and other obstructions, like a blue sky covered by clouds. These defilements are not the nature of our subtle body, but are temporary defilements. The method for transforming this impure body into a Buddha's Form Body is not conventional bodhichitta, but the ultimate bodhichitta of Highest Yoga Tantra, the union of great bliss and emptiness. This ultimate bodhichitta can directly transform our impure continuously residing body first into the pure illusory body and finally into the Form Body of a Buddha. Since Shantideva himself was a sincere Tantric practitioner, we can be certain that this was his intended meaning.

As already mentioned, to generate the bliss that possesses two special qualities we need to gather and dissolve our inner winds within our central channel. There are two ways to do this: by penetrating our own body or by penetrating another's body. We begin by penetrating our own body. Here, the term 'body' refers to our vajra body – our channels, drops and winds – and 'penetrate' to concentrating on our central channel, drops and winds. Meditation on the central channel is called the 'yoga of the central channel', meditation on the drops is called the 'yoga of the drop' and meditation on the winds is called the 'yoga of wind'. Penetrating another's body means relying upon an action mudra, or consort, and engaging in sexual intercourse. However, just penetrating another's body will not bring our inner winds into our central channel if we do not already have experience of and familiarity with

Phurchog Ngawang Jampa

the yoga of the central channel, the yoga of the drop and the yoga of wind. Only when we have such experience is it the right time to rely upon an action mudra. This order of practice is very important.

There are only ten doors through which the winds can enter the central channel. They are located along the central channel as follows:

(1) The upper tip of the central channel: the point between the eyebrows
(2) The lower tip: the tip of the sex organ
(3) The centre of the crown channel wheel: located in the apex of the cranium
(4) The centre of the throat channel wheel: located near the back of the throat
(5) The centre of the heart channel wheel: located between the two breasts
(6) The centre of the navel channel wheel
(7) The centre of the secret place channel wheel, four finger-widths below the navel
(8) The centre of the jewel channel wheel, located in the centre of the sex organ, near its tip
(9) The wheel of wind: the centre of the forehead channel wheel
(10) The wheel of fire: the centre of the channel wheel located midway between the throat and the heart channel wheels

Just as we can enter a house through any of the doors leading in from the outside, so the winds can enter the central channel through any of these ten doors.

The central channel is in reality one single channel, but it is divided into different sections: the central channel of the crown channel wheel, the central channel of the throat channel wheel, the central channel of the heart channel wheel, the central channel of the navel channel wheel and so forth. Because there are these different locations, when a practitioner wants to bring his or her winds into the central channel, he or she must choose one of these points at which to concentrate.

In the book *Clear Light of Bliss*, I explain how to bring the inner winds into the central channel through the sixth of the ten doors, the centre of the navel channel wheel. We do this by visualizing our inner heat inside our navel channel in the aspect of a short-AH and meditating on this. This is a common practice that accords with the tradition of the Six Yogas of Naropa. It was originally explained in *Hevajra Root Tantra* by Buddha Vajradhara, and since then has been used by many Kagyu practitioners such as Milarepa and his disciples, and later by practitioners in Je Tsongkhapa's tradition. However, within our tradition we have the uncommon Vajrayana Mahamudra practice of the oral lineage of the unequalled Virtuous Tradition. This is a very special practice of Vajrayana Mahamudra that Je Tsongkhapa received directly from Manjushri, who had received it directly from Buddha Vajradhara. The lineage of this practice was then passed to Togden Jampel Gyatso, Baso Chokyi Gyaltsen, Mahasiddha Dharmavajra and so on. A full list of the lineage Gurus of this special instruction is given in the sadhana *Great Liberation*, which can be found in Appendix II. These Lamas are the close lineage Gurus.

In this Vajrayana Mahamudra practice, we choose the heart channel wheel from among the ten doors into the central channel. This practice is indicated in the sadhana *Offering to the Spiritual Guide*, or *Lama Chopa*, which is the uncommon preliminary practice of Vajrayana Mahamudra according to Je Tsongkhapa's tradition. The sadhana says:

I seek your blessings, O Protector, that you may place
    your feet
On the centre of the eight-petalled lotus at my heart,
So that I may manifest within this life
The paths of illusory body, clear light, and union.

These words actually reveal that penetrating the central channel of the heart channel wheel, the indestructible drop and the indestructible wind – the three yogas explained below – are meditations on isolated body. These lead to the meditations on isolated speech and isolated mind, which in turn lead to the meditations on illusory body, clear light and union. All of these will be explained in this book.

Because penetrating and concentrating on the indestructible drop at the heart is a powerful method for attaining the realizations of completion stage, Buddha Vajradhara praises this method in *Ambhidana Tantra*, where he says:

Those who meditate on the drop
That always abides at the heart,
Single-pointedly and without change,
Will definitely attain realizations.

Mahasiddha Ghantapa also encouraged us to do this meditation. Therefore, our uncommon Vajrayana practice begins with meditating on the central channel of the heart channel wheel.

In the book *Clear Light of Bliss*, I explain only the common tradition, not our uncommon tradition. This is like a father who does not show his most precious family heirloom to anyone, but only to his close relatives and friends. It also indicates that, when we are engaging in an important practice such as Vajrayana Mahamudra, it is not sufficient simply to read the instructions in a book; we need to rely sincerely upon a qualified Spiritual Guide who can explain every aspect of the practice to us from his or her own experience.

The transmission, teachings and lineage of this instruction are not possessed by any other tradition. We can see from the list of lineage Gurus that they are all followers of Je Tsongkhapa. Togden Jampel Gyatso, Mahasiddha Dharmavajra, Gyalwa Ensapa and their many disciples all attained the Mahamudra that is the Union of No More Learning, or Buddhahood, within three years, joyfully and without any difficulties. They entered the path, progressed along it and completed it within three years. In ancient times, practitioners like Milarepa worked very hard before engaging in retreat. Milarepa experienced so many difficulties, and after entering retreat he spent a long time in very isolated places, but he was a very patient and determined practitioner, like an iron man. His heart was like an iron heart. Because of this, he attained high realizations; otherwise he would have found it very difficult. Why did he have to labour so long and hard when later Lamas such as Mahasiddha Dharmavajra and Gyalwa Ensapa were able to attain full enlightenment so quickly and easily? The only reason is that the later Lamas received these special instructions of Je Tsongkhapa, which are very simple and very blessed. For them, every problem was easily solved, and it was very easy for them to make progress and attain Buddhahood quickly. It is said that thousands of Je Tsongkhapa's disciples have attained a deathless vajra body without having to engage in hardships as Milarepa did. They all practised very joyfully and smoothly because of the special qualities of this practice.

Any special meditation for gathering and dissolving the winds within the central channel is called 'meditation on life exertion'. Here, 'life' refers to our inner winds and 'exertion' to a specific exertion for causing these winds to gather and dissolve within the central channel. There are four types of meditation on life exertion:

(1) Meditation on life exertion of isolated body
(2) Meditation on life exertion of isolated speech
(3) Meditation on life exertion of isolated mind
(4) Meditation on life exertion that is none of these three

According to the Guhyasamaja system, to do life exertion of isolated body we should meditate on a subtle drop inside the central channel at the tip of the sex organ, and thereby cause the winds to gather and dissolve within the central channel. According to the uncommon Vajrayana Mahamudra practice of Je Tsongkhapa's tradition, however, we should meditate on a subtle drop inside the central channel at the heart. It is this latter system that will be explained here.

THE ACTUAL EXPLANATION

For the uncommon practice of Vajrayana Mahamudra, there are two instructions:

1 An introduction to the central channel, drops and winds
2 The actual practice

AN INTRODUCTION TO THE CENTRAL CHANNEL,
DROPS AND WINDS

If we have no understanding of the central channel, the drops and the winds, there is no way we can penetrate them. Therefore, first we should try to understand these basic objects of knowledge clearly, and then we can practise the yoga of the central channel, the yoga of the drop and the yoga of wind.

Whenever we practise the yogas of the central channel, drop and wind, we are also practising tummo meditation because these yogas are methods for bringing the inner winds into the central channel. If we bring our inner winds into the central channel, our inner heat will naturally increase within the central channel, and this will cause bliss to arise naturally. Because these three yogas function to increase inner heat, indirectly they are tummo meditations. Directly or indirectly all completion stage meditations are tummo meditations.

Every completion stage meditation is related to the central channel. Meditation on the central channel is the life of Highest Yoga Tantra practice. It fulfils all the wishes of Highest Yoga Tantra practitioners and bestows upon them endless satisfaction, which is why the great Tibetan Yogi Longdol Lama said that it is like a wishfulfilling cow that bestows an endless stream of nourishment. However, to receive such benefits from meditating on the central channel, we must meditate with pure bodhichitta motivation.

In general, we need an understanding of the three main channels – the central channel, the right channel and the left channel – and the six principal channel wheels. The central channel is like the pole of an umbrella, running through the centre of each of the channel wheels, and the right and left channels run either side of it. The central channel is pale blue on the outside and has four attributes: (1) it is very straight, like the trunk of a plantain tree, (2) inside it is an oily red colour, like pure blood, (3) it is very clear and transparent, like a candle flame, and (4) it is very soft and flexible, like a lotus petal. The central channel is located exactly midway between the left and right halves of the body, but is closer to the back than the front. Immediately in front of the spine, there is the life channel, which is quite thick; and in front of this is the central channel. It begins at the point between the eyebrows, from where it ascends in an arch to the crown of the head, and then descends in a straight line to the tip of the sex organ.

Either side of the central channel, with no intervening space, are the right and left channels. The right channel is red in colour and the left is white. The right channel begins at the tip of the right nostril and the left channel at the tip of the left nostril. From there, they both ascend in an arch to the crown of the head, either side of the central channel. From the crown of the head down to the navel, these three main channels are straight and adjacent to one another. As the left channel continues down below the level of the navel, it curves a little to the right, separating slightly from the central channel and rejoining it at the tip of the sex organ. There it functions to hold and release sperm, blood and urine. As the right channel continues down below the level of the navel, it curves a little to the left and terminates at the tip of the anus, where it functions to hold and release faeces and so forth.

The right and left channels coil around the central channel at various places, thereby forming the so-called 'channel' knots. The four places at which these knots occur are, in ascending order, the navel channel wheel, the heart channel wheel, the throat channel wheel and the crown channel wheel. At each of these places, except at the heart level, there is a twofold knot formed by a single coil of the right channel and a single coil of the left. As the right and left channels ascend to these places, they coil around the central channel by crossing in front and then looping around it. They then continue upward to the level of the next knot. At the heart level, the same thing happens, except that here there is a sixfold knot formed by three overlapping loops of each of the flanking channels.

Because the uncommon tradition of Vajrayana Mahamudra is simpler than the common tradition, it is sufficient simply to have an understanding of what the three channels look like. Then we need to understand about the drops, particularly the indestructible drop. In this context, 'drop' is the essence of blood and sperm. As just explained, at the heart chakra there is a sixfold knot formed by the right and left channels coiling around the central channel and constricting it. This is the most difficult knot to loosen, but when it is loosened we will develop great power. Because the central channel at the heart is constricted by this sixfold knot, it is blocked like a tube of bamboo. Inside the central channel, at the centre of this knot, there is a very small vacuole, and inside this is a drop called the 'indestructible drop'. It is the size of a small pea, with the upper half white in colour and the lower half red. The substance of the white half is the very clear essence of sperm, and the substance of the red half is the very clear essence of blood. This drop, which is very pure and subtle, is the very essence of all drops. All the ordinary red and white drops throughout the body originally come from this drop.

The indestructible drop is rather like a small pea that has been cut in half, slightly hollowed out, and then rejoined. It is called the 'indestructible drop' because the two halves of this drop never separate until we die. When we die, all the inner winds dissolve into the indestructible drop, and this causes the drop to open. As the two halves separate, our consciousness immediately leaves our body and goes to the next life.

Inside the indestructible drop, there is the indestructible wind and mind, which is the union of the very subtle wind and the very subtle mind. This very subtle wind is our own body, or continuously residing body; and the very subtle mind is our own mind, or continuously residing mind. The union of these two is called the 'indestructible wind and mind'. This union has never separated since beginningless time, and it will never separate in the future. The potential of the combination of our very subtle body and mind to communicate is our very subtle speech, which is our own speech. This will become a Buddha's speech in the future. In short, inside the indestructible drop there is our own body, speech and mind.

As already explained, the indestructible wind is the very subtle inner wind. Inner winds are body, and they function as mounts for minds. There are three types of inner wind: gross, subtle and very subtle. These are explained in detail below, in the section on vajra recitation.

Practitioners of Vajrayogini always visualize the in-destructible wind and mind in the aspect of a letter BAM at the heart. They regard this letter BAM as the synthesis of all the thirty-seven Dakinis of the body mandala and their Spiritual Guide's omniscient wisdom. Because they always keep this recognition, when the time comes to do Vajrayana Mahamudra meditation they find it very easy to make progress, having already become very familiar with a similar practice.

Panchen Palden Yeshe

We should check what the central channel looks like, and what the indestructible drop looks like and where it is located, and become familiar with these. Then we can engage in the actual practice of the three meditations on life exertion of isolated body.

THE ACTUAL PRACTICE

This explanation has three parts:

1 The preliminary practices
2 The actual meditation
3 The results of the practice of this meditation

THE PRELIMINARY PRACTICES

When we engage in the actual practice, in each session we should always do the uncommon preliminary practices before engaging in the actual meditation on the central channel, drop and wind. Why is this? We can understand the relationship between these preliminary practices and the actual meditation by considering the analogy of a thangka painter. A thangka painter begins by making a rough outline and then he or she fills in the detail to complete the painting. In a similar fashion, the uncommon preliminary practices are like drawing the rough outline, and the completion stage meditation is like completing the picture. Vajrayogini practitioners, for example, begin by generating themselves as Vajrayogini and visualizing their environment, enjoyments, body, speech and mind as Vajrayogini's Pure Land, enjoyments, body, speech and mind. On the basis of this outline, they then complete the picture by meditating on the channels, drops and winds, and other completion stages. In this way, the actual development of Vajrayogini's environment, enjoyments, body, speech and mind are created anew. Without this first step, the outline, the second step, completion, is impossible.

As a preliminary practice, we can use the sadhana *Offering to the Spiritual Guide*, or the shorter sadhana *Great Liberation*. Generally, according to the unequalled Virtuous Tradition, *Offering to the Spiritual Guide* is used as the preliminary practice for Vajrayana Mahamudra meditation. It can be practised in conjunction with Heruka, Vajrayogini, or other Yidams. *Great Liberation* is specifically for Heruka and Vajrayogini practitioners to practise Vajrayana Mahamudra. Heruka practitioners can practise *Great Liberation of the Father*, and Vajrayogini practitioners can practise *Great Liberation of the Mother*. Besides self-generation, both these sadhanas also include the common preliminary practices of accumulating merit, purifying negativities and receiving the blessings of all the Buddhas through our Spiritual Guide. These sadhanas, together with a short explanation, can be found in Appendix II.

THE ACTUAL MEDITATION

This has three parts:

1 Meditation on the central channel – the yoga of the central channel
2 Meditation on the indestructible drop – the yoga of the drop
3 Meditation on the indestructible wind and mind – the yoga of wind

These will now be explained from the point of view of a Vajrayogini practitioner.

MEDITATION ON THE CENTRAL CHANNEL – THE YOGA OF THE CENTRAL CHANNEL

Having completed the preliminary practices according to *Great Liberation*, from going for refuge up to dissolving Guru Vajradhara into your mind in the aspect of a reddish-white letter BAM at your heart, you should now engage in the actual meditation as follows. With your mind, which is in the aspect of a letter BAM at your heart, you should check to see what the central channel looks like. You should think:

My central channel is located exactly midway between the left and right halves of my body, but is closer to the back than the front. Immediately in front of the spine, there is the life channel, which is quite thick; and in front of this is the central channel. It begins at the point between my eyebrows, from where it ascends in an arch to the crown of my head, and then descends in a straight line to the tip of my sex organ. It is pale blue in colour on the outside, and it is an oily red colour on the inside. It is clear and transparent and very soft and flexible.

At the very beginning you can, if you wish, visualize the central channel as being fairly wide, and then gradually visualize it as being thinner and thinner until finally you can visualize it as being the width of a drinking straw. You should contemplate like this repeatedly until you perceive a generic image of your main central channel. Then your mind should focus on the central channel at the level of your heart. You should feel that your mind is inside the

151

central channel at the heart and then meditate on this heart central channel single-pointedly. You should do many sessions of this meditation for months, or years. In each session you should repeat all the stages from the initial contemplation up to the final concentration on the heart central channel. The main object of this meditation is the heart central channel, but the concentration must possess two characteristics: (1) it perceives and holds the central channel at the heart level, and (2) it feels as if your mind is inside that central channel.

This meditation is called 'the yoga of the central channel'. Through continually practising this meditation, we can gather and dissolve our winds within the central channel. However, there are many levels to this dissolution, and to gain deeper experience we need to progress to the second meditation – meditation on the indestructible drop.

MEDITATION ON THE INDESTRUCTIBLE DROP – THE YOGA OF THE DROP

Having completed the preliminary practices as before, and dissolved Guru Vajradhara into your mind in the aspect of a reddish-white letter BAM, you should check and understand where the indestructible drop is located and what it looks like. You should think:

Inside my central channel at my heart level, there is a very small vacuole. Inside this is my indestructible drop. It is the size of a small pea, with the upper half white in colour and the lower half red. It is like a pea that has been cut in half, slightly hollowed out, and then rejoined. It is the very essence of all drops and is very pure and subtle. Even though it is the

substance of blood and sperm, it has a very clear nature, like
a tiny ball of crystal that radiates light.

You should contemplate like this repeatedly until you perceive a clear generic image of your indestructible drop and its location. When you perceive these two clearly, you should feel that your mind is inside the indestructible drop and then concentrate on the drop single-pointedly for as long as possible. The main object of this meditation is the indestructible drop, but the concentration must possess two characteristics: (1) it perceives and holds the indestructible drop and its location, and (2) it feels as if your mind is inside that drop.

This meditation is called 'the yoga of the drop'. We may need to practise it for many months or years. It causes us to experience an even deeper dissolution of the winds within the central channel than that accomplished by the first meditation. However, until we attain ultimate example clear light, we still need to improve our experience of this dissolution. For this reason, and to lay the foundation for the life exertion of isolated speech, we need to progress to the third meditation – meditation on the indestructible wind and mind.

MEDITATION ON THE INDESTRUCTIBLE WIND AND MIND – THE YOGA OF WIND

The main object of this meditation is the union of the indestructible wind and mind, which we visualize in the aspect of a letter BAM. Having dissolved Guru Vajradhara into your mind at your heart, you should try to perceive clearly the object of this meditation by contemplating as follows:

Inside my central channel at my heart is my indestructible drop.

Recall the location, size, shape, colour and nature of the drop, and then think:

Inside the indestructible drop is my indestructible wind and mind in the aspect of a tiny letter BAM, the size of a mustard seed. It is reddish-white in colour and radiates five-coloured rays of light. Its nature is my Guru, who is the synthesis of all the Buddhas, its substance is my indestructible wind and my own mind and its shape is that of a letter BAM, symbolizing Vajrayogini's mind.

You should think of the indestructible drop as being like a house, and of your actual mind in the aspect of a letter BAM as being like a person inhabiting that house. You should contemplate like this repeatedly until you perceive all together the tiny letter BAM, the indestructible drop and the location of the drop. Then, without forgetting the drop and its location, focus principally on the letter BAM inside the drop and, recognizing it as your actual mind, meditate on it single-pointedly for a while. This concentration must possess three characteristics: (1) it perceives and holds the tiny letter BAM, (2) it recognizes it as your actual mind, and (3) it does not forget the indestructible drop and its location.

If we train in this meditation repeatedly, we will gain an experience of our winds dissolving within the central channel that is deeper than that gained by the previous meditation, and we will attain the actual realization of isolated body of completion stage.

If you are a Heruka practitioner, you should practise these three meditations in exactly the same way as just explained, except that for your preliminary practices you can use *Great Liberation of the Father*, and instead of visualizing a letter BAM you should visualize a letter HUM, which is the nature of Heruka's mind. However, whether you are a Vajrayogini practitioner or a Heruka practitioner, you should visualize the letter as being reddish-white in colour. This symbolizes the red and white bodhichittas and reminds us to experience bliss.

THE RESULTS OF THE PRACTICE OF THIS MEDITATION

If we practise the above meditations sincerely and continually, we will definitely experience our inner winds entering, abiding and dissolving within our central channel. If, as a result of our meditation, the movement of the breath through both our nostrils becomes subtle, simultaneous and of equal strength, this is a sign that our winds have entered our central channel. Later, if, as a result of our meditation, the movement of the breath through both nostrils ceases, and at the same time abdominal movements and eye movements also cease, this is a sign that our winds are abiding within our central channel. After this, we will gradually experience the signs of our winds dissolving within our central channel as a result of our meditation.

Altogether there are seven different winds that dissolve sequentially within our central channel. They are: the earth element wind, the water element wind, the fire element wind, the wind element wind, the wind mounted by the mind of white appearance, the wind mounted by the mind of red increase and the wind mounted by the mind of black near-attainment. The first four are gross winds, and the last three are subtle winds. As each of these seven winds dissolves within the central channel, we experience a different sign.

The solid parts of our body, such as our bones, teeth and nails, are our earth element, and the wind that functions to support the increase of our earth element is our earth element wind. The fluid parts of our body, such as our blood, sperm and saliva, are our water element, and the wind that functions to support the increase of our water element is our water element wind. The inner heat of our body is our fire element, and the inner wind that functions to support the increase of our fire element is our fire element wind. Our earth element wind, water element wind and fire element wind are our wind element, and the wind that functions to support the increase of these winds is our wind element wind.

Once we have attained correct signs that our winds are abiding within our central channel, if, after continued meditation, we perceive the mirage-like appearance, this is the sign that our earth element wind has dissolved within our central channel. After this, if, through the force of meditation, we perceive the smoke-like appearance, this is the sign that our water element wind has dissolved. After this, if, through the force of meditation, we perceive the sparkling-fireflies-like appearance, this is the sign that our fire element wind has dissolved. After this, if, through the force of meditation, we perceive the candle-flame-like appearance, this is the sign that our wind element wind has started to dissolve.

These four signs are internal signs. Normally during the death process we perceive these four signs naturally, and we also experience corresponding external signs. The external signs of the dissolution of our earth element wind are that our body becomes thinner and its strength greatly diminishes. The external signs of the dissolution of our water element wind are that our saliva, blood and other bodily fluids dry up. The external sign of the dissolution of our fire element wind is that the warmth of our body diminishes. The external sign of the start of the dissolution of our wind element wind is that the strength of our bodily movements is greatly reduced.

Once we have attained the fourth internal sign, the candle-flame-like appearance, if, through the force of meditation, we perceive an appearance like white empty space, this is the sign that our wind element wind has completely dissolved. After this, if we perceive an appearance like red empty space, this is the sign that the wind mounted by the mind of white appearance has dissolved. After this, if we perceive an appearance like black empty space, this is the sign that the wind mounted by the mind of red increase has dissolved. After this, if we perceive an appearance like empty space pervaded by clear light, this is the sign that the wind mounted by the mind of black near-attainment has dissolved. A detailed description of these eight signs can be found in the book *Clear Light of Bliss*.

A mind that experiences the first of these last four appearances is called the 'mind of white appearance', a mind that experiences the second is called the 'mind of red increase', a mind that experiences the third is called the 'mind of black near-attainment', and a mind that experiences the fourth is called the 'mind of clear light'.

Through the force of the winds dissolving within the central channel, the inner heat within the central channel will increase, and because of this the white or red drops will melt and flow through the central channel. As a result of this, the practitioner will experience great bliss and attain the actual realization of clear light of isolated body. This is the result of these three meditations.

Khedrub Ngawang Dorje

HOW TO PRACTISE ISOLATED BODY OF COMPLETION
STAGE DURING THE MEDITATION BREAK

This practice is a powerful method for accumulating both the collection of merit and the collection of wisdom, as well as for overcoming ordinary appearance and ordinary conception, and so it enables us to accomplish quickly both the Form Body and the Truth Body of a Buddha. To practise isolated body during the meditation break, we need to refrain from ordinary appearance and ordinary conception by viewing all phenomena that appear to us as manifestations of bliss and emptiness, or in the aspect of Deities. This is the training in higher moral discipline according to Highest Yoga Tantra. By engaging in this practice, we can transform our normal activities such as working, shopping, cooking, eating, drinking, dancing, playing, kissing and sexual intercourse into a powerful method for accumulating merit and wisdom.

If we lack perfect knowledge of emptiness, or experience of the bliss of generation stage or completion stage, we will find it difficult to view all phenomena that appear to us as manifestations of bliss and emptiness. However, we can understand how all phenomena are manifestations of bliss and emptiness by considering the following explanation.

In the *Essence of Wisdom Sutra*, the *Heart Sutra*, it says:

Form is empty; emptiness is form.

'Form is empty' means that form lacks true existence – that the ultimate nature of form is the mere emptiness of form. 'Emptiness is form' means that this very emptiness appears as form, and so form is a manifestation of its own emptiness. Whenever a form appears to us, we need complete conviction

159

that this form is a manifestation of emptiness, and that, apart from its emptiness, there is no form existing from its own side.

The ultimate nature of form is the emptiness of form. Of all the many parts or aspects of form, only its emptiness is true. A wristwatch, for example, has many parts, but within the collection of all these parts only its emptiness is true and real. We can hold a wristwatch in our hands but, if we examine it more closely to find the 'real' watch, we cannot find anything at all. When we try to point to the watch, all we can ever point to are parts of the watch. The parts of the watch are not the watch itself, but, besides these parts, there is no watch. This very unfindability is the real nature of the watch. If the watch were truly existent, it would possess its own existence independent of other phenomena, and it would be possible mentally to remove all phenomena that are not the watch and be left with just the watch. The fact that this is not possible indicates that the watch lacks, or is empty of, true existence. The watch's lack of true existence is the real, or ultimate, nature of the watch. Since the emptiness of the watch is the real nature of the watch, the watch does not exist separately from its emptiness. The watch and its emptiness are two aspects of a single entity, like a gold coin and the gold of which it is made. The real nature of the watch is just its emptiness, but this very emptiness appears to us in the aspect of a watch.

If a monk with miracle powers manifested as a tiger, everyone would see a tiger and not a monk. In reality, however, the tiger is a manifestation of the monk. The tiger does not exist separately from the monk; it is the monk himself appearing in a different aspect. This analogy from the scriptures helps us to understand how things are manifestations of emptiness. If we find it difficult to believe in magical emanations, we can consider an actor. If a male actor puts on a wig and dresses in women's clothes he will appear to other people as a woman. The woman that people see is simply the actor in disguise; we could say that she is a manifestation of the actor. In a similar way, forms are like emptiness in disguise. Although forms appear to have their own characteristics and exist in their own right, if we examine them more closely we find only emptiness. This emptiness is their real nature, but it appears as form. Forms are therefore manifestations of emptiness.

If forms were not manifestations of emptiness, forms would be true, and when a Superior being placed his or her mind single-pointedly on the ultimate nature of form, form would appear to his or her mind. However, when Superior beings meditate on emptiness, forms do not appear. Why not? Because forms are not true, but are false objects. Forms are simply manifestations of emptiness.

Some people may think that teachings on the channels, drops and winds are very advanced, but I feel that teachings on emptiness and bodhichitta are much more advanced. It is not that difficult to focus the mind on a drop at the heart or to meditate on inner fire. In themselves, these practices have no great meaning; they become profound practices only when they are motivated by bodhichitta and conjoined with a realization of emptiness. Therefore, we need to make a special effort to understand emptiness. If we are intelligent, we should study extensive texts on the middle way such as the book *Ocean of Nectar*, but, if this seems too daunting a task, we should study the book *The New Heart of Wisdom*, or the ninth chapter of Shantideva's *Guide to the Bodhisattva's Way of Life* as explained in the book *Meaningful to Behold*, or the chapter on

Training in Ultimate Bodhichitta in the book *Modern Buddhism*. We also need to put effort into accumulating merit, purifying karmic obstructions and receiving the blessings of our Spiritual Guide. If we do all these things, we will not find it difficult to realize emptiness. The most important thing is to have faith in our Teacher and in Buddha's teachings. Even if our Teacher explains emptiness very clearly, if we have no faith in him or his teachings we will not understand them; our mind will be filled with doubts and confusion. On the other hand, if we have faith and create all the other necessary conditions, we will definitely attain a profound realization of emptiness.

In *The Three Principal Aspects of the Path*, Je Tsongkhapa says:

> Moreover, if you negate the extreme of existence
> By simply realizing that phenomena are just mere appearance,
> And if you negate the extreme of non-existence
> By simply realizing that all the phenomena you normally see or perceive do not exist,
>
> And if you realize how, for example, the emptiness of cause and effect
> Is perceived as cause and effect,
> Because there is no cause and effect other than emptiness,
> With these realizations you will not be harmed by extreme view.

The first three lines of the second verse reveal that all phenomena, such as causes and effects, are manifestations of emptiness. All functioning things are both causes and effects. A seed, for example, is a cause because it gives rise to a sprout, and an effect because it is produced from other causes such as its parent plant. Since a seed depends upon causes, it is empty of independent, inherent existence. This emptiness is the real nature of the seed. When a seed appears to us, in reality it is the emptiness of the seed appearing to us in the aspect of a seed. Apart from this emptiness, there is no seed. If a seed existed apart from its emptiness, it would be inherently existent, but an inherently existent seed is utterly impossible. If we search long enough, we may find a unicorn or a rabbit with horns, but we will never find an inherently existent seed! The real nature of a seed is just emptiness; not even an atom of the seed exists from its own side. Chandrakirti explains this in great detail in *Guide to the Middle Way*, where he reveals the absurdity of positing an inherently existent cause or effect.

Another point we need to understand is that the conventional and ultimate nature of an object are the same entity. This is the meaning of the statement in the *Essence of Wisdom Sutra*:

> Emptiness is not other than form; form also is not other than emptiness.

A seed and its emptiness, for example, are the same entity, but, due to our familiarity with grasping at true existence, whenever a seed appears to us, it appears as completely different from its emptiness. Instead of perceiving it as the same entity as its emptiness, we mistakenly perceive it as the same entity as its inherent existence. We need to overcome our innate tendency conceiving the two truths as different entities so that, instead of assenting to the appearance of inherent existence, we regard all phenomena as manifestations of emptiness. Je Tsongkhapa said:

Although many different conventional objects appear
to us, in truth it is their lack of inherent existence that is
appearing to us in different aspects.

For qualified practitioners, during their meditation on
bringing death into the path to the Truth Body, all their
appearances of conventional objects gather and dissolve
into emptiness. They feel that they experience a profound
bliss mixed with emptiness, as if emptiness and their mind
of bliss have become one entity. They meditate on this recognition repeatedly until they gain a special mindfulness
such that they never forget emptiness and their mind as
one entity. Once they have this experience, they simultaneously perceive any objects, such as forms, that appear to
them as manifestations both of emptiness and their mind of
bliss. Because they have a deep recognition of emptiness and
their mind of bliss as the same nature, they can view all phenomena that appear to their mind as manifestations of their
bliss, and this special way of looking at phenomena causes
them greatly to increase their experience of bliss, just as a fire
will increase if more fuel is added to it.

We can also consider what Buddha says many times in his
teachings, that all phenomena are like a dream. This means
that just as the things that appear in a dream are not truly existent but are mere aspects of the dream mind, so all phenomena
lack true existence and are mere aspects of mind. Phenomena
do not exist outside the mind, because they are mere appearances to mind. If they existed outside the mind, they would
exist inherently; but this is not the case. All phenomena exist
as mere aspects of mind, or as mere manifestations of mind.
Mere appearance to mind, mere aspect of mind and mere
manifestation of mind are synonyms.

Buddha also says in the Sutras:

External objects do not exist,
Mind appears as various things,
Such as bodies, enjoyments and places;
I explain these as only mind.

Here, 'only mind' means that everything is just a manifestation of mind – like things in a dream. If our mind becomes
full of bliss, all phenomena that appear to our mind are
mere manifestations of our mind of bliss; besides this they
do not exist at all. Generally, Highest Yoga Tantra is based
on the Madhyamika-Prasangika view but, unlike Sutra
Prasangika scholars, many Tantric Prasangikas also accept
the Chittamatra view that forms are the nature of mind.

To practise isolated body of completion stage, we first
generate a special bliss by dissolving our inner winds
within our central channel through the meditations on the
central channel, drop and wind explained above. We then
meditate on emptiness with this mind of bliss while one
part of our mind keeps a special recognition that our mind
of bliss and emptiness have become indivisible, like the
actual Truth Body or Dharmakaya. Once we have gained
this experience in meditation, when we are out of meditation
we should view all phenomena that appear to our mind as
just manifestations of our mind of bliss and emptiness. By
keeping this view day and night, we refrain from ordinary
appearance and ordinary conception and can enjoy objects of
desire to increase our bliss.

We can also view all phenomena as manifestations of
Deities. We view all aggregates of form as manifestations
of Buddha Vairochana, all aggregates of feeling as
manifestations of Buddha Ratnasambhava, all aggregates

of discrimination as manifestations of Buddha Amitabha, all aggregates of compositional factors as manifestations of Buddha Amoghasiddhi and all aggregates of consciousness as manifestations of Buddha Akshobya. We view the four elements as manifestations of the four Mothers – all earth elements as manifestations of Lochana, all water elements as manifestations of Mamaki, all fire elements as manifestations of Benzarahi and all wind elements as manifestations of Tara. In particular, we visualize all forms throughout the world in the aspect of Rupavajra Goddesses, all sounds in the aspect of Shaptavajra Goddesses, all smells in the aspect of Gändhavajra Goddesses, all tastes in the aspect of Rasavajra Goddesses, all tactile objects in the aspect of Parshavajra Goddesses and all other phenomena in the aspect of Dharmadhatuvajra Goddesses; and we enjoy these Goddesses and their offerings so as to increase our bliss.

A Rupavajra Goddess is a female Deity, white in colour and holding a mirror reflecting the whole universe, who is born from an omniscient wisdom that is indivisible from the emptiness of form. A Shaptavajra Goddess is a female Deity, blue in colour and holding a flute that spontaneously produces beautiful music, who is born from an omniscient wisdom that is indivisible from the emptiness of sound. A Gändhavajra Goddess is a female Deity, yellow in colour and holding a beautiful jewelled container filled with special perfumes whose fragrance pervades the whole world, who is born from an omniscient wisdom that is indivisible from the emptiness of smell. A Rasavajra Goddess is a female Deity, red in colour and holding a precious container filled with nectar possessing the three qualities – medicine-nectar that cures all disease, life-nectar that overcomes death and wisdom-nectar that destroys delusions – who is born from an omniscient wisdom that is indivisible from the emptiness of taste. A Parshavajra Goddess is a female Deity, green in colour and holding precious garments, who is born from an omniscient wisdom that is indivisible from the emptiness of touch. A Dharmadhatuvajra Goddess is a female Deity, white in colour and holding a phenomena source symbolizing emptiness, who is born from an omniscient wisdom that is indivisible from the emptiness of all other phenomena.

Each Goddess bestows the five types of bliss: bliss arisen from seeing her beautiful body, bliss arisen from hearing her beautiful songs, bliss arisen from smelling her pleasant fragrance, bliss arisen from tasting her kiss and bliss arisen from feeling the smoothness of her skin. We generate these five types of bliss and then meditate on emptiness, symbolized by the phenomena source. We should do this practice of subsequent attainment and the practice of meditative equipoise alternately until we become a Tantric Buddha.

Ngulchu Dharmabhadra

Isolated Speech and Isolated Mind

ISOLATED SPEECH

This is explained in three parts:

1 Definition and etymology of isolated speech
2 Divisions of isolated speech
3 How to practise isolated speech

DEFINITION AND ETYMOLOGY OF ISOLATED SPEECH

The definition of isolated speech is a completion stage yoga prior to isolated mind that functions to isolate the very subtle wind, the root of speech, from ordinary winds.

Speech depends upon the upward-moving wind, which is located principally at the throat and functions to enable us to speak. Like all gross winds, the upward-moving wind develops from the very subtle wind, so the real root of speech is the very subtle wind. The yoga of isolated speech functions to purify the very subtle wind by isolating it from the movements of ordinary winds.

DIVISIONS OF ISOLATED SPEECH

There are five types of isolated speech:

1 First empty of isolated speech

2 Second empty of isolated speech
3 Third empty of isolated speech
4 Fourth empty of isolated speech
5 Isolated speech that is none of these four

All the yogas of subsequent attainment of isolated speech are included within the fifth type.

The first empty is the mind of white appearance, the second empty the mind of red increase, the third empty the mind of black near-attainment and the fourth empty the mind of clear light. However, if something is one of the four empties, it is not necessarily one of the four empties of isolated speech. For example, the mind of white appearance that develops in dependence upon meditation on the indestructible drop prior to isolated speech is one of the four empties, but it is not isolated speech. For something to be isolated speech, it must have arisen through the force of loosening the knots of the heart channel wheel. An example of isolated speech is the mind of white appearance developed through the force of loosening the channel knots at the heart by means of vajra recitation, or other methods that have a similar function to vajra recitation.

According to Secret Mantra, it is very important to control the winds. All pure Dharma practitioners know how important it is to control the mind, but we cannot really control our mind without controlling our winds. As long as impure winds are flowing through our channels, we will continue to develop negative thoughts. Seeing how our states of mind depend upon the purity or impurity of our winds, Secret Mantra practitioners strive to control their winds. For a mind to function, it requires a wind to give it the power to move to its object. Thus, for as long as the defiled wind that acts as the mount for self-grasping ignorance flows through our channels, we will develop self-grasping ignorance, but, if we manage to subdue this wind, our self-grasping will have no power to grasp objects; it will not cause us to develop delusions, and it will not be able to act as the cause of samsara.

Recognizing the need to control the winds, Tantric Yogis consider the yoga of wind to be very important. Directly or indirectly, all completion stage yogas are yogas of wind because they are all methods for bringing the winds into the central channel. In *Vajra Rosary Tantra*, Vajradhara says that if Yogis meditate on wind they will accomplish the attainments swiftly, and in *Little Sambara Tantra*, he says:

> Those who do not know about the yoga of winds,
> Or do not meditate on it,
> Will be afflicted by various sufferings
> And will remain in samsara.

Of all winds, the most important is the very subtle wind. This is the basis of both samsara and Buddhahood. If we fail to control the very subtle wind, it will be the cause of rebirth in samsara, but, if we control it, it will become the substantial cause of the illusory body and the Form Body of a Buddha. Controlling the very subtle wind means stopping ordinary winds developing from it.

To understand how the very subtle wind is the foundation of both samsaric rebirth and liberation from samsara, we need to consider the process of death, intermediate state and rebirth. When we die, the winds dissolve within the central channel and we experience the very subtle mind of the clear light of death. When the very subtle mind of clear light is manifest, at the same time the very subtle wind is manifest.

The actual moment of death occurs when the clear light of death ceases. In the next moment, if we are going to be reborn as a human being we enter the intermediate state, or bardo, of a human being. We remain in the intermediate state until we see our future parents engaging in sexual intercourse, and then enter our future mother's womb. As we do so, the intermediate state being dies and experiences the clear light of death. The moment this clear light of death ceases and the mind of black near-attainment of reverse order manifests, the next life has begun. At the same time, the mounted wind of black near-attainment develops directly. Then the mounted winds of red increase and white appearance gradually develop. In the case of ordinary beings, because the mounted wind of the clear light of death of the intermediate state being is impure, the mounted wind of black near-attainment that manifests as they enter the womb is also impure. Since the source is impure, all the winds that develop from it are also impure. In dependence upon these impure winds, ordinary beings develop disturbing conceptual thoughts, such as self-grasping.

If, on the other hand, a person has purified and controlled his or her very subtle wind, all the winds that arise from it will also be pure. If the mounted wind of the clear light of death of the intermediate state is pure, the mounted wind of black near-attainment, and all the winds that develop from it, will also be pure. Such beings will attain high realizations naturally. Because only pure winds flow through their channels, it will be impossible for them to develop negative conceptions, and virtuous minds will arise effortlessly.

HOW TO PRACTISE ISOLATED SPEECH

This has three parts:

1 Meditation on the indestructible drop
2 Meditation on the indestructible wind and mind
3 Meditation on vajra recitation

The third of these is the actual practice of isolated speech. However, we first need to lay the foundation for vajra recitation through familiarity with meditation on the indestructible drop and the indestructible wind and mind. These two meditations make it easy for us to loosen the channel knots at the heart, but the actual method for directly loosening these knots is meditation on vajra recitation. Without loosening the knots of the heart channel wheel, we cannot attain the actual realizations of isolated speech. The first two meditations listed here have already been explained, and so there now follows an explanation of the third, meditation on vajra recitation.

MEDITATION ON VAJRA RECITATION

Vajra recitation is a yoga of wind that has two principal functions: (1) to loosen and untie the channel knots at the heart, and (2) to unite the winds with mantra, thereby stopping the ordinary movement of winds and transforming the very subtle wind into a wisdom wind. Vajra recitation will now be explained under the following three headings:

1 Definition and etymology of vajra recitation
2 Divisions of vajra recitation
3 How to practise vajra recitation

DEFINITION AND ETYMOLOGY OF VAJRA RECITATION

The definition of vajra recitation is a yoga in which wind and mantra are united, and which is the ultimate recitation of a person on completion stage. This definition has two parts. The first part describes the function of vajra recitation, which is to join the winds with mantra so that wind and mantra cannot be differentiated; and the second part indicates that vajra recitation is the ultimate mantra recitation. In general, there are three types of mantra recitation: verbal recitation, mental recitation and vajra recitation. Vajra recitation is neither verbal recitation nor mental recitation, but wind recitation.

The etymology of vajra recitation is as follows. 'Vajra' means 'indestructible' and refers to the indestructible union of wind and mantra, and 'recitation' indicates that vajra recitation is a practice of mantra recitation.

DIVISIONS OF VAJRA RECITATION

There are two types of vajra recitation:

1 Vajra recitation on the root winds
2 Vajra recitation on the branch winds

Since there are five root winds and five branch winds, we can further divide vajra recitation into ten types.

HOW TO PRACTISE VAJRA RECITATION

This is explained in three parts:

1 An explanation of the winds

2 An explanation of mantra
3 The actual meditation on vajra recitation

AN EXPLANATION OF THE WINDS

The definition of wind is any of the four elements that is light in weight and moving. Winds can be divided into external and internal winds, and into gross and subtle winds. Gross external wind is the wind we experience on a windy day. Subtle external wind is much more difficult to detect. It is the energy that makes plants grow and exists even inside rocks and mountains. It is with the help of subtle winds that plants draw up water, grow new leaves, and so forth. Such winds are the life-force of plants. Indeed, in some Tantric texts, wind is called 'life' or 'life-force'. Thus, although it is incorrect to say that plants are alive in the sense of being conjoined with consciousness, we can say that they are alive in this sense.

Internal winds are the winds in the continuum of a person that flow through the channels of the body. The main function of internal winds is to move the mind to its object. The function of the mind is to apprehend objects, but, without a wind to act as its mount, it cannot move towards, or establish a connection with, its object. Mind is sometimes likened to a lame person who can see, and wind to a blind person with legs. It is only by operating together with internal winds that minds can function.

There are many different winds flowing through the channels of the body, but all are included within the five root winds and the five branch winds. The five root winds are:

(1) The life-supporting wind
(2) The downward-voiding wind

(3) The upward-moving wind
(4) The equally-abiding wind
(5) The pervading wind

The life-supporting wind is called the 'Akshobya wind' because, when it is completely purified, it transforms into the nature of Akshobya. At the moment, our life-supporting wind is like the seed of Akshobya's Form Body, but not Akshobya himself. The main function of the life-supporting wind is to support life by maintaining the connection between body and mind. The stronger the life-supporting wind, the longer we will live. Another function of this wind is to support the water element of our body and to cause it to increase. The life-supporting wind is white in colour and its principal location is at the heart. When we exhale, it leaves from both nostrils, flowing gently downwards.

The downward-voiding wind is the seed of Ratnasambhava's Form Body and is associated with the earth element. It is yellow in colour and it functions to release urine, faeces, sperm and menstrual blood. Its principal locations are at the anus and the sex organ, and, when we exhale, it leaves horizontally from both nostrils, flowing heavily forwards.

The upward-moving wind is the seed of Amitabha's Form Body and is associated with the fire element. It is red in colour and it functions to enable us to swallow food and drink, to speak, to cough and so forth. Its principal location is at the throat, and, when we exhale, it leaves from the right nostril, flowing violently upwards.

The equally-abiding wind is the seed of Amoghasiddhi's Form Body and is associated with the wind element. It is greenish-yellow in colour and it functions to cause the inner fire to blaze, and to digest food and drink by separating the nutrients from waste matter. Its principal location is at the navel, and, when we exhale, it leaves from the left nostril, moving to the left and the right from the edge of the nostril.

The pervading wind is the seed of Vairochana's Form Body and is associated with the space element. It is pale blue in colour and, as its name suggests, it pervades the entire body, particularly the three hundred and sixty joints. It functions to enable the body to move. Without this wind, we would be completely immobile, like a stone. This wind does not flow through the nostrils except at the moment of death.

Generally speaking, at any one time, one of the winds is flowing more strongly through the nostrils than the other winds. If, for example, the life-supporting wind is flowing strongly, the other winds (except the pervading wind) are flowing gently. Unless we observe our breath very carefully, it is difficult to notice the different movements of the four winds, but they definitely flow through our nostrils whenever we breathe.

The five branch winds are:

(1) The moving wind
(2) The intensely-moving wind
(3) The perfectly-moving wind
(4) The strongly-moving wind
(5) The definitely-moving wind

The five branch winds are so called because they branch off from the life-supporting wind, which resides in the heart centre. The main location of these winds is in the four channel spokes of the heart channel wheel, from where they flow through our channels to the five doors of the sense powers. Because they function to enable sense awarenesses

Yangchen Drubpay Dorje

to develop, the five branch winds are also called the 'five winds of the sense powers'.

The first wind, the moving wind, flows from the heart through the door of the eyes to enable the eye awareness to move to its object, visual forms. Without the moving wind, eye awareness would be powerless to contact visual forms. The reason we cannot see when we are asleep is that the moving wind has withdrawn from the door of the eye sense power back to its seat at the heart.

The intensely-moving wind flows from the heart to the ears, enabling the ear awareness to move to sounds. The perfectly-moving wind flows from the heart to the nostrils, enabling the nose awareness to move to smells. The strongly-moving wind flows from the heart to the tongue, enabling the tongue awareness to move to tastes. The definitely-moving wind flows from the heart all over the body, enabling the body awareness to move to tactile objects.

The downward-voiding wind, the upward-moving wind, the equally-abiding wind, the pervading wind and the five branch winds are all gross internal winds. The life-supporting wind has three levels: gross, subtle and very subtle. Most mounted winds of conceptual thoughts are gross life-supporting winds; the mounted winds of the minds of white appearance, red increase and black near-attainment are subtle life-supporting winds; and the mounted wind of the mind of clear light is a very subtle life-supporting wind.

The life-supporting wind is very extensive. If a defiled life-supporting wind manifests, negative conceptual thoughts will develop, but if the life-supporting wind is purified, negative conceptual thoughts will be pacified. All meditations use the mental awareness, and the mounted wind of mental awareness is necessarily a life-supporting wind.

Each of the five winds of the sense powers and the gross life-supporting wind has two parts: a wind that develops the specific type of awareness, and a wind that moves the awareness towards its object. These twelve winds normally flow through the right and left channels and are the principal objects to be purified by means of vajra recitation. If we want to overcome distractions, it is very important to cause these twelve winds to enter, abide and dissolve within the central channel.

AN EXPLANATION OF MANTRA

There are many Deities of Highest Yoga Tantra, and each Deity has a number of different mantras, such as a root mantra, an essence mantra, a close essence mantra, an action mantra and mantras of retinue Deities. In the practice of Heruka, the root mantra, the essence mantra, the close essence mantra and the mantras of the armour Deities are particularly important, and are known as the 'four aspects of the precious ones'. All the great Mahasiddhas considered these mantras to be very precious. The three-OM mantra of Vajrayogini is another especially powerful mantra because it contains the root, essence and close essence mantras combined together. We receive great benefits from reciting the mantras of Heruka and Vajrayogini. It is even said that if we write these mantras in gold on paper and keep this on our body, we will not be harmed by humans or spirits.

All mantras are contained within the three letters: OM AH HUM. This short mantra is the mantra of all Buddhas. All Buddhas are contained within three groups: vajra body, vajra speech and vajra mind. The mantra of vajra body is OM, the mantra of vajra speech is AH and the mantra of vajra mind is HUM. If we recite these three letters, we receive the blessings of all mantras and all Buddhas. If this mantra is recited with strong faith, it is very powerful. There are three ways to recite OM AH HUM – verbally, mentally and by vajra recitation. Mental recitation is superior to verbal recitation, but vajra recitation is the supreme recitation.

The source of the three letters OM AH HUM, and of all mantras in general, is the sixteen Sanskrit vowels and the thirty-four Sanskrit consonants. The sixteen vowels are:

A, AA, I, II, U, UU, RI, RII, LI, LII, E, AI, O, AU, AM, AH

The thirty-four consonants are divided into seven groups as follows:

KA, KHA, GA, GHA, NGA,
CHA, CHHA, JA, JHA, NYA,
DA, THA, TA, DHA, NA,
DrA, THrA, TrA, DHrA, NA,
BA, PHA, PA, BHA, MA,
YA, RA, LA, WA,
SHA, KA, SA, HA, KYA

When we bless the inner offering in the sadhanas of Heruka and Vajrayogini, we visualize these vowels and consonants above the skullcup, and imagine them merging together and transforming into the three letters OM AH HUM. This demonstrates that the three letters in particular and all mantras in general are derived from the vowels and consonants.

When we say the vowels and consonants out loud they are the nature of sound, but what are they before they are spoken? Before they become speech, the fifty letters are the nature of inner winds within the channels of our body. When these winds reach our throat and meet other conditions, they transform into the sounds of the fifty letters. When we write letters down, they appear to us in the aspect of visual forms but, in reality, letters are not visual forms but expressive sounds. Similarly, all mantras are also originally the nature of wind, but they can be expressed verbally as sound or written down as form. There are four types of mantra: mantras that are mind, mantras that are wind, mantras that are sound and mantras that are form. The ultimate or definitive mantra is the mind of indivisible bliss and emptiness of all Buddhas, which is both mind and mantra; the mantras that exist in our channels before we speak or write them down are mantras that are wind; a spoken mantra is a mantra that is sound; and a written mantra is a mantra that is form.

'Mantra' literally means 'mind protection'. Since the mind of bliss and emptiness is the ultimate mind protection, it is mantra. An example of an ultimate mantra is the wisdom of bliss and emptiness of Heruka, which is the ultimate mantra of Heruka. When this wisdom appears as a root mantra, it is called the 'root mantra of Heruka'. Before the root mantra of Heruka is spoken, it abides as the nature of wind inside the channels, at which time it is both mantra and wind. When the root mantra is spoken, it becomes a mantra that is sound, and when it is written down, it becomes a mantra that is form.

The written letters of a mantra are a visible representation of the spoken mantra. Without the sound of the mantra, there would be no written mantra; and the sound of the mantra develops from wind. If there were no winds flowing in the channels, there would be no speech, and therefore no mantras that are sound. The inner nature of mantras is therefore wind. Since mantras are composed of the sixteen vowels and thirty-four consonants, the inner nature of these letters is also wind. When the fifty winds that are the inner nature of the fifty letters are purified, all winds are purified. Vajrayogini's garland of fifty skulls symbolizes the fifty purified winds – her fifty purified inner vowels and consonants appear in the aspect of a garland of human skulls.

In summary, the very subtle wind is the root of speech and the root of mantra. From the very subtle wind, gross winds develop, and from the gross winds the sound of mantra develops. Without wind, there is no mantra. Some scholars have raised the question: 'What is the real nature of scriptures?' This is very difficult to answer in terms of Sutra teachings alone. If we say scriptures are mind, then we have to explain how they can be communicated to others, but if we say scriptures are sound or visible form, we must explain how matter can express meanings. How can a sound, which is devoid of awareness, become an object-possessor? These problems can easily be resolved if we consider the Highest Yoga Tantra teachings on winds. The inner nature of scriptures is wind, which is conjoined with awareness. When the scriptures are recited they become sound, and when they are written down they become form.

The purpose of this discussion on winds and mantras is to dispel the misconception that mantras are just sound or form. To accomplish the aim of vajra recitation – to unite our winds with mantra – we need to understand that the inner nature of mantras is wind.

THE ACTUAL MEDITATION ON VAJRA RECITATION

We can meditate on vajra recitation at any time, but the best time is at dawn, when our mind is fresh. Dawn symbolizes clear light, so meditating on vajra recitation at dawn is auspicious for the swift attainment of the realization of clear light. The physical posture for doing vajra recitation is the seven-point posture of Vairochana, the object of meditation is inner wind, and the place where we focus our mind is principally at the heart. Vajra recitation is called 'life exertion on the drop of light' because the main object of vajra recitation is the very subtle wind endowed with rays of five-coloured lights.

If we have gained some familiarity with meditating on the indestructible drop and the indestructible wind and mind at the heart as explained above, we can begin the practice of vajra recitation. We focus on our indestructible wind and mind in the aspect of a tiny reddish-white letter BAM inside the indestructible drop, inside the central channel at the heart. From the nada of the letter BAM, we imagine that our life-supporting wind rises gently through our central channel, like white incense smoke. As it ascends, it makes the sound HUM. We should feel that the wind itself makes this sound and that our mind is simply listening to it. Gradually the life-supporting wind reaches the throat channel wheel. We hold it there for a while, still making the sound HUM, and then allow it to descend slowly. As it descends, it makes the sound OM. Finally it reaches the centre of the heart channel wheel and dissolves into the indestructible drop. It remains there for a short time, making the sound AH. Then again the life-supporting wind ascends to the throat making the sound HUM, descends making the sound OM and abides at the heart making the sound AH. We should repeat this cycle several times. Finally we concentrate single-pointedly only on the wind abiding at the heart and the sound AH.

When we have gained some familiarity with this medita-tion, we modify it as follows. We begin as before, but when the wind ascends, instead of it remaining at the throat we allow it to continue without interruption to the crown, all the time making the sound HUM. It remains at the crown very briefly and then descends slowly back to the heart making the sound OM. Then it abides at the heart for a while, making the sound AH. We repeat this cycle several times. Finally we concentrate only on the wind abiding at the heart and the sound AH.

When we have gained some familiarity with this second meditation, we imagine that the life-supporting wind rises from the indestructible wind and goes all the way to the nostrils without stopping at the throat or crown, and that as it ascends it makes the sound HUM. It remains at the nostrils very briefly and then returns slowly to the heart making the sound OM, and remains at the heart making the sound AH. We repeat this cycle several times and end by focusing single-pointedly on the sound of AH at the heart.

When we have gained some familiarity with this third meditation, we imagine that the wind rises from the heart, goes straight through the throat and crown chakras, leaves through the nostrils and reaches the hearts of all the Buddhas, whom we visualize in the space before us. All the time it is making the sound HUM. The wind receives the blessings of all the Buddhas and returns back through our nostrils to our heart, making the sound OM. The blessed wind dissolves into the indestructible drop and makes the sound AH. We repeat this cycle several times, all the time listening to the mantra sound of the wind.

When we have gained some familiarity with this meditation, we move to the fifth meditation. We begin as before. The life-supporting wind ascends and exits the nostrils, making the sound HUM. Then we imagine that the exhaled wind mixes with the external winds of countless world systems. The mixture of internal winds and external winds make the sound HUM. All the winds gather, becoming more and more subtle, enter our nostrils and descend to our heart, making the sound OM. Then they abide at our heart making the sound AH. While exhaling, inhaling and abiding at the heart, we should remain continuously mindful of the sounds OM AH HUM. Finally all internal and external winds become OM AH HUM.

Vajra recitation can also be done with the other four root winds and with the five branch winds. By doing this, we unite all our inner winds with mantra. In this way, impure winds will gradually cease and only pure winds will flow through our channels. A side-effect of this is that we will obtain clairvoyance and miracle powers. In the system of Secret Mantra, clairvoyance and miracle powers are obtained principally through the yoga of wind. For example, we can attain eye clairvoyance by doing vajra recitation on the moving wind, the wind that flows through the door of the eyes and supports eye awareness. Through uniting this wind with mantra, the wind becomes pure and, since pure winds support only pure minds, only pure appearances will appear to our eye awareness. We will see Pure Lands and other forms that ordinary beings cannot see.

At present our moving wind is impure, so we see only impure forms. The only reason we cannot see Pure Lands or pure beings, and the only reason even our Teachers appear to us as ordinary, is that our winds are impure. When we purify our winds, the minds mounted on these winds also become pure, and when the object-possessor is pure its objects are also pure. Objects exist only in relation to subjects, so the purity of the perceived object depends upon the purity of the perceiving subject. In *Ornament of Clear Realizations*, Maitreya says that the ability to see Buddha Lands depends upon the purity of our mind. When our mind becomes pure, then from our perspective everything is pure. When a human practitioner attains enlightenment, the place where he or she lives becomes his or her Pure Land. He does not need to travel elsewhere to attain Buddhahood. Ordinary people see only an ordinary, impure place, but for the practitioner himself it is a Pure Land. Purity and impurity depend upon the mind. We cannot clean our mind with soap and water, but we can purify it by purifying our inner winds through vajra recitation. We will then be able to see many subtle objects that cannot be seen by others.

The main function of vajra recitation is to loosen the channel knots at our heart. When these knots are loosened, the knots of the navel, throat and so on, naturally loosen. To facilitate the loosening of these other knots, it is also very helpful to do vajra recitation on a mixture of the life-supporting wind and the downward-voiding wind. How should we do this? First we try to attain a generic image of the indestructible drop at the heart. Inside the drop is the very subtle mind and wind in the aspect of a letter BAM. We imagine that all the life-supporting winds of the upper part of our body gather inwards, enter our central channel through the crown channel wheel and descend through the central channel making the sound OM. These winds are white in colour and are the nature of the sound OM. At the same time, we imagine that all the downward-voiding winds of the lower part of our body enter our central channel through the door of the sex organ and ascend making the sound OM. These winds are yellow in colour and also the nature of the sound OM. The life-supporting wind descends from the

Khedrub Tenzin Tsondru

crown, and the downward-voiding wind ascends from the sex organ, until finally the two winds reach the heart and dissolve into the indestructible drop. They abide in the drop making the sound AH. We remain with this experience for quite a long time. Then we imagine that the life-supporting wind ascends again to the crown while the downward-voiding wind descends to the sex organ, both winds making the sound HUM. The life-supporting wind reaches the very centre of the crown channel wheel, and at the same time the downward-voiding wind reaches the centre of the channel wheel of the sex organ. They then reverse direction and flow back to the heart once again, making the sound OM. They remain at the heart for some time, making the sound AH. The time we spend abiding at the heart should be longer than the time we spend ascending and descending.

During this meditation, when the downward-voiding wind passes through the navel channel wheel, or when the life-supporting wind passes through the throat channel wheel, we should imagine that they are very sharp and pass through the channel wheels without obstruction and with some force. The winds are the nature of light and sound, but they move through the channel wheels quite forcefully, effortlessly clearing them of obstructions. We imagine that the winds are freeing the knots of the sex organ, secret place, navel, heart, throat and crown channel wheels, as if we are clearing the blockages in a bamboo tube.

If we concentrate continually on vajra recitation in this way, the knots of the heart channel wheel will be loosened. As a result, the life-supporting wind and the downward-voiding wind will dissolve into the central channel at the heart, and we will experience the eight signs more clearly than before. The four empties – the last four of the eight signs of dissolution – attained through the force of freeing the heart channel knots through vajra recitation are the actual realizations of isolated speech. Through this practice, the very subtle wind, which is the root of speech, is separated from ordinary movement of the winds, and is thereby transformed into a wisdom wind. The clear light perceived at this time is the actual clear light. The clear light perceived through the force of isolated body is an artificial or facsimile clear light, not actual clear light.

Through practising the vajra recitation of mixing the life-supporting wind and downward-voiding wind, we will attain the actual realizations of isolated speech and transform the mind of clear light into spontaneous bliss. If we transform our very subtle mind into spontaneous bliss and learn to use it to meditate on emptiness, we will definitely attain Buddhahood in this life. This is the ultimate benefit of vajra recitation.

Temporary benefits of vajra recitation include the attainments of pacifying, increasing, controlling and wrathful actions. Moreover, because we are reciting the mantra of all Buddhas, the blessings of all Buddhas enter our body; and because the winds flowing in our channels are transformed into the nature of mantra, we attain miracle powers. When we complete the practice of vajra recitation, even external winds appear as the three mantra letters OM AH HUM. We can mix our internal winds with the external winds and gather them all into our heart. We gain power over external winds and other external elements such as fire, water and earth, so we cannot be harmed by these elements. Through gaining power over the wind element, we can fly in the sky, and through gaining power over the fire element, we are protected from harm by fire. It is said that once we have attained the realization of isolated speech, we can complete the practice of vajra recitation within six months.

ISOLATED MIND

This is explained in three parts:

1 Definition and etymology of isolated mind
2 Divisions of isolated mind
3 How to practise isolated mind

DEFINITION AND ETYMOLOGY OF ISOLATED MIND

The definition of isolated mind is a completion stage yoga prior to the attainment of illusory body that is developed principally through the force of completely releasing the heart channel knots, and that functions to isolate the very subtle mind from ordinary movements of mind. Another function of isolated mind is directly to purify ordinary death, intermediate state and rebirth, and to act as a direct cause of the attainment of the illusory body. The substantial cause of the illusory body is the mounted wind of isolated mind; isolated mind itself is the substantial cause of the mind of a person who possesses the illusory body. Without the realization of isolated mind, it is impossible to attain the illusory body, and without the illusory body it is impossible to attain the Form Body of a Buddha.

Isolated mind is the supreme condition for the attainment of Buddhahood because whoever attains isolated mind will definitely attain enlightenment without needing to undergo ordinary death ever again. There are two times when isolated mind can be attained: before death and at the time of death. Yogis who attain isolated mind in this life will soon attain the illusory body and will definitely attain enlightenment in this life. Some completion stage Yogis do not attain isolated mind while they are alive, but do so at the time of death by transforming the clear light of death into the wisdom of isolated mind. When the clear light of death ceases, instead of entering the ordinary intermediate state these Yogis or Yoginis arise in the form of the illusory body and then go on to attain enlightenment. It is said that they attain enlightenment in the intermediate state, but in reality the actual intermediate state has already been purified.

The mind of isolated mind is the substantial cause of the mind of a Buddha, and the mounted wind of isolated mind is the substantial cause of the body of a Buddha. The wisdom of isolated mind is both a collection of merit and a collection of wisdom. Simply by meditating on the wisdom of isolated mind the Yogi can complete both collections. He can meditate on isolated mind twenty-four hours a day, both while he is awake and while he is asleep. Such a person has no need to engage in external practices for accumulating merit such as making mandala offerings or prostrations, but can spend all day sleeping if he or she so wishes.

Isolated mind is so called because it is a yoga in which the very subtle mind is separated, or isolated, from ordinary movements of mind.

DIVISIONS OF ISOLATED MIND

There are five types of isolated mind:

1 Isolated mind of white appearance
2 Isolated mind of red increase

3 Isolated mind of black near-attainment
4 Isolated mind of clear light
5 Isolated mind that is none of these four

All the yogas of subsequent attainment of isolated mind are included within the fifth type.

In general, white appearance is called 'empty' because it is a subtle mental awareness that is empty of gross minds and winds. Red increase is called 'very empty' because it is empty of white appearance and its mounted wind. Black near-attainment is called 'great empty' because it is empty of red increase and its mounted wind. Clear light is called 'all empty' because it is empty of black near-attainment and its mounted wind, as well as all grosser minds and winds.

There are many levels of the four empties, such as the four empties of basic time and the four empties of path time. The four empties of basic time develop in ordinary beings during the death process, and facsimiles of them develop during sleep. The actual and facsimile four empties of basic time are causes of rebirth within samsara. Though ordinary people experience the four empties, they do not recognize them and so they cannot transform them into spiritual paths.

The four empties of path time include the four empties of isolated body, the four empties of isolated speech and the four empties of isolated mind. Like the four empties that develop during sleep, the four empties of isolated body are not actual four empties but facsimiles. The four empties of isolated speech are actual four empties but, compared with the four empties of isolated mind, they are not very qualified. The clearest experience of the four empties occurs when all the winds dissolve into the indestructible drop, which is possible only when the channel knots at the heart loosen completely.

This happens naturally during the death process through the force of karma, but a Yogi at the level of isolated mind experiences through the force of meditation a dissolution of winds as complete as that which occurs during the death process, and consequently has an equally clear experience of the four empties. The only difference is that the Yogi or Yogini retains mindfulness throughout the dissolutions (except during the deep swoon of the lower part of black near-attainment), and when the four empties manifest he or she transforms them into the nature of spontaneous bliss and uses them to meditate on emptiness. In this way, the four empties become the means for overcoming ordinary death. Such a person is free from death because, when he rises from the fourth empty of ultimate isolated mind, he will attain an illusory body. From then on, this will be his actual body, and it will never die.

It is important to understand the four empties precisely. The first empty and white appearance are synonyms, the second empty and red increase are synonyms, the third empty and black near-attainment are synonyms, and the fourth empty and clear light are synonyms. The definition of white appearance is a mental awareness that is manifest between the dissolution of the gross winds within the central channel and their re-emergence, that perceives an appearance like empty space pervaded by white light, similar to the light of the moon. There are two types of white appearance: basic time white appearance (including white appearance of the death process and white appearance of sleep), and path time white appearance (including white appearance of isolated body, isolated speech, isolated mind, and white appearance after isolated mind). Until we attain enlightenment, we will continue to develop the mind of white appearance.

When the gross winds dissolve within the central channel during the death process, the mind of white appearance becomes manifest and lasts until its mounted wind dissolves and the mind of red increase arises. Immediately after the clear light of death, we develop the mind of black near-attainment of reverse order, and then the mind of red increase of reverse order. Then, when the winds become slightly grosser, the mind of red increase ceases and we develop the mind of white appearance of reverse order. This subtle mind of an intermediate state being ceases when the gross winds re-emerge.

The definition of red increase is a mental awareness that is manifest between the dissolution of the gross winds within the central channel and their re-emergence, that perceives an appearance like empty space pervaded by red light, similar to the light of the setting sun. The definition of black near-attainment is a mental awareness that is manifest between the dissolution of the gross winds within the central channel and their re-emergence, that perceives an appearance like empty space pervaded by darkness. The definition of clear light is a mental awareness that is manifest between the dissolution of the mounted wind of black near-attainment within the central channel and its re-emergence, that perceives an appearance like empty space pervaded by clear light, similar to the light of dawn. Misled by the name, some people think that clear light is a kind of light, but this is completely wrong. In reality, the nature of clear light is awareness and, like all awarenesses, it is an object-possessor. The object of example clear light, for example, is emptiness.

Although we experience the four empties when we are asleep, it is difficult for us to know of their existence because, whenever they manifest, our mindfulness ceases to function and we cannot recognize them. Completion stage practitioners know the four empties through their own experience and do not need to rely upon reasons, but before this stage we can establish the existence of the four empties only by depending upon logical reasons. We can infer the existence of subtle minds by contemplating our present gross minds. All our minds are included within sense awarenesses and mental awarenesses. Sense awarenesses are necessarily gross minds. Mental awarenesses can be gross, subtle, or very subtle. Clear light is a very subtle mental awareness; black near-attainment, red increase and white appearance are subtle mental awarenesses; and the conceptual thoughts we have when we are awake are gross mental awarenesses. There are many levels of gross mind, depending upon the strength of movement of their mounted winds. For example, we develop strong anger when there is a strong movement of the mounted wind of anger, middling anger when there is a middling movement of wind and weak anger when there is a slight movement of wind. We should try to recognize these three levels of conceptual mind as they arise. Since gross minds arise from subtle minds, and we know through our own experience that there are three levels of gross mind, we can infer that there are three corresponding levels of subtle mind. Conceptual thoughts that depend upon strong movements of wind indicate the existence of the grossest level of subtle mind – the mind of white appearance. Conceptual thoughts that depend upon middling movements of wind indicate the mind of red increase. Conceptual thoughts that depend upon slight movements of wind indicate the mind of black near-attainment. The mind of white appearance is the source of the grossest level of conceptual thought, red increase is the source of the middling level of conceptual thought and black near-attainment is the source of the subtlest level of conceptual thought. If there were not three levels of subtle mind, there would not be three levels of gross mind. Thus, just as we can infer the cause, fire, by observing the effect, smoke, so we can infer the cause, the three levels of subtle mind, by observing the effect, the three levels of gross mind.

There are thirty-three conceptions indicative of the mind of white appearance, forty conceptions indicative of red increase and seven conceptions indicative of black near-attainment. These eighty indicative conceptions, which are listed in the book *Clear Light of Bliss*, are conclusive reasons indicating the existence of the first three empties. Until we can cause the winds to dissolve within the central channel through the force of meditation, we need to rely upon these conclusive reasons to understand these three empties.

HOW TO PRACTISE ISOLATED MIND

There are two methods for attaining the experience of isolated mind: an external method and an internal method. The external method is to rely upon an action mudra, or consort, and the internal method is to meditate on the process of absorption. There are two ways to meditate on the process of absorption: the absorption of subsequent destruction and the absorption of holding the body entirely. To practise the first, we imagine that the container (the world system) and the contents (its inhabitants) melt into light, which then gathers and dissolves into our body, which in turn dissolves into the indestructible mind and wind at our heart. We then meditate on the union of bliss and emptiness. To practise the absorption of holding the body entirely, we imagine that our body melts into light from below and above, and then dissolves into the indestructible mind and wind at our heart. We then meditate on bliss and emptiness. These two practices are sometimes called the 'absorptions of the two concentrations'. Through combining these with reliance upon an action mudra, the channel knots at the heart will be completely loosened and we will attain qualified realizations of isolated mind.

There are two levels of realization of isolated mind: the mere realization of isolated mind and the ultimate realization of isolated mind. We attain the mere realization of isolated mind when the four empties manifest through the force of the complete loosening of the heart channel knots through the practice of the methods explained above. This realization still needs to be improved because even though some winds have dissolved into the indestructible drop at the heart, there are still some that have not. Of the ten winds, it is particularly difficult to cause the pervading wind to gather and dissolve within the central channel, especially at the heart channel wheel. To accomplish this, we need to meditate on vajra recitation on the pervading wind. When the pervading wind completely gathers into the indestructible drop, at that time there are no gross winds flowing in the channels of our body, and we are left only with subtle minds. This happens naturally through the force of karma when we die but, to attain the ultimate realization of isolated mind through the force of meditation, we must cause the pervading wind to dissolve into the indestructible drop by engaging in vajra recitation on the pervading wind.

To do this vajra recitation, we begin by visualizing the seventy-two thousand channels of our body. Although we cannot see them clearly, we should try to gain a rough generic image of them. We imagine that the roots of all the channels radiate from the indestructible drop at the heart like the spokes of an umbrella radiating from the pole, and that the outer ends of the channels are between the skin and the flesh all over the body. The channels are like rays radiating everywhere from the indestructible drop, which is like a sun. Having visualized the seventy-two thousand channels in this way, we imagine that all the pervading winds are drawn inwards through the channels while making the sound OM. They gather and dissolve into the indestructible drop at the heart, making the sound AH, and then they return to their original places in the channels, making the sound HUM. We repeat this cycle several times, transforming the pervading wind into the nature of the mantra OM AH HUM. As we become familiar with this practice, the pervading wind will gradually gather and dissolve into the indestructible drop, and we will attain the ultimate clear light of isolated mind, the highest realization of isolated mind. This clear light is as subtle as the clear light of death. When an ordinary person develops such a subtle mind, he has no choice but to die; but when a Yogi of isolated mind develops such a subtle mind, instead of dying he or she attains the realization of deathlessness.

To attain the ultimate realization of isolated mind, we need to rely upon an action mudra. For qualified practitioners of isolated mind, relying upon an action mudra is a powerful method for completely releasing the heart channel knots and thereby transforming the four empties into the nature of spontaneous great bliss. To do this through meditation alone is difficult and time-consuming.

Some advanced practitioners choose not to use an action mudra but prefer to wait until the time of death, when the channel knots are completely loosened through the force of karma, and the pervading winds naturally dissolve into the indestructible drop. By retaining mindfulness throughout the death process, these practitioners transform the clear light of death into the ultimate clear light of isolated mind. In doing so, they purify ordinary death. When the clear light ceases, instead of entering the actual intermediate state they attain the illusory body. Yogis who attain the ultimate clear light of isolated mind by relying upon an action mudra will definitely attain enlightenment in that same life, and Yogis who attain this realization at the time of death will attain the illusory body and full enlightenment in the intermediate state.

Illusory Body, Clear Light and Union

ILLUSORY BODY

This is explained in three parts:

1 Definition and etymology of illusory body
2 Divisions of illusory body
3 How to attain the illusory body

DEFINITION AND ETYMOLOGY OF ILLUSORY BODY

The definition of illusory body is an actual divine body developed from its substantial cause, the mere mounted wind of clear light.

The illusory body is so called because, like a magician's illusion, it possesses arms, legs and so forth, but is insubstantial and not made of flesh and blood.

DIVISIONS OF ILLUSORY BODY

There are two types of illusory body:

1 Impure illusory body
2 Pure illusory body

Je Phabongkhapa Trinlay Gyatso

The definition of impure illusory body is an actual divine body developed from its substantial cause, the mere mounted wind of the ultimate example clear light of isolated mind. Impure illusory body and illusory body of the third of the five stages are synonyms. The definition of pure illusory body is an actual divine body developed from its substantial cause, the mere mounted wind of meaning clear light.

The impure illusory body has fifteen characteristics:

1 The characteristic of cause
2 The characteristic of time
3 The characteristic of location
4 The characteristic of nature
5 The characteristic of colour
6 The characteristic of shape
7 The characteristic of being seen
8 The characteristic of infinite light
9 The characteristic of enjoyment
10 The characteristic of motivation
11 The characteristic of good qualities
12 The characteristic of similes
13 The characteristic of names
14 The characteristic of definite words
15 The characteristic of duration

THE CHARACTERISTIC OF CAUSE

The substantial cause of our gross body is our parents' sperm and egg, and the substantial cause of the impure illusory body is the very subtle wind that is the mounted wind of ultimate example clear light. The dream body, the intermediate state body and the illusory body are all developed from the very subtle wind, but whereas the first two arise from an ordinary very subtle wind, the illusory body arises from a pure very subtle wind.

THE CHARACTERISTIC OF TIME

The time when the illusory body is attained is when the ultimate example clear light of isolated mind ceases and we attain the mind of black near-attainment of reverse order.

THE CHARACTERISTIC OF LOCATION

If we attain the illusory body before death, it will initially arise within the indestructible drop at the heart. After this, it can travel anywhere, like a dream body.

THE CHARACTERISTIC OF NATURE

The nature of the illusory body is wind. It is the nature of clear, unobstructed wisdom light.

THE CHARACTERISTIC OF COLOUR

The colour of the illusory body is white.

THE CHARACTERISTIC OF SHAPE

The shape of the illusory body is the shape of the Yogi's Yidam. When a Heruka practitioner attains the illusory body, its shape is the shape of Heruka. At the same time, he or she attains the actual mandala, retinue and enjoyments of Heruka.

THE CHARACTERISTIC OF BEING SEEN

Just as an intermediate state body can be seen by other intermediate state beings, but not by other beings, so the illusory body can be seen only by those who have an illusory body.

THE CHARACTERISTIC OF INFINITE LIGHT

A person who has attained the illusory body can radiate infinite light from his or her body that can illuminate the entire universe.

THE CHARACTERISTIC OF ENJOYMENT

A person who has attained the illusory body experiences only pure enjoyments. Because he has purified his five sense awarenesses and impure karma, he enjoys only pure forms, sounds, smells, tastes and tactile objects. Such a person has attained outer Dakini Land.

THE CHARACTERISTIC OF MOTIVATION

Before entering the meditative equipoise of the ultimate isolated mind, which focuses only on emptiness, the meditator develops the motivation to rise in the form of an illusory body as soon as this meditative equipoise ends. The illusory body rises through the power of this motivation and the great effort made over a long time.

THE CHARACTERISTIC OF GOOD QUALITIES

The illusory body has the major signs and minor indications. A person who has attained the illusory body can meet Buddhas face to face and receive empowerments from them. He can effortlessly obtain whatever resources and enjoyments he desires, simply by plucking them out of space.

THE CHARACTERISTIC OF SIMILES

There are twelve similes that help us to understand the illusory body. The illusory body is like an illusion, a reflection of the moon in water, the body's shadow, a mirage, a dream, an echo, a city of intermediate state beings, a manifestation, a rainbow, a bolt of lightning, a water bubble and a reflection in a mirror. These are explained in the book *Clear Light of Bliss*.

THE CHARACTERISTIC OF NAMES

To help us to understand the nature of the illusory body, Buddha Vajradhara gave the illusory body various names, such as 'blessed self', 'conventional truth' and 'vajra body'. He called it 'blessed self' because it is the basis of imputation of the subtle self. The basis of imputation of the subtle self is the very subtle mind and wind, and the illusory body is the very subtle wind transformed into a divine body. Why did Buddha call the illusory body 'conventional truth'? It is called 'conventional' because it is a conventional truth rather than an ultimate truth, and it is called 'truth' because it is a real rather than a fabricated divine body. Buddha called it 'vajra body' because it is indestructible and a person who has attained it will not experience death.

THE CHARACTERISTIC OF DEFINITE WORDS

Here, 'definite words' refers to the etymology of illusory body. The illusory body is so called because it resembles a magician's illusion. Just as a man created by a magician has the same shape as a real man but is not composed of flesh and blood, so the illusory body superficially resembles a solid body but is developed from inner wind rather than the sperm and egg of parents.

THE CHARACTERISTIC OF DURATION

The impure illusory body is first attained immediately after the cessation of the ultimate example clear light of isolated mind and lasts until the attainment of meaning clear light, when it disappears like a rainbow dissolving into the sky. When meaning clear light ceases, we attain the pure illusory body, which lasts until enlightenment.

When divided in terms of its basis, there are two types of impure illusory body: the impure illusory body that is related to the old aggregates (i.e. an illusory body attained before death), and the impure illusory body that is unrelated to the old aggregates (i.e. an illusory body attained after death). Examples of the first are the illusory bodies attained by Nagarjuna, Gyalwa Ensapa and Mahasiddha Dharmavajra before they died, which were like secret jewels contained within the gross bodies of these high Yogis. Their illusory body was related to their gross body in much the same way that our dream body is related to our physical body. We can know that our dream body is related to our gross body because we can observe experiences of the dream

207

body ripening on our gross body, such as when we wake up sweating and with our heart racing after a nightmare. The illusory body attained by means of transforming the clear light of death into the ultimate clear light of isolated mind is unrelated to the old aggregates, because such a person no longer has gross aggregates.

HOW TO ATTAIN THE ILLUSORY BODY

To attain the illusory body, we need to separate the subtle body from the gross body through the force of meditation. In general, the subtle and gross bodies of ordinary beings separate only during sleep or death. When we dream, our gross body remains on our bed but our dream body travels to various dream places, and when we die, the gross body remains behind but the subtle body goes to the next life. The difference between going to sleep and dying is that when we dream, the connection between the gross and subtle bodies is retained, whereas when we die it is completely severed.

Apart from these two occasions, most people cannot separate their gross body from their subtle body. Meditators, on the other hand, can separate their gross and subtle bodies through the force of meditation, and cause their subtle body to arise in a form with complete limbs. Even now while we are awake we have a subtle body, but it is only during dreams and the intermediate state that it manifests in an aspect with complete limbs.

As there are two types of mind – temporary gross minds and the continuously residing subtle mind that goes from life to life, so there are two types of body – a temporary gross body and a very subtle continuously residing body. As mentioned before, our gross body originally developed from our parents' sperm and egg, was formed in our mother's womb, and will eventually disintegrate at death. Although we regard it as our body, in reality it belongs to others. We did not make this body ourself and we cannot take it with us when we die. Our gross body is like a guesthouse in which our mind stays for a short time, and grasping onto it is like a guest grasping onto the guesthouse where he or she is staying. Though we grasp very tightly to our human body today, tomorrow we may already have lost it and moved into the body of an animal! Our gross body is very temporary and insecure.

Our very subtle body, on the other hand, will never disintegrate. The very subtle body is the very subtle wind that has existed since beginningless time and will continue to exist even after we have attained Buddhahood, when it will transform into the Enjoyment Body. At present, our very subtle body takes various shapes. When we are dreaming, our very subtle wind takes the shape of our dream body, and in the intermediate state it takes the shape of our intermediate state body. When we attain the illusory body, our very subtle wind takes the shape of our personal Deity.

Our real basis of imputation is our very subtle body and mind, which are the only stable basis, and the only basis we can really call our own. Our gross body and mind are temporary bases. Since there are two types of basis for imputing self – a temporary basis and an ultimate basis – there are two types of self – a gross self and a subtle self. The self that is imputed upon the very subtle mind and wind is the subtle self. Only those who have received Tantric teachings know about this self. The distinction between gross and subtle bodies, minds and selves is not made in Sutra teachings, so even Sutra Bodhisattvas do not know about the subtle self.

Death occurs when body and mind separate. Since the very subtle body and mind never separate, the subtle self never dies. Only the gross self can die. Thus, from one point of view there is no reason to fear death, because our real self will never die. Even though our gross self will die, if we do not grasp at it very strongly we will not be afraid when we die. Considering this, we might be tempted to think, 'If my subtle self is immortal, what is the point in practising Dharma?' The answer is that we need to practise Dharma because our subtle self carries the imprints of all our positive and negative actions. If we act negatively, our subtle self will descend to lower realms, but, if we perform only pure actions, our subtle self will go to a Pure Land. Therefore, we need to practise Dharma. If we do not practise Dharma, we cannot overcome our grasping at our gross body, and so we cannot overcome the fear of death. It is precisely because we have a subtle self that survives death that we need to be careful to act positively. If the imprints of our actions were left only on our gross self, our actions would have no consequences for us beyond this life; but this is not the case.

There are two ways to separate our subtle body from our gross body through the force of meditation. The first is through the force of vase breathing and forcefully ejecting our mind from our body, as in the practice of transference of consciousness. When people who have mastered this practice are about to die, they can transfer their mind directly to a Pure Land and thus avoid having to undergo the ordinary death process. A variation of the practice of transference of consciousness involves transferring our mind into a recently dead corpse and re-animating it. This practice is not very difficult and used to be quite widespread. In the book *Introduction to Buddhism*, for example, I tell the story of how Tarma Dode, the son of the Tibetan Master Marpa, transferred his consciousness into the body of a pigeon and then flew to India.

If we practise either type of transference of consciousness, we can separate our subtle body from our gross body, but this does not help us to attain the illusory body. To attain the illusory body, we need to practise a far more profound method for separating our gross and subtle bodies. We need to separate our gross and subtle bodies by completely dissolving all our inner winds into the indestructible drop at the heart through the force of meditation. When all the winds have dissolved into the indestructible drop during the death process and we have experienced the clear light of death, the indestructible drop opens and the subtle body leaves the gross body and transforms into the body of an intermediate state being. In a similar way, when we succeed in completely dissolving all our winds into the indestructible drop through the force of meditation, after we have experienced the ultimate example clear light of isolated mind our subtle body will separate from our gross body and become the illusory body.

Most of the completion stage yogas described above – particularly vajra recitation and the other life exertions at the heart – indirectly serve to separate the subtle body from the gross body because they help to gather and dissolve the winds within the central channel. When, through the force of meditation on isolated mind, we succeed in bringing all our winds into the central channel and dissolving them into the indestructible drop, the gross and subtle bodies separate naturally and we attain the illusory body. Thus, it is the yogas of isolated mind that are the direct methods for separating the subtle body from the gross body.

CLEAR LIGHT

This is explained in three parts:

1 Definition and etymology of meaning clear light
2 Divisions of meaning clear light
3 How to attain meaning clear light

DEFINITION AND ETYMOLOGY OF
MEANING CLEAR LIGHT

The definition of meaning clear light is a clear light that is the nature of spontaneous bliss and that realizes emptiness directly.

Meaning clear light is necessarily an uncontaminated mind and, according to Highest Yoga Tantra, an uncontaminated mind must be a mind of clear light. Even the subtle minds of white appearance, red increase and black near-attainment are contaminated by dualistic appearances, and so it goes without saying that all gross minds are contaminated minds. When we develop the mind of black near-attainment, for example, there is an appearance of a black vacuity, but this vacuity appears as truly existent. Similarly, when ordinary beings experience clear light there is an appearance like empty space, but this empty space appears as truly existent. All minds of clear light before the attainment of meaning clear light have dualistic appearance. Even the ultimate example clear light of isolated mind has dualistic appearance because it realizes emptiness by means of a generic image rather than directly, and so the appearance of emptiness is mixed with the appearance of the generic image of emptiness. Of all conceptual minds, ultimate example clear light of isolated mind is the most subtle.

To help us understand dualistic appearances, we can consider the following. Suppose I am reading a book while a radio is playing in the room. As long as my concentration is imperfect, there will be two appearances to my mind, the appearance of the book and the appearance of the sound; but, if my concentration improves, the appearance of the sound will gradually become weaker and weaker until it disappears completely, and only the book will appear to my mind. In a similar way, the minds of ordinary beings have two appearances, an appearance of the object and an appearance of the inherent existence of the object. This is true even when we meditate on emptiness: not only is there an appearance of emptiness to our mind, there is also an appearance of an inherently existent emptiness. Through concentrating on emptiness for a long time, however, the appearance of inherent existence gradually subsides until eventually we perceive only emptiness. Our mind is then free from dualistic appearances because only one thing appears to it – mere lack of inherent existence. Until we overcome dualistic appearances and see emptiness directly, we will be unable to abandon grasping at true existence. A mind that is free from dualistic appearances is an uncontaminated wisdom.

There are two etymologies of meaning clear light, one from the point of view of the object and one from the point of view of the object-possessor. From the point of view of the object, meaning clear light is so called because it directly realizes emptiness, the ultimate meaning of phenomena. From the point of view of the object-possessor, meaning clear light is that which is illustrated by example clear light: it is the meaning of the illustration. Example clear light is defined as a mind of clear light that realizes emptiness by means of a generic image. It has four types: example clear light at the time of isolated body, example clear light at the time of isolated speech, example clear light at the time of isolated mind, and example clear light at the time of the impure illusory body. A person who has attained any of these types of example clear light can use this experience as an example to help him understand meaning clear light.

Meaning clear light is a yogic direct perceiver. By meditating on emptiness repeatedly with example clear light, gradually the appearance of the generic image of emptiness becomes weaker and weaker and the appearance of emptiness itself becomes clearer and clearer. Finally the generic image disappears entirely and the mind sees emptiness directly. This mind is a yogic direct perceiver. The mind that realizes emptiness with a generic image can be used as a conclusive reason to establish the existence of a yogic direct perceiver that realizes emptiness directly. Thus, example clear light is a conclusive reason establishing the existence of meaning clear light.

Since the minds of white appearance, red increase, black near-attainment and clear light are not even mentioned in Sutra, a Bodhisattva who practises the Perfection Vehicle alone cannot attain meaning clear light. Such a Bodhisattva may reach the tenth Bodhisattva ground of the Sutra system but, according to the system of Secret Mantra, he or she is still on the level of the path of preparation and is still an ordinary being. He has realized emptiness directly only with a gross mind and so his meditative equipoise on emptiness does not have the power to overcome the subtle obstructions to omniscience. Only a direct realization of emptiness with the very subtle mind has the power to do this.

Since a tenth-ground Sutra Bodhisattva has very pure karma, he or she can see Buddhas face to face. These Buddhas explain to him that the paths he has been following until now do not have the power to lead to Buddhahood and that he needs to enter the path of Highest Yoga Tantra. Acting as that Bodhisattva's Spiritual Guide, at midnight these Buddhas will bestow upon him or her the third empowerment, the wisdom-mudra empowerment. Through receiving this empowerment, and with the help of an action mudra given to him by his Spiritual Guide, the Bodhisattva will gather and dissolve his winds within the central channel and develop the eight signs from the mirage-like appearance up to the clear light. When the mind of clear light develops, the Bodhisattva will meditate on emptiness for the rest of the night, and at dawn will attain meaning clear light. When he rises from meditative equipoise, he will simultaneously attain the pure illusory body, and after that he will attain the union that needs learning.

During the day, the Bodhisattva will practise one of the three types of enjoyment explained below. At midnight, he will receive instructions on the Union of No More Learning and, by relying upon an action mudra, develop the eight signs. Towards dawn, he will enter the vajra-like concentration of the path of meditation, the direct antidote to the very subtle obstructions to omniscience. With the break of dawn, he will abandon the very subtle dualistic appearances and their imprints, which together constitute the very subtle obstructions to omniscience, and he will attain Buddhahood, the Union of No More Learning that is the state possessing the seven pre-eminent qualities of embrace.

Such a Bodhisattva attains meaning clear light without having to meditate on generation stage, isolated body, isolated speech, isolated mind, or illusory body. This is possible because he is already on the tenth ground of Sutra, having accumulated merit for countless aeons by following the Sutra path. According to Tantra, this is the method of attaining enlightenment demonstrated by Buddha Shakyamuni at Bodh Gaya. The explanations given in Secret Mantra are Buddha's final intention. Of all Buddhist systems, the Madhyamika-Prasangika system is supreme, and the supreme interpretation of Madhyamika-Prasangika is that of Highest Yoga Tantra.

Meaning clear light is indispensable because a realization of emptiness with a gross mind does not have the power to remove the obstructions to omniscience; nor can a gross mind act as the substantial cause of the Truth Body. Meaning clear light is also necessary for the attainment of the Enjoyment Body. The highest type of form body explained in Sutra is a body that is the nature of mind. These are attained by Hinayana Foe Destroyers when they die and are reborn in one of the five pure abodes above the form realm, and also by Superior Bodhisattvas. According to Sutra, Superior Bodhisattvas do not have contaminated bodies but have uncontaminated bodies that are the nature of mind. According to Secret Mantra, however, these bodies that are the nature of mind cannot act as the substantial cause of Buddha's Enjoyment Body. The direct substantial cause of the Enjoyment Body is necessarily the pure illusory body that develops from the very subtle wind that is the mounted wind of meaning clear light. In summary, without meaning clear light it is impossible to attain the Truth Body because we cannot eliminate the obstructions to omniscience, and it is impossible to attain the Form Body because we cannot attain its direct substantial cause, the pure illusory body.

DIVISIONS OF MEANING CLEAR LIGHT

In general there are three types of meaning clear light:

1 Meaning clear light of the fourth stage
2 Meaning clear light of the union that needs learning
3 Meaning clear light of the Union of No More Learning

The definition of meaning clear light of the fourth stage is a meaning clear light arisen from the dissolution of the impure illusory body into clear light. Meaning clear light of the fourth stage is necessarily a path of seeing, and when we attain it we become a Superior being. Meaning clear light of the fourth stage can only manifest once the illusory body of the third stage dissolves. Why does the impure illusory body have to cease? The nature of the illusory body of the third stage is contaminated wind because its substantial cause, the mounted wind of ultimate example clear light of isolated mind, is a contaminated wind. This is because ultimate example clear light itself is a contaminated mind. To attain meaning clear light, a person with an impure illusory body meditates on emptiness with a mind of clear light. When dualistic appearances subside and he or she realizes emptiness directly, his or her mind of clear light transforms into the uncontaminated wisdom of meaning clear light. At the same time, the mounted wind of his clear light mind transforms into an uncontaminated wind. Since the impure illusory body depends upon a contaminated wind, and the mounted wind of meaning clear light is necessarily uncontaminated, the impure illusory body must cease before meaning clear light manifests.

From the point of view of nature, there are no divisions of meaning clear light, because all minds of meaning clear light are uncontaminated wisdoms realizing emptiness. From the point of view of time and function, however, meaning clear light is called 'external pacification' and 'internal pacification'. It is called 'external pacification' because the external time of its initial attainment is dawn, after the cessation of the three appearances. White appearance will cease during the day time, the appearance of red increase during the evening and the appearance of black near-attainment during the night. After these three appearances have ceased, meaning clear light is attained at dawn. We might ask, since we can attain other minds of clear light such as example clear light at any time, why do we have to wait until dawn to attain meaning clear light? This is something that can be understood only by those who have already gained some experience. Meaning clear light is also called 'internal pacification' because it is attained after the cessation of the three internal appearances – white appearance, red increase and black near-attainment.

HOW TO ATTAIN MEANING CLEAR LIGHT

To attain meaning clear light, a Yogi with an impure illusory body relies upon the external and internal methods mentioned previously to dissolve his or her impure illusory body into clear light, and then meditates on emptiness repeatedly with ultimate example clear light. Finally, even the subtlest dualistic appearances cease in meditation and the mind sees emptiness directly. The conceptual mind of ultimate example clear light transforms into the non-conceptual mind of meaning clear light, and the Yogi attains the path of seeing and becomes a Superior being.

According to Sutra, the path of seeing acts as the direct antidote to intellectually-formed delusions, but does not have the power to abandon innate delusions. The Highest Yoga Tantra path of seeing, however, abandons both intellectually-formed and innate delusions. This shows the superiority of the Tantric realization of emptiness. It is said that the merit and realizations of a Yogi with the impure illusory body are almost equal to those of a Sutra Bodhisattva on the tenth ground.

UNION

This is explained in three parts:

1 Definition and etymology of union
2 Divisions of union
3 How to attain union

DEFINITION AND ETYMOLOGY OF UNION

The definition of union is a yoga in which the pure illusory body and the good qualities of abandonment are united.

Union is so called because it is a union of a special body – the pure illusory body – and a special abandonment – the true cessation of innate delusions.

DIVISIONS OF UNION

There are two types of union:

1 Union of abandonment
2 Union of realization

An example of the first is the union that exists when the pure illusory body is first attained. When a Yogi first attains the pure illusory body, he has in his continuum the abandonment of delusion-obstructions. This is called the 'ordinary union' and is attained the moment meaning clear light of the path of seeing ceases and the mind of black near-attainment manifests. At the same time, the Yogi has abandoned the delusion-obstructions. Having attained this union, when the Yogi next enters the clear light he attains the union of realization, a union of meaning clear light and pure illusory body. This meaning clear light is the first level of the path of meditation and acts as the direct antidote to the big-big obstructions to omniscience.

Another way of dividing union is into the union that needs learning and the Union of No More Learning. All unions between the union of realization and Buddhahood are unions that need learning, and also paths of meditation that are included within the nine levels of the path of meditation. The Union of No More Learning is synonymous with the Union of a Buddha's Form Body and omniscient mind.

HOW TO ATTAIN UNION

When a Yogi or Yogini who has just attained meaning clear light is about to rise from meditative equipoise on clear light, there is a slight movement of wind, and then the clear light ceases and the black near-attainment of reverse order develops. At the same time, he or she attains the pure illusory body, abandons the delusion-obstructions, and attains the union of abandonment. The mounted wind of meaning clear light acts as the substantial cause of the pure illusory body, and meaning clear light itself acts as the contributory cause. When the Yogi attains this union, he or she has abandoned all delusion-obstructions, which include all ordinary conceptions.

HOW TO PROGRESS FROM THE LOWER STAGES TO THE HIGHER STAGES

A detailed explanation of this has already been given in the individual explanations of each of the six stages. What follows is just a summary.

To progress from the first stage, isolated body, to the second stage, isolated speech, the practitioner engages in a special meditation practice, such as vajra recitation, to loosen the heart channel knots. Once these knots are partially loosened, when the winds gather and dissolve within the central channel at the heart and the first empty develops, the practitioner has progressed to isolated speech. To progress from the second stage to the third stage, isolated mind, the Yogi or Yogini practises the internal and external methods to loosen the heart channel knots completely. When this has been accomplished, and the first empty manifests through any wind dissolving into the indestructible drop, the Yogi advances to isolated mind. To progress from the third stage to the fourth, the stage of illusory body, the Yogi meditates on emptiness with a mind of clear light until he attains ultimate example clear light. When ultimate example clear light ceases, its mounted wind transforms into the impure illusory body. To progress from the fourth stage to the fifth, meaning clear light, the Yogi repeatedly meditates on emptiness with the mind of ultimate example clear light until he realizes emptiness directly with his very subtle mind. The sixth stage, union, is attained as soon as meaning clear light of the path of seeing ceases. At this point, the Yogi simultaneously attains the pure illusory body and the abandonment of delusion-obstructions. Finally, to progress from the sixth stage to the Union of No More Learning, the Yogi has to abandon the nine levels of obstructions to omniscience by practising the three types of enjoyment: enjoyments with elaborations, enjoyments without elaborations and enjoyments completely without elaborations.

Here, 'enjoyments' means enjoying the five inner and outer objects of desire to improve the experience of the union of realization. We may ask why a person who has attained the union of realization needs to enjoy objects of desire? The answer is to increase his or her experience of spontaneous bliss. Spontaneous bliss depends upon the bodhichittas, the white or red drops, and the bodhichittas are increased by enjoying objects of desire.

The five inner objects of desire are the attractive forms, sounds, smells, tastes and touch of the action mudra or consort. The five outer objects of desire are external attractive forms, sounds, smells, tastes and tactile objects. A Yogi on the stage of union who enjoys the five inner and outer objects of desire elaborately, like in a royal wedding, is practising enjoyments with elaborations. A Yogi on the stage of union who practises with a consort, or action mudra, but who does not enjoy outer objects of desire in an elaborate way, is practising enjoyments without elaborations. A Yogi on the stage of union who practises only with a wisdom mudra, without depending upon an action mudra or elaborate outer objects of desire, is practising enjoyments completely without elaborations. Such Yogis or Yoginis tend to live like beggars and principally emphasize the clear light of sleep.

By practising any of these three types of enjoyment, the Yogi improves his or her experience of meaning clear light and gradually abandons the nine levels of obstructions to omniscience, from big-big obstructions to small-small. The meaning clear light that abandons small-small obstructions to omniscience is called the 'final clear light of the path of learning', or the 'vajra-like concentration of the path of meditation'. This, the last mind of a sentient being, acts as the direct antidote to the subtlest dualistic appearances. In the next moment the practitioner has completely abandoned the obstructions to omniscience and has attained the Union of No More Learning, the stage of Buddhahood.

At this point, the practitioner's mind of meaning clear light transforms into omniscient wisdom, and his or her pure illusory body transforms into the Enjoyment Body possessing the seven pre-eminent qualities of embrace. The Path of No More Learning is the resultant path. Although it is a path, it does not have a destination in the sense of it leading to any inner improvement – there is no more room for improvement!

Completion stage yogas can be divided into two: completion stage of the three isolations and completion stage of the two truths. Completion stage of the three isolations comprises isolated body, isolated speech and isolated mind. Completion stage of the two truths is divided into completion stage of the individual two truths and completion stage of the indivisibility of the two truths. With regard to completion stage of the individual two truths, the illusory body of the fourth of the six stages is called 'conventional truth' because it is a conventional truth, and the meaning clear light of the fifth of the six stages is called 'ultimate truth' because its principal object is ultimate truth. Completion stage of the indivisibility of the two truths refers to the principal union that needs learning – the union of realization – which is the union of meaning clear light and pure illusory body. A person's meaning clear light and pure illusory body are the same nature. The nature of the pure illusory body is the mounted wind of meaning clear light, which is the same nature as meaning clear light itself.

The Final Results

According to Chandrakirti's *Clear Lamp of the Five Stages*, there are three results of meditating on completion stage: the highest result, the middling result and the least result. The highest result is Buddhahood, the middling result is the eight great attainments, and the least result is the attainment of pacifying, increasing, controlling and wrathful actions. The principal goal of completion stage is the attainment of Buddhahood, but a secondary effect of meditating on completion stage is that we will naturally accomplish the eight great attainments and the four actions without needing to engage in any separate practices.

The foundation for attaining all three results is laid as soon as we begin practising generation stage meditations. For example, provided that we have received a Highest Yoga Tantra empowerment, if out of faith we do a single meditation on generation stage we will receive some benefits; our meditation will not be fruitless. However, just as we cannot expect to reap a harvest immediately after sowing seeds, so we cannot expect to experience the full effect of our meditation straight away. Nevertheless, we will definitely receive some blessings, and our merit and wisdom will increase. Through receiving blessings, our strong delusions and wrong views will be pacified. This is

Vajradhara Trijang Rinpoche Losang Yeshe

a pacifying attainment. The increase in our merit, wisdom and potential power for attaining spiritual experience are increasing attainments. Through the pacification of negative conceptions and an increase in merit and wisdom, we will gain the power to avert obstacles and will not be harmed by humans or non-humans. This is a controlling attainment. Finally, through strong divine pride in being the Deity, we will gradually accomplish wrathful attainments.

There are many levels of the four attainments, but the initial levels are not difficult to attain. Even now, we have some experience of them. For example, the fact that we now find it easy to believe in future lives, the law of karma, the existence of Buddhas and so forth, indicates that we have managed to pacify our delusions and wrong views to some degree.

The direct cause of the attainment of Buddhahood is the union that needs learning. It is said in the scriptures that a person who has attained the union that needs learning will attain Buddhahood within six months, but this is just a rough guide. Some Yogis require more time while others attain enlightenment in less than six months. In any case, after practising the three types of enjoyment for about six months, the Yogi or Yogini will receive certain signs. At midnight, in dependence upon external or internal methods, he or she will manifest meaning clear light. He will meditate on this throughout the night, and at dawn his meaning clear light will become the direct antidote to the very subtle obstructions to omniscience. In the next moment, these obstructions will be completely abandoned and the Yogi will become a Buddha with the four bodies of a Buddha – the two Form Bodies (the Enjoyment Body and the Emanation Body) and the two Truth Bodies (the Wisdom

Truth Body and the Nature Truth Body). All four bodies are attained simultaneously.

There are two definitions of Enjoyment Body, one according to Sutra and one according to Highest Yoga Tantra. The definition according to Sutra is an ultimate Form Body that possesses the five certainties. One of these certainties is certainty of place, which means that the Enjoyment Body resides continuously in the Pure Land of Akanishta. This definition is not accepted in Tantra because, according to Secret Mantra, it is possible (and indeed usual) to attain Buddhahood in the abodes of the desire realm. When a desire realm human attains Buddhahood, the initial location of his Enjoyment Body is in the abodes of the desire realm, not in Akanishta.

According to Highest Yoga Tantra, the definition of Enjoyment Body is a subtle Form Body of a Buddha possessing the seven pre-eminent qualities of embrace. The seven pre-eminent qualities are:

(1) A Form Body endowed with the major signs and minor indications
(2) Continuously in embrace with a wisdom knowledge consort
(3) A mind always abiding in a state of great bliss
(4) This mind of bliss always mixed with emptiness, the lack of inherent existence of all phenomena
(5) Endowed with great compassion that has abandoned the extreme of attachment to solitary peace
(6) Uninterruptedly manifesting Form Bodies that pervade the whole world
(7) Unceasingly performing enlightened deeds

There are three types of Enjoyment Body:

(1) An Enjoyment Body that is initially attained in the desire realm
(2) An Enjoyment Body that is initially attained in the form realm
(3) An Enjoyment Body that is initially attained in a Buddha Land

The definition of Emanation Body is a gross Form Body of a Buddha that can be seen by ordinary beings. How are Emanation Bodies attained? A Bodhisattva on the stage of union has two spiritual tasks: to become a Buddha by practising the three types of enjoyment, and to benefit others extensively by manifesting countless emanation bodies. When the Bodhisattva attains enlightenment, his or her actual body (i.e. his or her illusory body) will become the Enjoyment Body, and all his or her emanations will become Emanation Bodies. Previously these emanations were emanations of a Bodhisattva, but now they become emanations of a Buddha.

There are two types of Emanation Body:

(1) Supreme Emanation Body
(2) Ordinary Emanation Body

The first type can be seen only by those who have pure karma, and the second can be seen by anyone.

The definition of Truth Body is a Buddha's mind, or the ultimate nature of a Buddha's mind. There are two types of Truth Body:

(1) Wisdom Truth Body
(2) Nature Truth Body

The Wisdom Truth Body is the mind of a Buddha that is free from the two obstructions. The ultimate nature, or emptiness, of this mind is the Nature Truth Body. Because the emptiness of a mind is the same nature as that mind itself, when a person's mind is freed from the two obstructions, the emptiness of his or her mind is also freed from the two obstructions. The emptiness of Buddha's mind is endowed with two purities: purity from adventitious defilements and natural purity. Adventitious defilements are the two obstructions, which are adventitious because they are not intrinsic properties of the mind. 'Natural purity' means the mind's mere absence of inherent existence. No one except Buddhas can see a Buddha's Truth Body, because it is a very subtle body. Similarly, the Enjoyment Bodies cannot be seen by ordinary beings, because they are subtle Form Bodies.

Unlike our body and mind, all four bodies of a Buddha are the same entity or nature. Whatever is realized by Buddha's mind is also realized by his body, and whatever actions are performed by his body are also performed by his mind. A Buddha's good qualities are inconceivable. However, we can begin to understand them by contemplating the following explanation.

Buddhas possess ten forces. The definition of a force of a Buddha is an ultimate realization that is utterly victorious over all discordant conditions such as the two obstructions. The ten forces are:

(1) The force knowing source and non-source
(2) The force knowing full ripening of actions
(3) The force knowing the various desires
(4) The force knowing the various elements

(5) The force knowing supreme and non-supreme powers

(6) The force knowing all paths going everywhere

(7) The force knowing the mental stabilizations, concentrations of perfect liberation, concentrations, absorptions and so forth

(8) The force knowing recollections of previous lives

(9) The force knowing death and birth

(10) The force knowing the cessation of contaminations

These will now be briefly explained.

THE FORCE KNOWING SOURCE AND NON-SOURCE

Any cause from which an effect is definitely produced is called the 'source' of that effect. For example, a seed from which a sprout is produced is the source of that sprout. Thus, all causes are the sources of their effects, for example virtuous actions are the source of happiness, and non-virtuous actions are the source of suffering. On the other hand, wheat seeds, for example, are not the source of rice; non-virtuous actions are not the source of happiness; and virtuous actions are not the source of suffering. Because ordinary beings do not know the sources of happiness, they engage in actions that increase their suffering instead of increasing their happiness; and, because they do not know the sources of suffering, they continually create the causes of suffering for themselves, even though they have no wish to suffer. Therefore, it is essential to know what is a source and what is not a source. Only a Buddha can know directly everything that is a source and a non-source.

THE FORCE KNOWING FULL RIPENING OF ACTIONS

There are countless actions, such as virtuous actions, non-virtuous actions, actions that are a mixture of virtue and non-virtue, and uncontaminated actions that have abandoned non-virtue. Similarly, there is a great variety of effects of actions, such as fully ripened effects, environmental effects, effects similar to the cause, and bodies of the nature of mind that are effects of uncontaminated actions. Only a Buddha can directly understand all gross and subtle actions and their effects.

THE FORCE KNOWING THE VARIOUS DESIRES

Living beings have many desires: desires that arise through the force of delusions such as attachment and hatred, desires that arise through the force of virtuous minds such as faith and compassion, desires that arise through the force of imprints in the mind, and many others. Just one living being has countless desires. Some desires are inferior, others mid-dling and others superior. Since desire is an internal, mental phenomenon, it is difficult for an ordinary being to know others' desires. Only a Buddha knows all the desires of living beings directly.

THE FORCE KNOWING THE VARIOUS ELEMENTS

There are many divisions of elements, such as the six powers, the eye sense power and so forth; the six objects, forms and so forth; and the six consciousnesses, eye consciousness and so forth. Moreover, all the different types of emptiness are also elements. Thus, there are countless divisions of gross and subtle elements, and only a Buddha can know them all directly.

THE FORCE KNOWING SUPREME AND NON-SUPREME POWERS

Both supreme and non-supreme powers can be classified either from the point of view of persons or from the point of view of minds. Among persons, there are some who have very sharp powers, some who have middling powers and some who have dull powers. Among minds, those such as faith and wisdom are supreme powers because they are the powers that prevent delusions, whereas conceptualizations such as inappropriate attention are inferior powers because they are the powers that generate delusions.

From another point of view, there are twenty-two types of power:

    (1) Eye sense power
    (2) Ear sense power
    (3) Nose sense power
    (4) Tongue sense power
    (5) Body sense power
    (6) Mental power
    (7) The power of life
    (8) Male power
    (9) Female power
  (10) The power of pleasant feeling
  (11) The power of mental happiness
  (12) The power of unpleasant feeling
  (13) The power of mental unhappiness
  (14) The power of neutral feeling

(15) The power of faith
(16) The power of effort
(17) The power of mindfulness
(18) The power of concentration
(19) The power of wisdom
(20) The power that causes knowledge of all
(21) The power that knows all
(22) The power that possesses all knowledge

The first six are powers that produce their own consciousnesses; the seventh is the power that sustains life; the eighth is the power that determines a person as male; the ninth is the power that determines a person as female; the tenth, which is bodily feeling, and the eleventh, which is mental feeling, are the powers that generate attachment in ordinary beings; the twelfth, which is bodily feeling, and the thirteenth, which is mental feeling, are the powers that generate hatred in ordinary beings; the fourteenth is the power that generates confusion in ordinary beings; the fifteenth through to the nineteenth are the powers that generate the path of seeing; the twentieth, which is the path of seeing, is the power that generates the path of meditation; the twenty-first, which is the path of meditation, is the power that generates the Path of No More Learning; and the last, which is the Path of No More Learning, is the power that generates a nirvana without remainder. Only a Buddha can know directly all the powers, as well as their ability to support each other.

THE FORCE KNOWING ALL PATHS
GOING EVERYWHERE

In general, there are two types of path: external paths and internal paths. The paths that concern the spiritual practitioner are internal paths, and these are more difficult to understand. Internal paths are either correct or incorrect. Correct internal paths lead to liberation or enlightenment. Some, such as the five Mahayana paths, lead to great enlightenment, or Buddhahood; and some, such as the five Hinayana paths, lead to the enlightenment of a Solitary Realizer or the enlightenment of a Hearer. Incorrect internal paths, on the other hand, lead not to liberation but to samsara. Some, such as the ten non-virtuous actions, lead to the hell realms, the hungry ghost realms, or the animal realms; and some, such as contaminated virtuous actions, lead to the god realms or the human realms. Since there are so many different paths, only a Buddha can know them all directly.

THE FORCE KNOWING THE MENTAL STABILIZATIONS,
CONCENTRATIONS OF PERFECT LIBERATION,
CONCENTRATIONS, ABSORPTIONS AND SO FORTH

There are many different types of Yogi and Yogini throughout limitless worlds, each of whom has attained different meditative concentrations, such as the four mental stabilizations, the eight concentrations of perfect liberation, the various concentrations that are tranquil abidings, and the absorptions of the nine successive abidings. Since there are countless different concentrations, some of which are mundane and some of which are supramundane, only a Buddha can know them all directly.

THE FORCE KNOWING RECOLLECTIONS
OF PREVIOUS LIVES

For as long as they have confusion, living beings will remain in samsara. In the past, the countless samsaric beings including ourself have already taken countless rebirths in countless different places of birth, each in a different body with different characteristics, friends, possessions and so forth. Only a Buddha can know all these directly.

THE FORCE KNOWING DEATH AND BIRTH

Because the realms of all the worlds are as extensive as space, the living beings inhabiting them are countless. Each and every living being experiences uncontrolled death and birth, one after the other without cessation, as the effects of their accumulated actions. However, ordinary beings do not know how or where they died in the past, how or where they were born in the past, how or where they will die in this life, or how and where they will be born and die in future lives. The many varieties of death and birth of each and every living being can be known directly only by a Buddha.

THE FORCE KNOWING THE CESSATION OF
CONTAMINATIONS

There are three types of enlightenment: great, middling and small. Buddhas attain a great enlightenment by abandoning all delusions together with their imprints, Solitary Realizers attain a middling enlightenment by abandoning all delusions and Hearers attain a small enlightenment also by abandoning all delusions. Each of these three enlightenments is known as a 'cessation of contaminations'. Only a Buddha knows all these directly and reveals them to disciples.

Besides the ten forces, Buddhas also possess four fearlessnesses. The definition of a fearlessness of a Buddha is an utterly firm, ultimate realization that is entirely free from fear in expounding Dharma. There are four types: fearlessness in revealing the Dharma of renunciation, fearlessness in revealing the Dharma of overcoming obstructions, fearlessness in revealing the Dharma of excellent abandonments, and fearlessness in revealing the Dharma of excellent realizations.

Buddhas also possess four correct, specific cognizers. The definition of correct, specific cognizer is an ultimate realization that knows the entities, divisions and so forth of all phenomena without error. There are four types: correct cognizers of specific phenomena, correct cognizers of specific meanings, correct cognizers of specific, definite words, and correct cognizers of specific confidence. An example of the first is a wisdom of a Buddha that realizes the specific, uncommon signs of all phenomena. An example of the second is a wisdom of a Buddha that realizes the specific divisions of all phenomena. An example of the third is a wisdom of a Buddha that realizes the specific etymological explanations of all phenomena. An example of the fourth is a wisdom of a Buddha that experiences inexhaustible confidence in revealing Dharma.

Buddhas also possess many other excellent qualities. For example, there is the great love of a Buddha, which is defined as an ultimate love that bestows benefit and happiness upon all living beings; the great compassion

237

of a Buddha, which is defined as an ultimate compassion completely protecting suffering beings; the great joy of a Buddha, which is defined as an ultimate joy that is supremely joyful in leading all living beings to a state of happiness; and the great equanimity of a Buddha, which is defined as an ultimate realization unmixed with attachment or hatred.

Buddhas also possess eighteen unshared qualities. The definition of an unshared quality of a Buddha is an uncommon quality of the body, speech, or mind of a Buddha that is not possessed by other Superior beings. There are eighteen unshared qualities: six unshared activities, six unshared realizations, three unshared deeds and three unshared exalted awarenesses. The six unshared activities are: not possessing mistaken activities of body, not possessing mistaken activities of speech, not possessing mistaken activities of mind, not possessing a mind not in meditative equipoise, not possessing conceptuality, and not possessing neutrality. The six unshared realizations are: not possessing degeneration of aspiration, not possessing degeneration of effort, not possessing degeneration of mindfulness, not possessing degeneration of concentration, not possessing degeneration of wisdom, and not possessing degeneration of perfect liberation. The three unshared deeds are: deeds of body preceded by and followed by exalted awareness, deeds of speech preceded by and followed by exalted awareness, and deeds of mind preceded by and followed by exalted awareness. The three unshared exalted awarenesses are: unobstructed exalted awareness that knows all the past directly and without obstruction, unobstructed exalted awareness that knows all the future directly and without obstruction, and unobstructed exalted awareness that knows all the present directly and without obstruction.

We should contemplate the good qualities of a Buddha, such as those briefly described here, and pray that we can attain the same good qualities by completing all the grounds and paths of Secret Mantra.

Dorjechang Kelsang Gyatso Rinpoche

Dedication

We should pray:

To *accomplish all the purposes of living beings,*
By this virtue may I quickly attain
The seven pre-eminent qualities of embrace:
A Form Body endowed with the major signs and minor
    indications
Continuously in embrace with a wisdom knowledge consort,
A mind always abiding in a state of great bliss,
This mind of bliss always mixed with emptiness, the lack of
    inherent existence of all phenomena,
Endowed with great compassion that has abandoned the
    extreme of attachment to solitary peace,
Uninterruptedly manifesting Form Bodies that pervade the
    whole world,
And unceasingly performing enlightened deeds.

May everything be auspicious.

This book, *Tantric Grounds and Paths*, is the teachings of
Venerable Geshe Kelsang Gyatso Rinpoche. These
teachings were recorded and transcribed, and then
edited principally by him and some of his senior students.

Appendix I:
The Condensed Meaning
of the Text

The Condensed Meaning
of the Text

Tantric Grounds and Paths is presented in three parts:

1 Introduction
2 The good qualities of Secret Mantra
3 The four classes of Tantra

The good qualities of Secret Mantra has six parts:

1 Secret Vehicle
2 Mantra Vehicle
3 Effect Vehicle
4 Vajra Vehicle
5 Method Vehicle
6 Tantric Vehicle

The four classes of Tantra has four parts:

1 Action Tantra
2 Performance Tantra
3 Yoga Tantra
4 Highest Yoga Tantra

Action Tantra has six parts:

1 Receiving empowerments, the method for ripening our mental continuum

2 Observing the vows and commitments
3 Engaging in close retreat, the method for attaining realizations
4 How to accomplish the common and uncommon attainments once we have experience of the four concentrations
5 How to progress through the grounds and paths in dependence upon Action Tantra
6 The families of Action Tantra Deities

Engaging in close retreat, the method for attaining realizations, has four parts:

1 Concentration of the four-limbed recitation
2 Concentration of abiding in fire
3 Concentration of abiding in sound
4 Concentration of bestowing liberation at the end of sound

Concentration of the four-limbed recitation has four parts:

1 Accomplishing the self base
2 Accomplishing the other base
3 Accomplishing the mind base
4 Accomplishing the sound base

Accomplishing the self base has six parts:

1 The Deity of emptiness
2 The Deity of sound
3 The Deity of letters
4 The Deity of form
5 The Deity of the mudra
6 The Deity of signs

How to accomplish the common and uncommon attainments once we have experience of the four concentrations has two parts:

    1 Accomplishing the common attainments
    2 Accomplishing the uncommon attainments

Accomplishing the common attainments has eight parts:

    1 The attainment of pills
    2 The attainment of eye-lotion
    3 The attainment of seeing beneath the ground
    4 The attainment of the sword
    5 The attainment of flying
    6 The attainment of invisibility
    7 The attainment of longevity
    8 The attainment of youth

The families of Action Tantra Deities has three parts:

    1 The Tathagata family
    2 The Lotus family
    3 The Vajra family

Highest Yoga Tantra has four parts:

    1 The five paths and the thirteen grounds of Highest Yoga Tantra
    2 The Tantric vows and commitments
    3 Generation stage
    4 Completion stage

The five paths and the thirteen grounds of Highest Yoga Tantra has two parts:

    1 The five paths of Highest Yoga Tantra
    2 The thirteen grounds of Highest Yoga Tantra

The five paths of Highest Yoga Tantra has five parts:

1 The path of accumulation of Highest Yoga Tantra
2 The path of preparation of Highest Yoga Tantra
3 The path of seeing of Highest Yoga Tantra
4 The path of meditation of Highest Yoga Tantra
5 The Path of No More Learning of Highest Yoga Tantra

The thirteen grounds of Highest Yoga Tantra has thirteen parts:

1 Very Joyful
2 Stainless
3 Luminous
4 Radiant
5 Difficult to Overcome
6 Approaching
7 Gone Afar
8 Immovable
9 Good Intelligence
10 Cloud of Dharma
11 Without Examples
12 Possessing Exalted Awareness
13 Holding the Vajra

The Tantric vows and commitments has two parts:

1 The commitments of the individual five Buddha families
2 The commitments of the five Buddha families in common

The commitments of the individual five Buddha families has five parts:

1 The six commitments of the family of Buddha Vairochana
2 The four commitments of the family of Buddha Akshobya
3 The four commitments of the family of Buddha Ratnasambhava
4 The three commitments of the family of Buddha Amitabha
5 The two commitments of the family of Buddha Amoghasiddhi

The six commitments of the family of Buddha Vairochana has six parts:

1 To go for refuge to Buddha
2 To go for refuge to Dharma
3 To go for refuge to Sangha
4 To refrain from non-virtue
5 To practise virtue
6 To benefit others

The four commitments of the family of Buddha Akshobya has four parts:

1 To keep a vajra to remind us to emphasize the development of great bliss through meditation on the central channel
2 To keep a bell to remind us to emphasize meditation on emptiness
3 To generate ourself as the Deity while realizing all things that we normally see do not exist

4 To rely sincerely upon our Spiritual Guide who leads us to the practice of the pure moral discipline of the Pratimoksha, Bodhisattva and Tantric vows

The four commitments of the family of Buddha Ratnasambhava has four parts:

1 To give material help
2 To give Dharma
3 To give fearlessness
4 To give love

The three commitments of the family of Buddha Amitabha has three parts:

1 To rely upon the teachings of Sutra
2 To rely upon the teachings of the two lower classes of Tantra
3 To rely upon the teachings of the two higher classes of Tantra

The two commitments of the family of Buddha Amoghasiddhi has two parts:

1 To make offerings to our Spiritual Guide
2 To strive to maintain purely all the vows we have taken

The commitments of the five Buddha families in common has four parts:

1 The fourteen root downfalls of the Secret Mantra vows
2 The branch commitments
3 The gross downfalls of the Secret Mantra vows
4 The uncommon commitments of Mother Tantra

The fourteen root downfalls of the Secret Mantra vows has fourteen parts:

1 Abusing or scorning our Spiritual Guide
2 Showing contempt for the precepts
3 Criticizing our vajra brothers and sisters
4 Abandoning love for any being
5 Giving up aspiring or engaging bodhichitta
6 Scorning the Dharma of Sutra or Tantra
7 Revealing secrets to an unsuitable person
8 Abusing our body
9 Abandoning emptiness
10 Relying upon malevolent friends
11 Not recollecting the view of emptiness
12 Destroying others' faith
13 Not maintaining commitment objects
14 Scorning women

The branch commitments has three parts:

1 The commitments of abandonment
2 The commitments of reliance
3 The additional commitments of abandonment

The commitments of abandonment are to abandon negative actions, especially killing, stealing, sexual misconduct, lying and taking intoxicants.

The commitments of reliance are to rely sincerely upon our Spiritual Guide, to be respectful towards our vajra brothers and sisters, and to observe the ten virtuous actions.

The additional commitments of abandonment are to abandon the causes of turning away from the Mahayana, to avoid scorning gods and to avoid stepping over sacred objects.

The gross downfalls of the Secret Mantra vows has eleven parts:

1 Relying upon an unqualified mudra
2 Engaging in union without the three recognitions
3 Showing secret substances to an unsuitable person
4 Fighting or arguing during a tsog offering ceremony
5 Giving false answers to questions asked out of faith
6 Staying seven days in the home of someone who rejects the Vajrayana
7 Pretending to be a Yogi while remaining imperfect
8 Revealing holy Dharma to those with no faith
9 Engaging in mandala actions without completing a close retreat
10 Needlessly transgressing the Pratimoksha or Bodhisattva precepts
11 Acting in contradiction to the *Fifty Verses on the Spiritual Guide*

The uncommon commitments of Mother Tantra has eight parts:

1 To perform all physical actions first with our left, to make offerings to our Spiritual Guide, and never to abuse him
2 To abandon union with those unqualified
3 While in union, not to be separated from the view of emptiness
4 Never to lose appreciation for the path of attachment
5 Never to forsake the two kinds of mudra
6 To strive mainly for the external and internal methods

7 Never to release seminal fluid; to rely upon pure behaviour

8 To abandon repulsion when tasting bodhichitta

Generation stage has five parts:

1 Definition and etymology of generation stage
2 Divisions of generation stage
3 How to practise actual generation stage meditation
4 The measurement of having completed generation stage
5 How to advance from generation stage to completion stage

Divisions of generation stage has two parts:

1 Gross generation stage
2 Subtle generation stage

How to practise actual generation stage meditation has two parts:

1 Training in gross generation stage meditation
2 Training in subtle generation stage meditation

Training in gross generation stage meditation has two parts:

1 Training in divine pride
2 Training in clear appearance

Training in clear appearance has two parts:

1 Training in clear appearance on the general aspect
2 Training in clear appearance on specific aspects

The measurement of having completed generation stage has four parts:

1 Beginners
2 Practitioners in whom some wisdom has descended
3 Practitioners with some power over wisdom
4 Practitioners with complete power over wisdom

Completion stage has four parts:

1 Definition and etymology of completion stage
2 Divisions of completion stage
3 How to progress from the lower stages to the higher stages
4 The final results of completion stage

Divisions of completion stage has six parts:

1 Isolated body of completion stage
2 Isolated speech
3 Isolated mind
4 Illusory body
5 Clear light
6 Union

Isolated body of completion stage has three parts:

1 Definition and etymology of isolated body of completion stage
2 Divisions of isolated body of completion stage
3 How to practise isolated body of completion stage

Divisions of isolated body of completion stage has two parts:

1 Isolated body of completion stage that is meditative equipoise
2 Isolated body of completion stage that is subsequent attainment

How to practise isolated body of completion stage has two parts:

1 How to practise isolated body of completion stage during the meditation session
2 How to practise isolated body of completion stage during the meditation break

How to practise isolated body of completion stage during the meditation session has two parts:

1 A preliminary explanation
2 The actual explanation

The actual explanation has two parts:

1 An introduction to the central channel, drops and winds
2 The actual practice

The actual practice has three parts:

1 The preliminary practices
2 The actual meditation
3 The results of the practice of this meditation

The actual meditation has three parts:

1 Meditation on the central channel – the yoga of the central channel
2 Meditation on the indestructible drop – the yoga of the drop
3 Meditation on the indestructible wind and mind – the yoga of wind

Isolated speech has three parts:

1 Definition and etymology of isolated speech
2 Divisions of isolated speech
3 How to practise isolated speech

Divisions of isolated speech has five parts:

1 First empty of isolated speech
2 Second empty of isolated speech
3 Third empty of isolated speech
4 Fourth empty of isolated speech
5 Isolated speech that is none of these four

How to practise isolated speech has three parts:

1 Meditation on the indestructible drop
2 Meditation on the indestructible wind and mind
3 Meditation on vajra recitation

Meditation on vajra recitation has three parts:

1 Definition and etymology of vajra recitation
2 Divisions of vajra recitation
3 How to practise vajra recitation

Divisions of vajra recitation has two parts:

1 Vajra recitation on the root winds
2 Vajra recitation on the branch winds

How to practise vajra recitation has three parts:

1 An explanation of the winds
2 An explanation of mantra
3 The actual meditation on vajra recitation

Isolated mind has three parts:

1 Definition and etymology of isolated mind
2 Divisions of isolated mind
3 How to practise isolated mind

Divisions of isolated mind has five parts:

1 Isolated mind of white appearance
2 Isolated mind of red increase
3 Isolated mind of black near-attainment
4 Isolated mind of clear light
5 Isolated mind that is none of these four

Illusory body has three parts:

1 Definition and etymology of illusory body
2 Divisions of illusory body
3 How to attain the illusory body

Divisions of illusory body has two parts:

1 Impure illusory body
2 Pure illusory body

Impure illusory body has fifteen parts:

1 The characteristic of cause
2 The characteristic of time
3 The characteristic of location
4 The characteristic of nature
5 The characteristic of colour
6 The characteristic of shape
7 The characteristic of being seen
8 The characteristic of infinite light
9 The characteristic of enjoyment
10 The characteristic of motivation
11 The characteristic of good qualities
12 The characteristic of similes
13 The characteristic of names
14 The characteristic of definite words
15 The characteristic of duration

The characteristic of similes has twelve parts:

1 Like an illusion
2 Like a reflection of the moon in water
3 Like the body's shadow
4 Like a mirage
5 Like a dream
6 Like an echo
7 Like a city of intermediate state beings
8 Like a manifestation
9 Like a rainbow
10 Like a bolt of lightning
11 Like a water bubble
12 Like a reflection in a mirror

Clear light has three parts:

1 Definition and etymology of meaning clear light
2 Divisions of meaning clear light
3 How to attain meaning clear light

Divisions of meaning clear light has three parts:

1 Meaning clear light of the fourth stage
2 Meaning clear light of the union that needs learning
3 Meaning clear light of the Union of No More Learning

Union has three parts:

1 Definition and etymology of union
2 Divisions of union
3 How to attain union

Divisions of union has two parts:

1 Union of abandonment
2 Union of realization

Appendix II:
The Preliminary Practices

CONTENTS

Liberating Prayer
Praise to Buddha Shakyamuni   263

**A Handbook for the Daily Practice of Bodhisattva
Vows and Tantric Vows**   265

Great Liberation of the Mother
Preliminary Prayers for Mahamudra Meditation
in conjunction with Vajrayogini Practice   281

Great Liberation of the Father
Preliminary Prayers for Mahamudra Meditation
in conjunction with Heruka Practice   293

An Explanation of the Practice   305

Liberating Prayer

PRAISE TO BUDDHA SHAKYAMUNI

O Blessed One, Shakyamuni Buddha,
Precious treasury of compassion,
Bestower of supreme inner peace,

You, who love all beings without exception,
Are the source of happiness and goodness;
And you guide us to the liberating path.

Your body is a wishfulfilling jewel,
Your speech is supreme, purifying nectar,
And your mind is refuge for all living beings.

With folded hands I turn to you,
Supreme unchanging friend,
I request from the depths of my heart:

Please give me the light of your wisdom
To dispel the darkness of my mind
And to heal my mental continuum.

Please nourish me with your goodness,
That I in turn may nourish all beings
With an unceasing banquet of delight.

Through your compassionate intention,
Your blessings and virtuous deeds,
And my strong wish to rely upon you,

May all suffering quickly cease
And all happiness and joy be fulfilled;
And may holy Dharma flourish for evermore.

Colophon: This prayer was composed by Venerable Geshe Kelsang Gyatso Rinpoche and is recited at the beginning of teachings, meditations and prayers in Kadampa Buddhist Centres throughout the world.

A Handbook for the Daily
Practice of Bodhisattva Vows
and Tantric Vows

Introduction

Those who have received Bodhisattva vows and Tantric vows should know that the commitments of these vows are the basic foundation upon which the realizations of Mahayana and Vajrayana will grow. If we neglect these commitments our practice of Mahayana and Vajrayana will be powerless. Je Tsongkhapa said:

The two attainments both depend on
My sacred vows and my commitments
Bless me to understand this clearly
And keep them at the cost of my life.

The two attainments are the common attainments – the real-izations of Sutra – and the uncommon attainments – the realizations of Tantra.

The *Perfection of Wisdom Sutras* and Lamrim teachings explain extensively the practice of the six perfections as the commitment of the Bodhisattva vows. The six perfections are the practices of giving, moral discipline, patience, effort, concentration and wisdom motivated by the compassionate mind of bodhichitta. Through sincerely engaging in the practice of the six perfections we can fulfil all the commitments of our Bodhisattva vows, including the commitments to abandon the eighteen root and forty-six secondary downfalls.

In the practice of giving love, if we sincerely cherish all living beings there is no basis for incurring any downfalls of the Bodhisattva and Tantric vows because these downfalls are necessarily motivated by self-cherishing.

Although there are many commitments of Tantric vows, such as abandoning many downfalls, especially the fourteen root downfalls, through sincerely practising the nineteen commitments of the five Buddha families we can fulfil all the commitments of Tantric vows. Through fulfilling our commitments of the Pratimoksha, Bodhisattva and Tantric vows we can make quick progress on the path to enlightenment.

We should know that in truth our commitments of the Pratimoksha, Bodhisattva and Tantric vows are the only method to solve our own and others' problems and the only method to make ourself and others happy. This is what we really need. We should never think that our commitments are like heavy luggage but always think that they are a wishfulfilling jewel that has been given to us by Buddha, and we should keep them purely at the cost of our life.

Geshe Kelsang Gyatso
2007

A Handbook for the Daily Practice of Bodhisattva Vows and Tantric Vows

PART ONE:
THE PRACTICE OF BODHISATTVA VOWS

Visualizing Guru Buddha Shakyamuni

In the space before me is the living Buddha Shakyamuni surrounded by all the Buddhas and Bodhisattvas, like the full moon surrounded by stars.

Taking Bodhisattva Vows

With strong faith place your two hands at your heart in the gesture of prostration. Verbally or mentally recite the following ritual prayer three times, while concentrating on its meaning.

O Guru Buddha Shakyamuni please listen to what I now say.
From this time forth until I attain enlightenment
I go for refuge to the Three Jewels – Buddha, Dharma and Sangha –
And confess individually all negative actions.

This means: I will apply effort to purify all negative actions together with their roots, the delusions.

I rejoice in the virtues of all beings,

> *This means: I rejoice and engage in the practice of the Bodhisattva's way of life, that is, the practice of the six perfections. This is the way of practising the Bodhisattva vows.*

And promise to accomplish a Buddha's enlightenment.

> *This means: I promise to accomplish a Buddha's enlightenment in order to liberate all living beings permanently from suffering.*

In this ritual practice you have promised to accomplish a Buddha's enlightenment in order to liberate all living beings permanently from suffering. This promise is your Bodhisattva vow. To fulfil your promise you need to engage in the Bodhisattva's way of life, the practice of the six perfections, which are the commitments of the Bodhisattva vow. In this way you can make progress on the path to enlightenment, from the path of accumulation to the path of preparation, path of seeing, path of meditation and the Path of No More Learning, which is enlightenment.

The six perfections are the practices of giving, moral discipline, patience, effort, concentration and wisdom motivated by bodhichitta. You should recognize that the six perfections are your daily practice, as the commitments of your Bodhisattva vow.

In the practice of **giving** you should practise:

1 giving material help to those in poverty, including giving food to animals;
2 giving practical help to those sick or physically weak;

3 giving protection by always trying to save others'
   lives, including those of insects;
4 giving love, learning to cherish all living beings by
   always believing that their happiness and freedom
   are important; and
5 giving Dharma, helping to solve the problems
   of anger, attachment and ignorance by giving
   Dharma teachings or meaningful advice.

In the practice of **moral discipline** you should abandon
any inappropriate actions including those that cause others
suffering. By doing this your actions of body, speech and
mind will be pure so that you will become a pure being. This
is the basic foundation upon which all spiritual realizations
will grow.

In the practice of **patience** you should never allow
yourself to become angry or discouraged, by temporarily
accepting any difficulties or harm from others. This is the
practice of patience. Anger destroys your merit, or good fortune, so that you will continually experience many obstacles,
and because of lacking good fortune it will be difficult to
fulfil your wishes, especially your spiritual aims. There is
no greater evil than anger. With the practice of patience you
can accomplish any spiritual aim; there is no greater virtue
than patience.

In the practice of **effort** you should rely upon irreversible
effort to accumulate the great collections of merit and wisdom, which are the main causes of the attainment of Buddha's
Form Body (Rupakaya) and Truth Body (Dharmakaya), and
especially you should emphasize contemplation and meditation on emptiness, the way things really are. By doing this
you can easily make progress on the path to enlightenment.

With effort you can accomplish your aim; with laziness you cannot achieve anything.

In the practice of **concentration**, at this stage you should emphasize accomplishing the concentration of tranquil abiding observing emptiness. Through the power of this concentration, when you experience a special wisdom called 'superior seeing' that realizes the emptiness of all phenomena very clearly, you will have progressed from being a Bodhisattva on the path of accumulation to being a Bodhisattva on the path of preparation.

In the practice of **wisdom**, at this stage you need to emphasize increasing the power of your wisdom of superior seeing by continually meditating on the emptiness of all phenomena with bodhichitta motivation. Through this, when your superior seeing transforms into the path of seeing, which is the direct realization of the emptiness of all phenomena, you will have progressed from being a Bodhisattva on the path of preparation to being a Bodhisattva on the path of seeing. The moment you attain the path of seeing you are a Superior Bodhisattva who no longer experiences samsara's sufferings. Even if someone cuts your body piece by piece with a knife you have no pain because you have the direct realization of the way things really are.

Having completed the path of seeing, to make further progress you need to engage continually in meditation on the emptiness of all phenomena with bodhichitta motivation. This meditation is called the 'path of meditation'. When you reach this stage you have progressed from being a Bodhisattva on the path of seeing to being a Bodhisattva on the path of meditation.

Having completed the path of meditation, when your wisdom of the path of meditation transforms into an omniscient wisdom that experiences the permanent cessation of mistaken appearances, this omniscient wisdom is called the 'Path of No More Learning', which is actual enlightenment. When you reach this stage you have progressed from being a Bodhisattva on the path of meditation to being an enlightened being, a Buddha. You have completed the ultimate goal of living beings.

More detail on the Bodhisattva vows can be found in the book *The Bodhisattva Vow*.

Tantric commitment objects:
inner offering in kapala, vajra, bell, damaru, action vase, mala

PART TWO:
THE PRACTICE OF TANTRIC VOWS

Visualizing Guru Buddha Shakyamuni

In the space before me is the living Buddha Shakyamuni surrounded by all the Buddhas and Bodhisattvas, like the full moon surrounded by stars.

Taking Tantric Vows

With strong faith place your two hands at your heart in the gesture of prostration. Verbally or mentally recite the following ritual prayer three times, while concentrating on its meaning.

O Guru Buddha Shakyamuni please listen to what I now say.
From this time forth until I attain enlightenment,
For the sake of all living beings
I shall maintain the general and individual vows and commitments of the five Buddha families,
I shall deliver those not delivered from lower rebirth,
Liberate those not liberated from samsaric rebirth,
Give breath – the spiritual life of Vajrayana – to those unable to engage in the Vajrayana path,
And lead all beings to a state beyond sorrow, the state of enlightenment.

In this ritual practice you have promised to maintain the nineteen commitments of the Highest Yoga Tantric vows, to liberate all living beings from lower rebirth and from samsaric rebirth, and to lead them to the Vajrayana path, which quickly leads all beings to the state of enlightenment. This promise is your Tantric vow. To fulfil your promise you need to engage in the practice of the nineteen commitments of the five Buddha families. The nineteen commitments are:

The six commitments of the family of Buddha Vairochana:

1 To go for refuge to Buddha
2 To go for refuge to Dharma
3 To go for refuge to Sangha
4 To refrain from non-virtue
5 To practise virtue
6 To benefit others

The four commitments of the family of Buddha Akshobya:

1 To keep a vajra to remind us to emphasize the development of great bliss through meditation on the central channel
2 To keep a bell to remind us to emphasize meditation on emptiness
3 To generate ourself as the Deity while realizing all things that we normally see do not exist
4 To rely sincerely upon our Spiritual Guide who leads us to the practice of the pure moral discipline of the Pratimoksha, Bodhisattva and Tantric vows

The four commitments of the family of Buddha Ratnasambhava:

1 To give material help
2 To give Dharma
3 To give fearlessness
4 To give love

The three commitments of the family of Buddha Amitabha:

1 To rely upon the teachings of Sutra
2 To rely upon the teachings of the two lower classes of Tantra
3 To rely upon the teachings of the two higher classes of Tantra

Since Lamrim is the main body of Buddhadharma, if we sincerely rely upon Kadam Lamrim we fulfil these three commitments.

The two commitments of the family of Buddha Amoghasiddhi:

1 To make offerings to our Spiritual Guide
2 To strive to maintain purely all the vows we have taken

As Buddha Vajradhara said, you should remember these nineteen commitments six times every day, which means every four hours. This is called *'Six Session Yoga'*. To fulfil this commitment, you should verbally or mentally recite the following condensed six session yoga six times every day, while concentrating on its meaning:

I go for refuge to the Guru and Three Jewels.
Holding vajra and bell I generate as the Deity and make
　　offerings.
I rely upon the Dharmas of Sutra and Tantra and refrain
　　from all non-virtuous actions.
Gathering all virtuous Dharmas, I help all living beings
　　through the practice of the four givings.

All nineteen commitments are referred to in this verse. The
words, '*I go for refuge to the . . . Three Jewels*', refer to the first
three commitments of the family of Buddha Vairochana – to
go for refuge to Buddha, to go for refuge to Dharma, and
to go for refuge to Sangha. The word, '*Guru*', refers to the
fourth commitment of the family of Buddha Akshobya – to
rely sincerely upon our Spiritual Guide.

The words, '*Holding vajra and bell I generate as the Deity*',
refer to the first three commitments of the family of Buddha
Akshobya – to keep a vajra to remind us of great bliss, to
keep a bell to remind us of emptiness, and to generate ourself
as the Deity. The words, '*and make offerings*', refer to the first
commitment of the family of Buddha Amoghasiddhi – to
make offerings to our Spiritual Guide.

The words, '*I rely upon the Dharmas of Sutra and Tantra*',
refer to the three commitments of the family of Buddha
Amitabha – to rely upon the teachings of Sutra, to rely upon
the teachings of the two lower classes of Tantra, and to rely
upon the teachings of the two higher classes of Tantra. The
words, '*and refrain from all non-virtuous actions*', refer to the
fourth commitment of the family of Buddha Vairochana – to
refrain from non-virtue.

The words, '*Gathering all virtuous Dharmas*', refer to the
fifth commitment of the family of Buddha Vairochana – to

practise virtue. The words, *'I help all living beings'*, refer to the sixth commitment of the family of Buddha Vairochana – to benefit others. The words, *'through the practice of the four givings'*, refer to the four commitments of the family of Buddha Ratnasambhava – to give material help, to give Dharma, to give fearlessness, and to give love.

Finally, the entire verse refers to the second commitment of the family of Buddha Amoghasiddhi – to strive to maintain purely all the vows we have taken.

Colophon: This practice and explanation was prepared from traditional sources by Venerable Geshe Kelsang Gyatso Rinpoche.

Great Liberation of the Mother

PRELIMINARY PRAYERS FOR MAHAMUDRA
MEDITATION IN CONJUNCTION WITH
VAJRAYOGINI PRACTICE

Great Liberation of the Mother

Going for refuge

In the space before me appear Guru Chakrasambara
Father and Mother, surrounded by the assembly of root
and lineage Gurus, Yidams, Three Jewels, Attendants and
Protectors.

Imagining yourself and all living beings going for refuge,
recite three times:

I and all sentient beings, the migrators as extensive as
    space, from this time forth until we reach the essence of
    enlightenment,
Go for refuge to the glorious, sacred Gurus,
Go for refuge to the complete Buddhas, the Blessed Ones,
Go for refuge to the sacred Dharmas,
Go for refuge to the superior Sanghas.

Generating bodhichitta

Generate bodhichitta and the four immeasurables while
reciting three times:

Once I have attained the state of a complete Buddha, I
shall free all sentient beings from the ocean of samsara's
suffering and lead them to the bliss of full enlightenment.
For this purpose I shall practise the stages of Vajrayogini's
path.

Receiving blessings

Now with your palms pressed together recite:

I prostrate and go for refuge to the Gurus and Three Precious Jewels. Please bless my mental continuum.

Due to reciting this:

The objects of refuge before me melt into the form of white, red and dark blue rays of light. These dissolve into me and I receive their blessings of body, speech and mind.

GENERATING ONESELF AS VAJRAYOGINI

Bringing death into the path to the Truth Body

All worlds and their beings melt into light and dissolve
      into me.
I too melt into light and dissolve into emptiness.
I am the actual Truth Body Buddha Vajrayogini.

Bringing the intermediate state into the path to the Enjoyment Body

In my place, upon a lotus and sun seat,
My mind appears as a cubit of red light.
I am the actual Enjoyment Body Buddha Vajrayogini.

Bringing rebirth into the path to the Emanation Body

These completely transform,
And I arise as the Emanation Body Buddha Vajrayogini,
Together with my Pure Land.

GURU YOGA

Blessing the environment and offering substances

Light rays from the letter BAM at my heart
Purify all worlds and their beings.
Everything becomes immaculately pure,
Completely filled with a vast array of offerings,
The nature of exalted wisdom, and bestowing
    uncontaminated bliss.

Visualization

In the space before me is the living Buddha Vajradhara,
who is inseparable from my root Guru, surrounded by
all the Mahamudra lineage Gurus, Yidams, Buddhas,
Bodhisattvas, Dakas, Dakinis and Dharma Protectors.

Prayer of seven limbs

With my body, speech and mind, humbly I prostrate,
And make offerings both set out and imagined.
I confess my wrong deeds from all time,
And rejoice in the virtues of all.
Please stay until samsara ceases,
And turn the Wheel of Dharma for us.
I dedicate all virtues to great enlightenment.

Offering the mandala

OM VAJRA BHUMI AH HUM
Great and powerful golden ground,
OM VAJRA REKHE AH HUM
At the edge the iron fence stands around the outer circle.

In the centre Mount Meru the king of mountains,
Around which are four continents:
In the east, Purvavideha, in the south, Jambudipa,
In the west, Aparagodaniya, in the north, Uttarakuru.
Each has two sub-continents:
Deha and Videha, Tsamara and Abatsamara,
Satha and Uttaramantrina, Kurava and Kaurava.
The mountain of jewels, the wish-granting tree,
The wish-granting cow, and the harvest unsown.
The precious wheel, the precious jewel,
The precious queen, the precious minister,
The precious elephant, the precious supreme horse,
The precious general, and the great treasure vase.
The goddess of beauty, the goddess of garlands,
The goddess of song, the goddess of dance,
The goddess of flowers, the goddess of incense,
The goddess of light, and the goddess of scent.
The sun and the moon, the precious umbrella,
The banner of victory in every direction.
In the centre all treasures of both gods and men,
An excellent collection with nothing left out.
I offer this to you my kind root Guru and lineage Gurus,
To all of you sacred and glorious Gurus;
Please accept with compassion for migrating beings,
And having accepted please grant us your blessings.

O Treasure of Compassion, my Refuge and Protector,
I offer you the mountain, continents, precious objects,
    treasure vase, sun and moon,
Which have arisen from my aggregates, sources and
    elements
As aspects of the exalted wisdom of spontaneous bliss and
    emptiness.

I offer without any sense of loss
The objects that give rise to my attachment, hatred and
    confusion,
My friends, enemies and strangers, our bodies and
    enjoyments;
Please accept these and bless me to be released directly
    from the three poisons.

IDAM GURU RATNA MANDALAKAM NIRYATAYAMI

Prayers of request to the Mahamudra lineage Gurus

O Conqueror Vajradhara, Manjushri,
Je Tsongkhapa Losang Dragpa, Togden Jampel Gyatso,
Baso Chokyi Gyaltsen, Mahasiddha Dharmavajra,
Ensapa Losang Dondrub and Khedrub Sangye Yeshe,
I request you please to grant me your blessings
So that I may cut the clinging of self-grasping within my
    mental continuum,
Train in love, compassion and bodhichitta,
And swiftly accomplish the Mahamudra that is the Union
    of No More Learning.

O Venerable Losang Chogyen, Mahasiddha Gendun
    Gyaltsen,
Drungpa Tsondru Gyaltsen, Konchog Gyaltsen,
Panchen Losang Yeshe, Losang Trinlay,
Drubwang Losang Namgyal and Kachen Yeshe Gyaltsen,
I request you please to grant me your blessings
So that I may cut the clinging of self-grasping within my
    mental continuum,
Train in love, compassion and bodhichitta,
And swiftly accomplish the Mahamudra that is the Union
    of No More Learning.

O Phurchog Ngawang Jampa, Panchen Palden Yeshe,
Khedrub Ngawang Dorje, Ngulchu Dharmabhadra,
Yangchen Drubpay Dorje, Khedrub Tenzin Tsondru,
Phabongkhapa Trinlay Gyatso and Trijang Dorjechang
    Losang Yeshe,
I request you please to grant me your blessings
So that I may cut the clinging of self-grasping within my
    mental continuum,
Train in love, compassion and bodhichitta,
And swiftly accomplish the Mahamudra that is the Union
    of No More Learning.

O Venerable Kelsang Gyatso Rinpoche,
Who through your compassion and with your great skill
Explain to fortunate disciples
The instructions of your Guru and the profound lineage,
I request you please to grant me your blessings
So that I may cut the clinging of self-grasping within my
    mental continuum,
Train in love, compassion and bodhichitta,
And swiftly accomplish the Mahamudra that is the Union
    of No More Learning.

Please grant me your blessings
So that I may see the venerable Guru as a Buddha,
Overcome attachment for the abodes of samsara,
And having assumed the burden of liberating all migrators,
Accomplish the common and uncommon paths,
And swiftly attain the Union of the Mahamudra.

This body of mine and your body, O Father,
This speech of mine and your speech, O Father,
This mind of mine and your mind, O Father,
Through your blessings may they become inseparably one.

Special request

Recite three times:

I request you my precious Guru Vajradhara, the essence
of all Buddhas, please bless my mental continuum and
pacify all outer and inner obstacles so that I may progress
in the training on the profound path of the Mahamudra
meditations, and swiftly attain the Mahamudra that is the
union of bliss and emptiness.

Receiving blessings

All the other holy beings dissolve into my root Guru,
Vajradhara, in the centre. My root Guru too, out of
affection for me, melts into the form of blue light and,
entering through the crown of my head, mixes inseparably
with my mind in the aspect of a letter BAM at my heart.

*At this point, we engage in the actual training in
Mahamudra meditation. We can do either the common
Vajrayana Mahamudra meditations as explained in the
commentary* Clear Light of Bliss, *or the uncommon
Vajrayana Mahamudra meditations as explained in
the commentaries* Mahamudra Tantra, The Oral
Instructions of Mahamudra *and* Tantric Grounds and
Paths. *Through this, we accomplish the Mahamudra that
is the union of bliss and emptiness, the Mahamudra that
is the union of the two truths, and the Mahamudra that is
the resultant Union of No More Learning.*

Dedication

By this virtue, may I see the venerable Guru as a Buddha,
Overcome attachment for the abodes of samsara,
And, having assumed the burden of liberating all
    migrators,
Accomplish the common and uncommon paths
And swiftly attain the Union of the Mahamudra.

In short, may I never be parted from you, Venerable
    Guru Dakini,
But always come under your care
And, swiftly completing the grounds and paths,
Attain the great Dakini state.

Prayers for the Virtuous Tradition

So that the tradition of Je Tsongkhapa,
The King of the Dharma, may flourish,
May all obstacles be pacified
And may all favourable conditions abound.

Through the two collections of myself and others
Gathered throughout the three times,
May the doctrine of Conqueror Losang Dragpa
Flourish for evermore.

The nine-line *Migtsema* prayer

Tsongkhapa, crown ornament of the scholars of the Land
    of the Snows,
You are Buddha Shakyamuni and Vajradhara, the source
    of all attainments,
Avalokiteshvara, the treasury of unobservable compassion,

Manjushri, the supreme stainless wisdom,

And Vajrapani, the destroyer of the hosts of maras.

O Venerable Guru-Buddha, synthesis of all Three Jewels,

With my body, speech and mind, respectfully I make
   requests:

Please grant your blessings to ripen and liberate myself
   and others,

And bestow the common and supreme attainments.

(3x)

Colophon: This sadhana or ritual prayer for spiritual attainments
was compiled by Venerable Geshe Kelsang Gyatso Rinpoche and
translated under his compassionate guidance.
The verse of request to Venerable Geshe Kelsang Gyatso Rinpoche
was composed by the glorious Dharma Protector, Duldzin Dorje
Shugden, at the request of Venerable Geshe Kelsang's faithful
disciples, and has been included in this sadhana at their request.

Great Liberation of the Father

PRELIMINARY PRAYERS FOR MAHAMUDRA
MEDITATION IN CONJUNCTION WITH
HERUKA PRACTICE

Great Liberation of the Father

Visualizing the objects of refuge

In the space before me is Guru Heruka Father and Mother,
surrounded by the assembly of lineage Gurus, Yidams,
Buddhas, Bodhisattvas, Heroes, Dakinis and Dharma
Protectors.

Going for refuge and generating aspiring bodhichitta

Eternally I shall go for refuge
To Buddha, Dharma and Sangha.
For the sake of all living beings
I shall become Heruka.   (3x)

Generating engaging bodhichitta

To lead all mother sentient beings to the state of ultimate
    happiness,
I shall attain as quickly as possible, in this very life,
The state of the Union of Buddha Heruka;
For this purpose I shall practise the stages of Heruka's path.

    (3x)

Receiving blessings

Guru Heruka Father and Mother together with all the
other objects of refuge dissolve into me, and I receive their
blessings.

GENERATING ONESELF AS HERUKA

Bringing death into the path to the Truth Body

All worlds and their beings melt into light and dissolve
    into me.
I too melt into light and dissolve into emptiness.
I am the actual Truth Body Buddha Heruka.

Bringing the intermediate state into the path to the Enjoyment Body

In my place, upon a lotus and sun seat,
My mind appears as a cubit of blue light.
I am the actual Enjoyment Body Buddha Heruka.

Bringing rebirth into the path to the Emanation Body

These completely transform,
And I arise as the Emanation Body Buddha Heruka,
Together with my Pure Land.

GURU YOGA

Blessing the environment and offering substances

Light rays from the letter HUM at my heart
Purify all worlds and their beings.
Everything becomes immaculately pure,
Completely filled with a vast array of offerings,
The nature of exalted wisdom, and bestowing
    uncontaminated bliss.

Visualization

In the space before me is the living Buddha Vajradhara,
who is inseparable from my root Guru, surrounded by
all the Mahamudra lineage Gurus, Yidams, Buddhas,
Bodhisattvas, Dakas, Dakinis and Dharma Protectors.

Prayer of seven limbs

With my body, speech and mind, humbly I prostrate,
And make offerings both set out and imagined.
I confess my wrong deeds from all time,
And rejoice in the virtues of all.
Please stay until samsara ceases,
And turn the Wheel of Dharma for us.
I dedicate all virtues to great enlightenment.

Offering the mandala

OM VAJRA BHUMI AH HUM
Great and powerful golden ground,
OM VAJRA REKHE AH HUM
At the edge the iron fence stands around the outer circle.
In the centre Mount Meru the king of mountains,
Around which are four continents:
In the east, Purvavideha, in the south, Jambudipa,
In the west, Aparagodaniya, in the north, Uttarakuru.
Each has two sub-continents:
Deha and Videha, Tsamara and Abatsamara,
Satha and Uttaramantrina, Kurava and Kaurava.
The mountain of jewels, the wish-granting tree,
The wish-granting cow, and the harvest unsown.
The precious wheel, the precious jewel,
The precious queen, the precious minister,

297

The precious elephant, the precious supreme horse,
The precious general, and the great treasure vase.
The goddess of beauty, the goddess of garlands,
The goddess of song, the goddess of dance,
The goddess of flowers, the goddess of incense,
The goddess of light, and the goddess of scent.
The sun and the moon, the precious umbrella,
The banner of victory in every direction.
In the centre all treasures of both gods and men,
An excellent collection with nothing left out.
I offer this to you my kind root Guru and lineage Gurus,
To all of you sacred and glorious Gurus;
Please accept with compassion for migrating beings,
And having accepted please grant us your blessings.

O Treasure of Compassion, my Refuge and Protector,
I offer you the mountain, continents, precious objects,
    treasure vase, sun and moon,
Which have arisen from my aggregates, sources and
    elements
As aspects of the exalted wisdom of spontaneous bliss and
    emptiness.

I offer without any sense of loss
The objects that give rise to my attachment, hatred and
    confusion,
My friends, enemies and strangers, our bodies and
    enjoyments;
Please accept these and bless me to be released directly
    from the three poisons.

IDAM GURU RATNA MANDALAKAM NIRYATAYAMI

Prayers of request to the Mahamudra lineage Gurus

O Conqueror Vajradhara, Manjushri,
Je Tsongkhapa Losang Dragpa, Togden Jampel Gyatso,
Baso Chokyi Gyaltsen, Mahasiddha Dharmavajra,
Ensapa Losang Dondrub and Khedrub Sangye Yeshe,
I request you please to grant me your blessings
So that I may cut the clinging of self-grasping within my
    mental continuum,
Train in love, compassion and bodhichitta,
And swiftly accomplish the Mahamudra that is the Union
    of No More Learning.

O Venerable Losang Chogyen, Mahasiddha Gendun
    Gyaltsen,
Drungpa Tsondru Gyaltsen, Konchog Gyaltsen,
Panchen Losang Yeshe, Losang Trinlay,
Drubwang Losang Namgyal and Kachen Yeshe Gyaltsen,
I request you please to grant me your blessings
So that I may cut the clinging of self-grasping within my
    mental continuum,
Train in love, compassion and bodhichitta,
And swiftly accomplish the Mahamudra that is the Union
    of No More Learning.

O Phurchog Ngawang Jampa, Panchen Palden Yeshe,
Khedrub Ngawang Dorje, Ngulchu Dharmabhadra,
Yangchen Drubpay Dorje, Khedrub Tenzin Tsondru,
Phabongkhapa Trinlay Gyatso and Trijang Dorjechang
    Losang Yeshe,
I request you please to grant me your blessings
So that I may cut the clinging of self-grasping within my
    mental continuum,

Train in love, compassion and bodhichitta,
And swiftly accomplish the Mahamudra that is the Union
   of No More Learning.

O Venerable Kelsang Gyatso Rinpoche,
Who through your compassion and with your great skill
Explain to fortunate disciples
The instructions of your Guru and the profound lineage,
I request you please to grant me your blessings
So that I may cut the clinging of self-grasping within my
   mental continuum,
Train in love, compassion and bodhichitta,
And swiftly accomplish the Mahamudra that is the Union
   of No More Learning.

Please grant me your blessings
So that I may see the venerable Guru as a Buddha,
Overcome attachment for the abodes of samsara,
And having assumed the burden of liberating all migrators,
Accomplish the common and uncommon paths,
And swiftly attain the Union of the Mahamudra.

This body of mine and your body, O Father,
This speech of mine and your speech, O Father,
This mind of mine and your mind, O Father,
Through your blessings may they become inseparably one.

Special request

   Recite three times:

I request you my precious Guru Vajradhara, the essence
of all Buddhas, please bless my mental continuum and
pacify all outer and inner obstacles so that I may progress
in the training on the profound path of the Mahamudra

meditations, and swiftly attain the Mahamudra that is the union of bliss and emptiness.

Receiving blessings

All the other holy beings dissolve into my root Guru, Vajradhara, in the centre. My root Guru too, out of affection for me, melts into the form of blue light and, entering through the crown of my head, mixes inseparably with my mind in the aspect of a letter HUM at my heart.

At this point, we engage in the actual training in Mahamudra meditation. We can do either the common Vajrayana Mahamudra meditations as explained in the commentary Clear Light of Bliss, *or the uncommon Vajrayana Mahamudra meditations as explained in the commentaries* Mahamudra Tantra, The Oral Instructions of Mahamudra *and* Tantric Grounds and Paths. *Through this, we accomplish the Mahamudra that is the union of bliss and emptiness, the Mahamudra that is the union of the two truths, and the Mahamudra that is the resultant Union of No More Learning.*

Dedication

By this virtue, may I see the venerable Guru as a Buddha,
Overcome attachment for the abodes of samsara,
And, having assumed the burden of liberating all
    migrators,
Accomplish the common and uncommon paths
And swiftly attain the Union of the Mahamudra.

In short, may I never be parted from you, Venerable Guru
    Heruka,
But always come under your care
And, swiftly completing the grounds and paths,
Attain the state of the Union of Buddha Heruka.

Prayers for the Virtuous Tradition

So that the tradition of Je Tsongkhapa,
The King of the Dharma, may flourish,
May all obstacles be pacified
And may all favourable conditions abound.

Through the two collections of myself and others
Gathered throughout the three times,
May the doctrine of Conqueror Losang Dragpa
Flourish for evermore.

The nine-line *Migtsema* prayer

Tsongkhapa, crown ornament of the scholars of the Land
    of the Snows,
You are Buddha Shakyamuni and Vajradhara, the source
    of all attainments,
Avalokiteshvara, the treasury of unobservable compassion,
Manjushri, the supreme stainless wisdom,
And Vajrapani, the destroyer of the hosts of maras.
O Venerable Guru-Buddha, synthesis of all Three Jewels,
With my body, speech and mind, respectfully I make
    requests:
Please grant your blessings to ripen and liberate myself
    and others,
And bestow the common and supreme attainments.

(3x)

Colophon: This sadhana or ritual prayer for spiritual attainments was compiled by Venerable Geshe Kelsang Gyatso Rinpoche and translated under his compassionate guidance.
The verse of request to Venerable Geshe Kelsang Gyatso Rinpoche was composed by the glorious Dharma Protector, Duldzin Dorje Shugden, at the request of Venerable Geshe Kelsang's faithful disciples, and has been included in this sadhana at their request.

An Explanation of the Practice

The following explanation is based on *Great Liberation of the Mother*, but *Great Liberation of the Father* can be understood in the same way. We begin the preliminary practices by going for refuge and generating bodhichitta. In the space before us, we visualize the principal objects of refuge – Guru Chakrasambara Father and Mother, surrounded by the assembly of root and lineage Gurus, Yidams, and Three Jewels. We then go for refuge to the Guru, Buddha, Dharma, and Sangha while reciting the prayer from the sadhana and concentrating on its meaning. This practice makes our subsequent meditation on the channels, drops and winds a Buddhist path.

After going for refuge, we generate bodhichitta while reciting the appropriate prayer from the sadhana. This makes our meditation a Mahayana path, which is the main path to full enlightenment. In particular, when we recite:

For this purpose I shall practise the stages of Vajrayogini's path

we generate a special Tantric bodhichitta, and this makes our meditation a Vajrayana path, which is the quick path to full enlightenment. We should not neglect the practices of going for refuge and generating bodhichitta just because we are now practising Tantra. On the contrary, for Tantric practitioners the basic meditations on Lamrim and Lojong are even more important. According to Je Tsongkhapa's tradition, the more we practise Highest Yoga Tantra, the more we appreciate and practise Lamrim and Lojong. A more extensive explanation of these practices of refuge and bodhichitta can be found in the book *The New Guide to Dakini Land*.

After going for refuge and generating bodhichitta, we dissolve the objects of refuge into us and receive their blessings, while reciting the words from the sadhana:

The objects of refuge before me melt into the form of white, red, and dark blue rays of light. These dissolve into me and I receive their blessings of body, speech and mind.

Here, the explanation is a little different from that given in the book *The New Guide to Dakini Land*. For the purposes of this practice, we imagine that all the other objects of refuge dissolve into the principal object of refuge, Guru Chakrasambara Father and Mother in the centre. Chakrasambara, or Heruka, is a manifestation of the great bliss of all the Buddhas, whereas Vajrayogini, or Vajravarahi, is a manifestation of the wisdom of all the Buddhas. The former is method and the latter is wisdom. Because the great bliss and wisdom of a Buddha are one nature, Father Mother Heruka and Vajrayogini are also one nature, not different people like man and wife! Therefore, when we are accomplishing Heruka we are also accomplishing Vajrayogini, and when we are accomplishing Vajrayogini we are accomplishing Heruka. We never think of these two holy beings as different persons.

The purpose of these preliminary practices is to prepare the basic outline for our subsequent completion stage meditation, just as a thangka painter first prepares a rough outline of the thangka and then completes it by filling in the detail. At this stage, we are preparing a rough experience of bliss and emptiness in our mind. As mentioned in the commentary, we first need to train in these two separately, and then train in the union of bliss and emptiness. To begin with, we train in bliss, and so our principal object of concentration should be Heruka, whom we recognize as a manifestation of the great bliss of all the Buddhas.

After all the other holy beings have dissolved into Heruka, we imagine that Heruka, who is the nature of the great bliss of all the Buddhas, melts into light, enters through our crown, descends through our central channel, and dissolves into our indestructible wind and mind inside the central channel at our heart. We imagine that our mind becomes inseparable from Guru Heruka. Because Guru Heruka has dissolved into the union of our indestructible wind and mind, our mind now becomes the nature of great bliss. We imagine very strongly that our own mind has become the spontaneous great bliss of all the Buddhas, and meditate on this experience of bliss for a while. At first our experience of bliss will not be very strong but, if we develop familiarity with this meditation, we will gradually develop a special feeling of bliss. We should maintain this experience and keep our own subtle mind focused on this feeling single-pointedly. While one part of our mind remains single-pointedly on this feeling of bliss, another part should remain aware that its nature is Guru Heruka's mind.

This generation stage practice is a method for ripening the bliss of completion stage. It helps us to receive powerful blessings, because all the other holy beings dissolve into Guru Heruka, and Guru Heruka then dissolves into our own mind. If we receive all Buddha's blessings through our Guru, our spiritual development, and particularly our practice of Sutra and Tantra, will progress very easily. We will experience fewer obstacles, and our good intention, faith, and pure view will naturally improve month by month, year by year. With blessings, our mind will become more and more happy and confident, but without blessings our mind is like a dry seed from which nothing good will grow. Without blessings, we will experience many obstacles and we will find it difficult to develop and maintain any positive states of mind. Therefore, the practice of receiving the blessings of all the Buddhas into our mind is of utmost importance.

After meditating on the experience of bliss for a while, we begin the practice of generating ourself as Vajrayogini by bringing death into the path to the Truth Body. We recite:

All worlds and their beings melt into light and dissolve into me.

Without forgetting the experience of bliss previously generated, we imagine that all worlds and the beings who inhabit them melt into light and dissolve into us. We should make a very strong decision that nothing is left except ourself, and completely stop the appearance of other things. We then think:

I too melt into light and dissolve into emptiness.

We strongly recognize that everything has now become one with emptiness, remember that all phenomena are empty of true existence, and concentrate on this knowledge. We are now training in emptiness. At this point, we should recall whatever understanding of emptiness we have and mix our mind thoroughly with the meaning of emptiness. We should come to a clear conclusion that everything is finally one nature in emptiness, and then perceive nothing other than emptiness. Then we should meditate on this emptiness single-pointedly.

Having trained in bliss and emptiness separately, we now need to train in the union of bliss and emptiness. When we recite:

I am the actual Truth Body Buddha Vajrayogini.

we should think that our mind of bliss has mixed with emptiness and they have become one nature. We develop this recognition strongly, and hold it with concentration. This is training in the union of bliss and emptiness. Because this is generation stage, we have to imagine that our mind of bliss becomes one with emptiness, mixing inseparably with emptiness like water mixing with water. We hold this union of bliss and emptiness without forgetting, and meditate on it single-pointedly.

We then use this union of bliss and emptiness as the basis for imputing I. When the union of bliss and emptiness becomes permanent and unchanging, it becomes the Dharmakaya, or Truth Body, of a Buddha. Therefore, we now strongly believe that our mind of bliss is mixed with emptiness in a permanent and unchanging union, and we take this permanent union as our basis for imputing I. In this way, we develop the divine pride thinking, 'I am the Truth Body.' Now our basis for imputing I is our own body, which is our very subtle body, and our own mind, which is our very subtle mind. This is a special method for causing our very subtle body and mind to manifest. If this meditation goes well, later we will find it very easy to do completion stage meditation and to realize the Mahamudra that is the actual union of bliss and emptiness.

This meditation is a collection of wisdom and a cause of the attainment of a Buddha's Truth Body. We should try to become very familiar with this practice before we die. If we can do this practice while we are dying, we will definitely be reborn in Vajrayogini's Dakini Land. We will then have purified ordinary death. If we can transform the clear light of death into this feeling of the union of bliss and emptiness, regarding it as the Truth Body, then, as Khedrub Rinpoche said, this practice becomes a supreme practice of transference of consciousness. Practitioners of bringing death into the path to the Truth Body do not need to practise any separate instruction of transference of consciousness – this meditation alone is sufficient.

The next stage is to practise bringing the intermediate state into the path to the Enjoyment Body, and then bringing rebirth into the path to the Emanation Body. Detailed explanations of these practices and the previous practice of bringing death into the path to the Truth Body can be found in the book *The New Guide to Dakini Land*. At this stage, we imagine that we have generated ourself as Vajrayogini with Vajrayogini's body, speech, mind and enjoyments; the environment as Dakini Land with the phenomena source palace; and all the beings as Heroes and Heroines in the Pure Land. This is the basic outline for our subsequent completion stage meditations. When we attain the pure illusory body, all this will become a reality.

At the beginning, when we are meditating on ourself as Vajrayogini in the Pure Land, we do not need to visualize everything very clearly. It is sufficient to have a rough idea of how it looks. We should think:

I am born now into the Pure Land of Vajrayogini. I myself am Vajrayogini, and around me are the thirty-six Dakinis and other Dakas and Dakinis. The entire pure environment, all the other beings and myself as Vajrayogini are all newly developed.

We meditate on this rather like a dream. We should try to stop all distraction and hold strongly to this rough idea until we attain a generic image. We simply try to accomplish an appearance of our own Pure Land, pure enjoyments, pure body, pure speech and pure mind of Vajrayogini, all of which are newly developed.

We then proceed with the practice of Guru yoga. The purpose of this practice is to receive blessings and accumulate merit. Here, the principal Field for Accumulating Merit is Guru Vajradhara, surrounded by the lineage Gurus of Vajrayana Mahamudra and other holy beings. We offer the practice of the seven limbs and the mandala. The main offering is the mandala offering. When we are offering the mandala, we are offering the whole universe transformed into a pure world, into a pure object of offering. We should try to familiarize our mind with this. More information on this practice can be found in the book *The New Guide to Dakini Land*.

Finally, we make requests to the lineage Gurus, and then a special request:

I request you my precious Guru Vajradhara, the essence of all Buddhas, please bless my mental continuum and pacify all outer and inner obstacles so that I may progress in the training on the profound path of the Mahamudra meditations, and swiftly attain the Mahamudra that is the union of bliss and emptiness.

We imagine that all the holy beings and lineage Gurus dissolve into Guru Vajradhara. He melts into the form of blue light, enters through the crown of our head, comes down through our central channel, and mixes with our very subtle mind inside the indestructible drop within the central channel at our heart. We imagine that our own very subtle body, speech and mind become inseparable from Guru Vajradhara's body, speech and mind, and that this union appears in the aspect of a letter BAM, which is white with a tint of red. We meditate briefly on this experience.

We now proceed to the actual completion stage meditation as explained in the main commentary. At the end of the meditation, we conclude our session by reciting the dedication prayers sincerely.

Glossary

Absorption of cessation An uncontaminated wisdom focused single-pointedly on emptiness in dependence upon the actual absorption of peak of samsara. See *Ocean of Nectar*.

Akshobya The manifestation of the aggregate of consciousness of all Buddhas. He has a blue-coloured body.

Amitabha The manifestation of the aggregate of discrimination of all Buddhas. He has a red-coloured body. See *The New Eight Steps to Happiness*.

Amitayus A Buddha who increases our lifespan, merit and wisdom. He is the Enjoyment Body aspect of Buddha Amitabha.

Amoghasiddhi The manifestation of the aggregate of compositional factors of all Buddhas. He has a green-coloured body.

Analytical meditation The mental process of investigating a virtuous object – analyzing its nature, function, characteristics and other aspects. See *Joyful Path of Good Fortune* and *The New Meditation Handbook*.

Anger A deluded mental factor that observes its contaminated object, exaggerates its bad qualities, considers it to be undesirable and wishes to harm it. See *How to Understand the Mind* and *How to Solve our Human Problems*.

Appearing object In general, an object that appears to a mind. In the context of generation stage meditation, the appearing object is the mandala and Deities. See *How to Understand the Mind*.

Atisha (982-1054 CE) A famous Indian Buddhist scholar and meditation master. He was Abbot of the great Buddhist monastery of Vikramashila at a time when Mahayana Buddhism was flourishing in India. He was later invited to Tibet where he reintroduced pure Buddhism. He is the author of the first text on the stages of the path, *Lamp for the Path*. His tradition later became known as the 'Kadampa Tradition'. See *Joyful Path of Good Fortune* and *Modern Buddhism*.

Attachment   A deluded mental factor that observes a contaminated object, regards it as a cause of happiness and wishes for it. See *Joyful Path of Good Fortune* and *How to Understand the Mind*.

Avalokiteshvara   The embodiment of the compassion of all the Buddhas. At the time of Buddha Shakyamuni, he manifested as a Bodhisattva disciple. 'Chenrezig' in Tibetan. See *Living Meaningfully, Dying Joyfully*.

Basis of imputation   All phenomena are imputed upon their parts, therefore, any of the individual parts, or the entire collection of the parts, of any phenomenon is its basis of imputation. A phenomenon is imputed by mind in dependence upon its basis of imputation appearing to that mind. See *The New Heart of Wisdom* and *Ocean of Nectar*.

Blessing   The transformation of our mind from a negative state to a positive state, from an unhappy state to a happy state, or from a state of weakness to a state of strength, through the inspiration of holy beings such as our Spiritual Guide, Buddhas and Bodhisattvas.

Body mandala   The transformation into a Deity of any part of the body of a self-generated or in-front-generated Deity. See *Essence of Vajrayana, Great Treasury of Merit, The New Guide to Dakini Land* and *Modern Buddhism*.

Buddha family   There are five main Buddha families: the families of Vairochana, Ratnasambhava, Amitabha, Amoghasiddhi and Akshobya. They are the five purified aggregates: the aggregates of form, feeling, discrimination, compositional factors and consciousness, respectively; and the five exalted wisdoms: the exalted mirror-like wisdom, the exalted wisdom of equality, the exalted wisdom of individual realization, the exalted wisdom of accomplishing activities and the exalted wisdom of the Dharmadhatu, respectively. See *Great Treasury of Merit*.

Buddha nature   The root mind of a sentient being, and its ultimate nature. Buddha nature, Buddha seed and Buddha lineage are synonyms. All sentient beings have Buddha nature and therefore have the potential to attain Buddhahood. See *Mahamudra Tantra*.

Chandrakirti   (circa 7th century CE) A great Indian Buddhist scholar and meditation master who composed, among many other books, the well-known *Guide to the Middle Way*, in which he clearly elucidates the view of the Madhyamika-Prasangika school according to Buddha's teachings given in the *Perfection of Wisdom Sutras*. See *Ocean of Nectar*.

Chittamatra   The lower of the two schools of Mahayana tenets. 'Chittamatra' means 'mind only'. According to this school, all phenomena are the same nature as the mind that apprehends them. They also assert that dependent phenomena are truly existent but do not exist external to the mind. A Chittamatrin is a proponent of Chittamatra tenets. See *Meaningful to Behold* and *Ocean of Nectar*.

Clairvoyance   Abilities that arise from special concentration. There are five principal types of clairvoyance: the clairvoyance of divine eye (the ability to see subtle and distant forms), the clairvoyance of divine ear (the ability to hear subtle and distant sounds), the clairvoyance of miracle powers (the ability to emanate various forms by mind), the clairvoyance of knowing previous lives and the clairvoyance of knowing others' minds. Some beings, such as bardo beings and some human beings and spirits, have contaminated clairvoyance that is developed due to karma, but these are not actual clairvoyance.

Collection of merit   A virtuous action motivated by bodhichitta that is a main cause of attaining the Form Body of a Buddha. Examples are: making offerings and prostrations to holy beings with bodhichitta motivation, and the practice of the perfections of giving, moral discipline and patience.

Collection of wisdom   A virtuous mental action motivated by bodhichitta that is a main cause of attaining the Truth Body of a Buddha. Examples are: listening to, contemplating and meditating on emptiness with bodhichitta motivation.

Commitment being A visualized Buddha or ourself visualized as a Buddha. A commitment being is so called because in general it is the commitment of all Buddhists to visualize or remember Buddha, and in particular it is a commitment of those who have received an empowerment into Highest Yoga Tantra to generate themselves as a Deity.

Conceived object The apprehended object of a conceptual mind. It need not be an existent object. For example, the conceived object of the view of the transitory collection is an inherently existent I, but this does not exist. See *How to Understand the Mind*.

Concentration A mental factor that makes its primary mind remain on its object single-pointedly. See *Joyful Path of Good Fortune* and *Clear Light of Bliss*.

Conceptual mind A thought that apprehends its object through a generic, or mental, image. See *How to Understand the Mind*.

Contaminated aggregate Any of the aggregates of form, feeling, discrimination, compositional factors and consciousness of a samsaric being. See *Joyful Path of Good Fortune* and *The New Heart of Wisdom*.

Conventional nature See *Ultimate nature*.

Damaru A small hand-drum used in Tantric rituals. Playing the damaru symbolizes the gathering of the outer Dakinis into our body, and the manifestation of the inner Dakini (the mind of clear light) within our mind through the blazing of inner fire. It is also used as a music offering to the Buddhas.

Deity body Divine body. When a practitioner attains an illusory body, he or she attains an actual divine body, or Deity body, but not a Deity's body. A Deity's body is necessarily a body of a Tantric enlightened being. See also *Divine body*.

Deluded pride A deluded mental factor that, through considering and exaggerating one's own good qualities or possessions, feels arrogant. See *Joyful Path of Good Fortune* and *How to Understand the Mind*.

Delusion A mental factor that arises from inappropriate attention and functions to make the mind unpeaceful and uncontrolled. There are three main delusions: ignorance, desirous attachment and anger. From these arise all the other delusions, such as jealousy, pride and deluded doubt. See also Innate delusions and Intellectually-formed delusions. See *Joyful Path of Good Fortune* and *How to Understand the Mind*.

Desire realm The environment of hell beings, hungry ghosts, animals, human beings, demi-gods and the gods who enjoy the five objects of desire.

Dharma Buddha's teachings and the inner realizations that are attained in dependence upon practising them. 'Dharma' means 'protection'. By practising Buddha's teachings, we protect ourself from suffering and problems.

Dharmakirti (circa 6th to 7th century CE) A great Indian Buddhist Yogi and scholar who composed *Commentary to Valid Cognition*, a commentary to *Compendium of Valid Cognition*, which was written by his Spiritual Guide, Dignaga. See *How to Understand the Mind*.

Divine body A subtle body arising from the mounted wind of ultimate example clear light or meaning clear light. See also *Deity body*.

Empowerment A special potential power to attain any of the four Buddha bodies that is received by a Tantric practitioner from his or her Guru, or from other holy beings, by means of Tantric ritual. It is the gateway to the Vajrayana. See *Mahamudra Tantra*.

Essence of Wisdom Sutra One of several *Perfection of Wisdom Sutras* that Buddha taught. Although much shorter than the other *Perfection of Wisdom Sutras*, it contains explicitly or implicitly their entire meaning. Also known as the *Heart Sutra*. For a full translation and commentary, see *The New Heart of Wisdom*.

Expressive sound An object of hearing that makes its expressed object understood.

Faith A naturally virtuous mind that functions mainly to oppose the perception of faults in its observed object. There are three types of faith: believing faith, admiring faith and wishing faith. See *Joyful Path of Good Fortune*, *Modern Buddhism* and *How to Transform Your Life*.

317

Field for Accumulating Merit   Generally, this refers to the Three Jewels. Just as external seeds grow in a field of soil, so the virtuous internal seeds produced by virtuous actions grow in dependence upon Buddha Jewel, Dharma Jewel and Sangha Jewel. Also known as 'Field of Merit'.

Formless realm   The environment of the gods who do not possess form. See *Ocean of Nectar*.

Four Mothers   Lochana, Mamaki, Benzarahi and Tara. The consorts of Vairochana, Ratnasambhava, Amitabha and Amoghasiddhi respectively.

Functioning thing   A phenomenon that is produced and disintegrates within a moment. Synonymous with impermanent phenomenon, thing and product.

Guide to the Bodhisattva's Way of Life   A classic Mahayana Buddhist text composed by the great Indian Buddhist Yogi and scholar Shantideva, which presents all the practices of a Bodhisattva from the initial generation of bodhichitta through to the completion of the practice of the six perfections. For a translation, see *Guide to the Bodhisattva's Way of Life*. For a full commentary, see *Meaningful to Behold*.

Guide to the Middle Way   A classic Mahayana Buddhist text composed by the great Indian Buddhist Yogi and scholar Chandrakirti, which provides a comprehensive explanation of the Madhyamika-Prasangika view of emptiness as taught in the *Perfection of Wisdom Sutras*. For a full commentary, see *Ocean of Nectar*.

Guru yoga   A special way of relying upon our Spiritual Guide in order to receive his or her blessings. See *Joyful Path of Good Fortune*, *Great Treasury of Merit* and *Heart Jewel*.

Hearer   One of two types of Hinayana practitioner. Both Hearers and Solitary Conquerors are Hinayanists, but they differ in their motivation, behaviour, merit and wisdom. In all these respects, Solitary Conquerors are superior to Hearers. See *Ocean of Nectar*.

Heart Sutra   See *Essence of Wisdom Sutra*.

Hell realm   The lowest of the six realms of samsara. See *Joyful Path of Good Fortune*.

Ignorance   A mental factor that is confused about the ultimate nature of phenomena. See also *Self-grasping*. See *How to Understand the Mind*.

Imputation, mere   According to the Madhyamika-Prasangika school, all phenomena are merely imputed by conception in dependence upon their basis of imputation. Therefore, they are mere imputations and do not exist from their own side in the least. See *The New Heart of Wisdom* and *Ocean of Nectar*.

Imputed object   An object imputed onto its basis of imputation. See *The New Heart of Wisdom* and *Ocean of Nectar*.

Innate delusions   Delusions that are not the product of intellectual speculation, but that arise naturally. See *How to Understand the Mind*.

Intellectually-formed delusions   Delusions that arise as a result of relying upon incorrect reasoning or mistaken tenets. See *How to Understand the Mind*.

Intermediate state   'Bardo' in Tibetan. The state between death and rebirth. It begins the moment the consciousness leaves the body, and ceases the moment the consciousness enters the body of the next life. See *Joyful Path of Good Fortune* and *Living Meaningfully, Dying Joyfully*.

Jealousy   A deluded mental factor that feels displeasure when observing others' enjoyments, good qualities or good fortune. See *How to Understand the Mind*.

Je Tsongkhapa   (1357-1419 CE) An emanation of the Wisdom Buddha Manjushri, whose appearance in fourteenth-century Tibet as a monk, and the holder of the lineage of pure view and pure deeds, was prophesied by Buddha. He spread a very pure Buddhadharma throughout Tibet, showing how to combine the practices of Sutra and Tantra, and how to practise pure Dharma during degenerate times. His tradition later became known as the 'Gelug', or 'Ganden Tradition'. See *Heart Jewel* and *Great Treasury of Merit*.

Kadampa   A Tibetan word in which 'Ka' means 'word' and refers to all Buddha's teachings, 'dam' refers to Atisha's special Lamrim instructions known as the 'stages of the path to enlightenment', and 'pa' refers to a follower of Kadampa Buddhism who integrates all the teachings of Buddha that they know into their Lamrim practice. See also *Kadampa Buddhism* and *Kadampa Tradition*.

Kadampa Buddhism A Mahayana Buddhist school founded by the great Indian Buddhist Master Atisha (982-1054 CE). See *Modern Buddhism*. See also *Kadampa* and *Kadampa Tradition*.

Kadampa Tradition The pure tradition of Buddhism established by Atisha. Followers of this tradition up to the time of Je Tsongkhapa are known as 'Old Kadampas', and those after the time of Je Tsongkhapa are known as 'New Kadampas'. See also *Kadampa* and *Kadampa Buddhism*.

Karma Sanskrit word referring to 'action'. Through the force of intention, we perform actions with our body, speech and mind, and all of these actions produce effects. The effect of virtuous actions is happiness and the effect of negative actions is suffering. See *Joyful Path of Good Fortune* and *Modern Buddhism*.

Khatanga A ritual object symbolizing the sixty-two Deities of Heruka. See *The New Guide to Dakini Land*.

Khedrubje (1385-1438 CE) One of the principal disciples of Je Tsongkhapa, who did much to promote the tradition of Je Tsongkhapa after he passed away. See *Great Treasury of Merit*.

Lamrim A Tibetan term, literally meaning 'stages of the path'. A special arrangement of all Buddha's teachings that is easy to understand and put into practice. It reveals all the stages of the path to enlightenment. For a full commentary, see *Joyful Path of Good Fortune*.

Letter A vocalization that is a basis for the composition of names and phrases.

Lineage A line of instruction that has been passed down from Spiritual Guide to disciple, with each Spiritual Guide in the line having gained personal experience of the instruction before passing it on to others.

Lineage Gurus The line of Spiritual Guides through whom a particular instruction has been passed down.

Lojong   A Tibetan term, literally meaning 'training the mind'. A special lineage of instructions that came from Buddha Shakyamuni through Manjushri and Shantideva to Atisha and the Kadampa Geshes, which emphasizes the generation of bodhichitta through the practices of equalizing and exchanging self with others combined with taking and giving. See *Universal Compassion* and *The New Eight Steps to Happiness*.

Madhyamika   A Sanskrit word, literally meaning 'Middle Way'. The higher of the two schools of Mahayana tenets. The Madhyamika view was taught by Buddha in the Perfection of Wisdom Sutras during the second turning of the Wheel of Dharma and was subsequently elucidated by Nagarjuna and his followers. There are two divisions of this school, Madhyamika-Svatantrika and Madhyamika-Prasangika, of which the latter is Buddha's final view. See *Meaningful to Behold* and *Ocean of Nectar*.

Mahasiddha   Sanskrit word for 'Greatly Accomplished One', which is used to refer to Yogis or Yoginis with high attainments.

Maitreya   The embodiment of the loving kindness of all the Buddhas. At the time of Buddha Shakyamuni he manifested as a Bodhisattva disciple. In the future, he will manifest as the fifth founding Buddha.

Manjushri   The embodiment of the wisdom of all the Buddhas. At the time of Buddha Shakyamuni he manifested as a Bodhisattva disciple. See *Great Treasury of Merit* and *Heart Jewel*.

Mental awareness   All minds are included within the five sense awarenesses and mental awareness. The definition of mental awareness is an awareness that is developed in dependence upon its uncommon dominant condition, a mental power. There are two types of mental awareness: conceptual mental awareness and non-conceptual mental awareness. Conceptual mental awareness and conceptual mind are synonyms. See *How to Understand the Mind*.

Merit   The good fortune created by virtuous actions. It is the potential power to increase our good qualities and produce happiness.

Mind That which is clarity and cognizes. Mind is clarity because it always lacks form and because it possesses the actual power to perceive objects. Mind cognizes because its function is to know or perceive objects. See *Clear Light of Bliss* and *How to Understand the Mind*.

Nagarjuna A great Indian Buddhist scholar and meditation master who revived the Mahayana in the first century CE by bringing to light the teachings on the *Perfection of Wisdom Sutras*. See *Ocean of Nectar* and *The New Heart of Wisdom*.

New Kadampa Tradition-International Kadampa Buddhist Union (NKT-IKBU) The union of Kadampa Buddhist Centres, an international association of study and meditation centres that follow the pure tradition of Mahayana Buddhism derived from the Buddhist meditators and scholars Atisha and Je Tsongkhapa, introduced into the West by the Buddhist teacher Venerable Geshe Kelsang Gyatso Rinpoche.

Nine mental abidings Nine levels of concentration leading to tranquil abiding: placing the mind, continual placement, replacement, close placement, controlling, pacifying, completely pacifying, single-pointedness and placement in equipoise. See *Joyful Path of Good Fortune* and *Clear Light of Bliss*.

Observed object Any object upon which the mind is focused. See *How to Understand the Mind*.

Offering to the Spiritual Guide *Lama Chopa* in Tibetan. A special Guru yoga of Je Tsongkhapa, in which our Spiritual Guide is visualized in the aspect of Lama Losang Tubwang Dorjechang. The instruction for this practice was revealed by Buddha Manjushri in the *Kadam Emanation Scripture* and written down by the first Panchen Lama (1570-1662 CE). It is an essential preliminary practice for Vajrayana Mahamudra. For a full commentary, see *Great Treasury of Merit*.

Pratimoksha Sanskrit word for 'individual liberation'. See *The Bodhisattva Vow*.

Pure Land A pure environment in which there are no true sufferings. There are many Pure Lands. For example, Tushita is the Pure Land of Buddha Maitreya, Sukhavati is the Pure Land of Buddha Amitabha, and Dakini Land, or Keajra, is the Pure Land of Buddha Vajrayogini and Buddha Heruka. See *Living Meaningfully, Dying Joyfully*.

Purification Generally, any practice that leads to the attainment of a pure body, speech or mind. More specifically, a practice for purifying negative karma by means of the four opponent powers. See *Joyful Path of Good Fortune* and *The Bodhisattva Vow*.

Ratnasambhava The manifestation of the aggregate of feeling of all Buddhas. He has a yellow-coloured body.

Samsara This can be understood in two ways: as uninterrupted rebirth without freedom or control, or as the aggregates of a being who has taken such a rebirth. Samsara, sometimes known as 'cyclic existence', is characterized by suffering and dissatisfaction. There are six realms of samsara. Listed in ascending order according to the type of karma that causes rebirth in them, they are the realms of the hell beings, hungry ghosts, animals, human beings, demi-gods and gods. The first three are lower realms or unhappy migrations, and the second three are higher realms or happy migrations. Although from the point of view of the karma that causes rebirth there, the god realm is the highest realm in samsara, the human realm is said to be the most fortunate realm because it provides the best conditions for attaining liberation and enlightenment. See *Joyful Path of Good Fortune*.

Saraha One of the first Mahasiddhas, and the Teacher of Nagarjuna. See *Essence of Vajrayana*.

Seed-letter The sacred letter from which a Deity is generated. Each Deity has a particular seed-letter. For example, the seed-letter of Manjushri is DHI, of Tara is TAM, of Vajrayogini is BAM and of Heruka is HUM. To accomplish Tantric realizations, we need to recognize that Deities and their seed-letters are the same nature.

Self-grasping A conceptual mind that holds any phenomenon to be inherently existent. The mind of self-grasping gives rise to all other delusions, such as anger and attachment. It is the root cause of all suffering and dissatisfaction. See *The New Heart of Wisdom*, *Modern Buddhism* and *Ocean of Nectar*.

Sense awareness All minds are included within sense awareness and mental awareness. The definition of sense awareness is an awareness that is developed in dependence upon its uncommon dominant condition, a sense power possessing form. There are five types of sense awareness: eye awareness, ear awareness, nose awareness, tongue awareness and body awareness. See *How to Understand the Mind*.

Sense power An inner power located in the very centre of a sense organ that functions directly to produce a sense awareness. There are five sense powers, one for each type of sense awareness – the eye awareness and so forth. See *How to Understand the Mind*.

Seven-point posture of Vairochana A special posture for meditation, in which parts of our body adopt a particular position: (1) sitting on a comfortable cushion with the legs crossed in the vajra posture (in which the feet are placed upon the opposite thighs), (2) the back straight, (3) the head inclined slightly forward, (4) the eyes remaining open slightly, gazing down the nose, (5) the shoulders level, (6) the mouth gently closed, and (7) the right hand placed upon the left, palms up, four finger widths below the navel with the two thumbs touching just above the navel.

Shakyamuni, Buddha The fourth of one thousand founding Buddhas who are to appear in this world during this Fortunate Aeon. The first three were Krakuchchanda, Kanakamuni and Kashyapa. The fifth Buddha will be Maitreya. See *Introduction to Buddhism*.

Shantideva (687-763 CE) A great Indian Buddhist scholar and meditation master. He composed *Guide to the Bodhisattva's Way of Life*. See *Guide to the Bodhisattva's Way of Life* and *Meaningful to Behold*.

Solitary Conqueror One of two types of Hinayana practitioner. Also known as 'Solitary Realizer'. See also *Hearer*.

Spiritual Guide 'Guru' in Sanskrit, 'Lama' in Tibetan. A Teacher who guides us along the spiritual path. See *Joyful Path of Good Fortune* and *Great Treasury of Merit*.

Stream Enterer A type of Hearer. See *Ocean of Nectar*.

Subsequent attainment The period between meditation sessions. See *Joyful Path of Good Fortune* and *The New Meditation Handbook*.

Superior being 'Arya' in Sanskrit. A being who has a direct realization of emptiness. There are Hinayana Superiors and Mahayana Superiors.

Superior seeing A special wisdom that sees its object clearly, and that is maintained by tranquil abiding and the special suppleness that is induced by investigation. See *Joyful Path of Good Fortune*.

Sutra The teachings of Buddha that are open to everyone to practise without the need for empowerment. These include Buddha's teachings of the three turnings of the Wheel of Dharma.

Tranquil abiding A concentration that possesses the special bliss of physical and mental suppleness that is attained in dependence upon completing the nine mental abidings. See *Joyful Path of Good Fortune*, *Clear Light of Bliss* and *Meaningful to Behold*.

Trijang Rinpoche, Vajradhara (1901-1981 CE) A special Tibetan Lama of the twentieth century who was an emanation of Buddha Shakyamuni, Heruka, Atisha, Amitabha and Je Tsongkhapa. Also known as 'Kyabje Trijang Rinpoche' and 'Losang Yeshe'.

Tsog offering An offering made by an assembly of Heroes and Heroines. See *The New Guide to Dakini Land* and *Great Treasury of Merit*.

Tummo Tibetan word for 'inner fire'. An inner heat located at the centre of the navel channel wheel. See *Clear Light of Bliss*.

Twelve dependent-related links Dependent-related ignorance, compositional actions, consciousness, name and form, six sources, contact, feeling, craving, grasping, existence, birth, and ageing and death. These twelve links are causes and effects that keep ordinary beings bound within samsara. See *Joyful Path of Good Fortune* and *The New Heart of Wisdom*.

Two truths Conventional truth and ultimate truth. See *Meaningful to Behold* and *Ocean of Nectar*.

Ultimate nature All phenomena have two natures: a conventional nature and an ultimate nature. In the case of a table, for example, the table itself, and its shape, colour and so forth are all the conventional nature of the table. The ultimate nature of the table is the table's lack of inherent existence. The conventional nature of a phenomenon is a conventional truth, and its ultimate nature is an ultimate truth. See *The New Heart of Wisdom, Modern Buddhism* and *Ocean of Nectar*.

Vairochana   The manifestation of the aggregate of form of all Buddhas. He has a white-coloured body.

Vajradhara   The founder of Vajrayana. He is the same mental continuum as Buddha Shakyamuni but displays a different aspect. Buddha Shakyamuni appears in the aspect of an Emanation Body, and Conqueror Vajradhara appears in the aspect of an Enjoyment Body. See *Great Treasury of Merit*.

Vajrayana Spiritual Guide   A fully qualified Tantric Spiritual Guide. See *Great Treasury of Merit*.

Valid cognizer   A cognizer that is non-deceptive with respect to its engaged object. There are two types: inferential valid cognizers and direct valid cognizers. See *The New Heart of Wisdom* and *How to Understand the Mind*.

Wisdom   A virtuous, intelligent mind that makes its primary mind realize its object thoroughly. A wisdom is a spiritual path that functions to release our mind from delusions or their imprints. An example of wisdom is the correct view of emptiness. See *The New Heart of Wisdom* and *How to Understand the Mind*.

Wisdom being   An actual Buddha, especially one who is invited to unite with a visualized commitment being.

Wrong awareness   A cognizer that is mistaken with respect to its engaged object. See *How to Understand the Mind*.

Wrong view   An intellectually-formed wrong awareness that denies the existence of an object that it is necessary to understand to attain liberation or enlightenment – for example, denying the existence of enlightened beings, karma or rebirth. See *Joyful Path of Good Fortune*.

Yoga   A term used for various spiritual practices that entail maintaining a special view, such as Guru yoga and the yogas of eating, sleeping, dreaming and waking. 'Yoga' also refers to union, such as the union of tranquil abiding and superior seeing. See *The New Guide to Dakini Land*.

Yogic direct perceiver A direct perceiver that realizes a subtle object directly, in dependence upon its uncommon dominant condition, a concentration that is a union of tranquil abiding and superior seeing. See *How to Understand the Mind*.

Bibliography

Venerable Geshe Kelsang Gyatso Rinpoche is a highly respected meditation master and scholar of the Mahayana Buddhist tradition founded by Je Tsongkhapa. Since arriving in the West in 1977, Venerable Geshe Kelsang has worked tirelessly to establish pure Buddhadharma throughout the world. Over this period he has given extensive teachings on the major scriptures of the Mahayana. These teachings provide a comprehensive presentation of the essential Sutra and Tantra practices of Mahayana Buddhism.

Books

The following books by Venerable Geshe Kelsang Gyatso Rinpoche are all published by Tharpa Publications.

The Bodhisattva Vow A practical guide to helping others. (2nd. edn., 1995)

Clear Light of Bliss A Tantric meditation manual. (3rd. edn., 2014)

Essence of Vajrayana The Highest Yoga Tantra practice of Heruka body mandala. (2nd. edn., 2017)

Great Treasury of Merit How to rely upon a Spiritual Guide. (2nd. edn., 2015)

Guide to the Bodhisattva's Way of Life How to enjoy a life of great meaning and altruism. (A translation of Shantideva's famous verse masterpiece.) (2nd. edn., 2018)

Heart Jewel The essential practices of Kadampa Buddhism. (2nd. edn., 1997)

How to Solve Our Human Problems The four noble truths. (2005)

How to Transform Your Life A blissful journey. (3rd. edn., 2016)

How to Understand the Mind The nature and power of the mind. (4th. edn., 2014)

Introduction to Buddhism An explanation of the Buddhist way of life. (2nd. edn., 2001)

Joyful Path of Good Fortune The path to the supreme happiness of enlightenment. (3rd. edn., 2016)

Living Meaningfully, Dying Joyfully The profound practice of transference of consciousness. (1999)

Mahamudra Tantra The supreme Heart Jewel nectar. (2005)

Meaningful to Behold Becoming a friend of the world. (6th. edn., 2016)

The Mirror of Dharma with Additions How to find the real meaning of human life. (2nd. edn., 2019)

Modern Buddhism The path of compassion and wisdom. (2nd. edn., 2013)

The New Eight Steps to Happiness The Buddhist way of loving kindness. (3rd. edn., 2016)

The New Guide to Dakini Land The Highest Yoga Tantra practice of Buddha Vajrayogini. (3rd. edn., 2012)

The New Heart of Wisdom Profound teachings from Buddha's heart (An explanation of the *Heart Sutra*). (5th. edn., 2012)

The New Meditation Handbook Meditations to make our life happy and meaningful. (5th. edn., 2013)

Ocean of Nectar The true nature of all things. (2nd. edn., 2017)

The Oral Instructions of Mahamudra The very essence of Buddha's teachings of Sutra and Tantra. (2nd. edn., 2016)

Tantric Grounds and Paths How to enter, progress on, and complete the Vajrayana path. (2nd. edn., 2016)

Universal Compassion Inspiring solutions for difficult times. (5th. edn., 2018)

Sadhanas and Other Booklets

Venerable Geshe Kelsang Gyatso Rinpoche has also supervised the translation of a collection of essential sadhanas, or ritual prayers for spiritual attainments, available in booklet or audio formats.

Avalokiteshvara Sadhana Prayers and requests to the Buddha of Compassion.

The Blissful Path The condensed self-generation sadhana of Vajrayogini.

The Bodhisattva's Confession of Moral Downfalls The purification practice of the *Mahayana Sutra of the Three Superior Heaps*.

Condensed Long Life Practice of Buddha Amitayus.

Dakini Yoga The middling self-generation sadhana of Vajrayogini.

Drop of Essential Nectar A special fasting and purification practice in conjunction with Eleven-faced Avalokiteshvara.

Essence of Good Fortune Prayers for the six preparatory practices for meditation on the stages of the path to enlightenment.

Essence of Vajrayana Heruka body mandala self-generation sadhana according to the system of Mahasiddha Ghantapa.

Feast of Great Bliss Vajrayogini self-initiation sadhana.

Great Liberation of the Father Preliminary prayers for Mahamudra meditation in conjunction with Heruka practice.

Great Liberation of the Mother Preliminary prayers for Mahamudra meditation in conjunction with Vajrayogini practice.

The Great Mother A method to overcome hindrances and obstacles by reciting the *Essence of Wisdom Sutra* (the *Heart Sutra*).

A Handbook for the Daily Practice of Bodhisattva and Tantric Vows.

Heart Jewel The Guru yoga of Je Tsongkhapa combined with the condensed sadhana of his Dharma Protector.

Heartfelt Prayers Funeral service for cremations and burials.

Heruka Body Mandala Burning Offering.

The Hundreds of Deities of the Joyful Land According to Highest Yoga Tantra The Guru yoga of Je Tsongkhapa as a Preliminary Practice for Mahamudra.

The Kadampa Way of Life The essential practice of Kadam Lamrim.

Keajra Heaven The essential commentary to the practice of *The Uncommon Yoga of Inconceivability*.

Lay Pratimoksha Vow Ceremony.

Liberating Prayer Praise to Buddha Shakyamuni.

Liberation from Sorrow Praises and requests to the Twenty-one Taras.

Mahayana Refuge Ceremony and Bodhisattva Vow Ceremony.

Medicine Buddha Prayer A method for benefiting others.

Medicine Buddha Sadhana A method for accomplishing the attainments of Medicine Buddha.

Meditation and Recitation of Solitary Vajrasattva.

Melodious Drum Victorious in all Directions The extensive fulfilling and restoring ritual of the Dharma Protector, the great king Dorje Shugden, in conjunction with Mahakala, Kalarupa, Kalindewi and other Dharma Protectors.

The New Essence of Vajrayana Heruka body mandala self-generation practice, an instruction of the Ganden Oral Lineage.

Offering to the Spiritual Guide (*Lama Chopa*) A special way of relying upon a Spiritual Guide.

Path of Compassion for the Deceased Powa sadhana for the benefit of the deceased.

Pathway to the Pure Land Training in powa – the transference of consciousness.

Powa Ceremony Transference of consciousness for the deceased.

Prayers for Meditation Brief preparatory prayers for meditation.

Prayers for World Peace.

A Pure Life The practice of taking and keeping the eight Mahayana precepts.

Quick Path to Great Bliss The extensive self-generation sadhana of Vajrayogini.

Request to the Holy Spiritual Guide Venerable Geshe Kelsang Gyatso Rinpoche from his Faithful Disciples.

Request to the Lord of All Lineages Request prayer for practising Lamrim – the Stages of the Path to Enlightenment, Lojong – Training the Mind, Generation Stage and Completion Stage.

The Root Tantra of Heruka and Vajrayogini Chapters One & Fifty-one of the *Condensed Heruka Root Tantra*.

The Root Text: Eight Verses of Training the Mind.

Treasury of Wisdom The sadhana of Venerable Manjushri.

The Uncommon Yoga of Inconceivability The special instruction of how to reach the Pure Land of Keajra with this human body.

Union of No More Learning Heruka body mandala self-initiation sadhana.

Vajrayogini Burning Offering.

The Vows and Commitments of Kadampa Buddhism.

Wishfulfilling Jewel The Guru yoga of Je Tsongkhapa combined with the sadhana of his Dharma Protector.

The Yoga of Buddha Amitayus A special method for increasing lifespan, wisdom and merit.

The Yoga of Buddha Heruka The essential self-generation sadhana of Heruka body mandala & Condensed six-session Yoga.

The Yoga of Buddha Maitreya Self-generation sadhana.

The Yoga of Buddha Vajrapani Self-generation sadhana.

The Yoga of Enlightened Mother Arya Tara Self-generation sadhana.

The Yoga of Great Mother Prajnaparamita Self-generation sadhana.

The Yoga of Thousand-armed Avalokiteshvara Self-generation sadhana.

The Yoga of White Tara, Buddha of Long Life.

To order any of our publications, or to request a catalogue, please visit www.tharpa.com or contact your nearest Tharpa office listed on pages 340-341.

Study Programmes of
Kadampa Buddhism

Kadampa Buddhism is a Mahayana Buddhist school founded by the great Indian Buddhist Master Atisha (982-1054 CE). His followers are known as 'Kadampas'. 'Ka' means 'word' and refers to Buddha's teachings, and 'dam' refers to Atisha's special Lamrim instructions known as 'the stages of the path to enlightenment'. By integrating their knowledge of all Buddha's teachings into their practice of Lamrim, and by integrating this into their everyday lives, Kadampa Buddhists are encouraged to use Buddha's teachings as practical methods for transforming daily activities into the path to enlightenment. The great Kadampa Teachers are famous not only for being great scholars but also for being spiritual practitioners of immense purity and sincerity.

The lineage of these teachings, both their oral transmission and blessings, was then passed from Teacher to disciple, spreading throughout much of Asia, and now to many countries throughout the world. Buddha's teachings, which are known as 'Dharma', are likened to a wheel that moves from country to country in accordance with changing conditions and people's karmic inclinations. The external forms of presenting Buddhism may change as it meets with different cultures and societies, but its essential authenticity is ensured through the continuation of an unbroken lineage of realized practitioners.

Kadampa Buddhism was first introduced to the modern world in 1977 by the renowned Buddhist Master, Venerable Geshe Kelsang Gyatso Rinpoche. Since that time, he has worked tirelessly to spread Kadampa Buddhism throughout the world by giving extensive teachings, writing many profound texts on Kadampa Buddhism, and founding the New Kadampa Tradition – International Kadampa Buddhist Union (NKT-IKBU), which now has over 1200 Kadampa Buddhist Centres worldwide. Each Centre offers study programmes on Buddhist psychology, philosophy and meditation instruction, as well as retreats for all levels of practitioner. The emphasis is on integrating Buddha's teachings into daily life to solve our human problems and to spread lasting peace and happiness throughout the world.

The Kadampa Buddhism of the NKT-IKBU is an entirely independent Buddhist tradition and has no political affiliations. It is an association of Buddhist Centres and practitioners that derive their inspiration and guidance from the example of the ancient Kadampa Buddhist Masters and their teachings, as presented by Venerable Geshe Kelsang.

There are three reasons why we need to study and practise the teachings of Buddha: to develop our wisdom, to cultivate a good heart, and to maintain a peaceful state of mind. If we do not strive to develop our wisdom, we will always remain ignorant of ultimate truth – the true nature of reality. Although we wish for happiness, our ignorance leads us to engage in non-virtuous actions, which are the main cause of all our suffering. If we do not cultivate a good heart, our selfish motivation destroys harmony and good relationships with others. We have no peace, and no chance to gain pure happiness. Without inner peace, outer peace is impossible. If we do not maintain a peaceful state of mind, we are not happy even if we have ideal conditions. On the other hand, when our mind is peaceful, we are happy, even if our external conditions are unpleasant. Therefore, the development of these qualities is of utmost importance for our daily happiness.

Venerable Geshe Kelsang, or 'Geshe-la' as he is affectionately called by his students, has designed three special spiritual programmes for the systematic study and practice of Kadampa Buddhism that are especially suited to the modern world – the General Programme (GP), the Foundation Programme (FP), and the Teacher Training Programme (TTP).

GENERAL PROGRAMME

The General Programme provides a basic introduction to Buddhist view, meditation and practice that is suitable for beginners. It also includes advanced teachings and practice from both Sutra and Tantra.

FOUNDATION PROGRAMME

The Foundation Programme provides an opportunity to deepen our understanding and experience of Buddhism through a systematic study of six texts:

1 *Joyful Path of Good Fortune* – a commentary to Atisha's Lamrim instructions, the stages of the path to enlightenment.
2 *Universal Compassion* – a commentary to Bodhisattva Chekhawa's *Training the Mind in Seven Points*.
3 *The New Eight Steps to Happiness* – a commentary to Bodhisattva Langri Tangpa's *Eight Verses of Training the Mind*.
4 *The New Heart of Wisdom* – a commentary to the *Heart Sutra*.
5 *Meaningful to Behold* – a commentary to Bodhisattva Shantideva's *Guide to the Bodhisattva's Way of Life*.
6 *How to Understand the Mind* – a detailed explanation of the mind, based on the works of the Buddhist scholars Dharmakirti and Dignaga.

The benefits of studying and practising these texts are as follows:

(1) *Joyful Path of Good Fortune* – we gain the ability to put all Buddha's teachings of both Sutra and Tantra into practice. We can easily make progress on, and complete, the stages of the path to the supreme happiness of enlightenment. From a practical point of view, Lamrim is the main body of Buddha's teachings, and the other teachings are like its limbs.

(2) and (3) *Universal Compassion* and *The New Eight Steps to Happiness* – we gain the ability to integrate Buddha's teachings into our daily life and solve all our human problems.

(4) *The New Heart of Wisdom* – we gain a realization of the ultimate nature of reality. By gaining this realization, we can eliminate the ignorance of self-grasping, which is the root of all our suffering.

(5) *Meaningful to Behold* – we transform our daily activities into the Bodhisattva's way of life, thereby making every moment of our human life meaningful.

(6) *How to Understand the Mind* – we understand the relationship between our mind and its external objects. If we understand that objects depend upon the subjective mind, we can change the way objects appear to us by changing our own mind. Gradually, we will gain the ability to control our mind and in this way solve all our problems.

TEACHER TRAINING PROGRAMME

The Teacher Training Programme is designed for people who wish to train as authentic Dharma Teachers. In addition to completing the study of fourteen texts of Sutra and Tantra, which include the six texts mentioned above, the student is required to observe certain commitments with regard to behaviour and way of life, and to complete a number of meditation retreats.

A Special Teacher Training Programme is also held at Manjushri Kadampa Meditation Centre, Ulverston, England, and can be studied either by attending the classes at the centre or by correspondence. This special meditation and study programme consists of twelve courses based on the books of Venerable Geshe Kelsang Gyatso Rinpoche: *How to Understand the Mind*; *Modern Buddhism*; *The New Heart of Wisdom*; *Tantric Grounds and Paths*; Shantideva's *Guide to the Bodhisattva's Way of Life* and its commentary, *Meaningful to Behold*; *Ocean of Nectar*; *The New Guide to Dakini Land*; *The Oral Instructions of Mahamudra; The New Eight Steps to Happiness; The Mirror of Dharma with Additions; Essence of Vajrayana;* and *Joyful Path of Good Fortune.*

All Kadampa Buddhist Centres are open to the public. Every year we celebrate Festivals in many countries throughout the world, including two in England, where people gather from around the world to receive special teachings and empowerments and to enjoy a spiritual holiday. Please feel free to visit us at any time!

For further information about NKT-IKBU study programmes or to find your nearest centre visit www.kadampa.org, or please contact:

NKT-IKBU Central Office
Conishead Priory
Ulverston, Cumbria,
LA12 9QQ, UK
Tel: +44 (0) 01229-588533
Email: info@kadampa.org
Website: www.kadampa.org

or

US NKT-IKBU Office
KMC New York
47 Sweeney Road
Glen Spey, NY 12737, USA
Tel: +1 845-856-9000
or 877-523-2672 (toll-free)
Fax: +1 845-856-2110
Email: info@kadampanewyork.org
Website: www.kadampanewyork.org

Tharpa Offices Worldwide

Tharpa books are currently published in English (UK and US), Chinese, French, German, Italian, Japanese, Portuguese and Spanish. Most languages are available from any Tharpa office listed below.

Tharpa UK
Conishead Priory,
ULVERSTON
Cumbria,
LA12 9QQ, UK
Tel: +44 (0)1229-588599
Web: tharpa.com/uk
E-mail: info.uk@tharpa.com

Tharpa US
47 Sweeney Road
GLEN SPEY,
NY 12737, USA
Tel: +1 845-856-5102
Toll-free: 888-741-3475
Fax: +1 845-856-2110
Web: tharpa.com/us
E-mail: info.us@tharpa.com

Tharpa Asia
1st Floor Causeway Tower,
16-22 Causeway Road,
Causeway Bay,
HONG KONG
Tel: +(852) 2507 2237
Web: tharpa.com/hk-en
E-mail: info.asia@tharpa.com

Tharpa Australia
25 McCarthy Road,
MONBULK, VIC 3793, AU
Tel: +61 (0)3 9756 7203
Web: tharpa.com/au
E-mail: info.au@tharpa.com

Tharpa Brasil
Rua Artur de Azevedo 1360
Pinheiros, 05404-003
SÃO PAULO, SP, BR
Tel: +55 (11) 3476-2328
Web: tharpa.com.br
E-mail: info.br@tharpa.com

Tharpa Canada (English)
631 Crawford St.,
TORONTO, ON, M6G 3K1, CA
Tel: (+1) 416-762-8710
Toll-free: 866-523-2672
Fax: (+1) 416-762-2267
Web: tharpa.com/ca
E-mail: info.ca@tharpa.com

Tharpa Canada (Français)
835 Laurier est Montréal H2J
    1G2, CA
Tel: (+1) 514-521-1313
Web: tharpa.com/ca-fr/
E-mail: info.ca-fr@tharpa.com

Tharpa Chile
Av. Seminario 589, Providencia,
SANTIAGO, CL
Tel: +56 (9) 6650 6535
Web: tharpa.com/cl
E-mail: info.cl@tharpa.com

Tharpa Deutschland (Germany)
Chausseestraße 108,
10115 BERLIN, DE
Tel: +49 (030) 430 55 666
Web: tharpa.com/de
E-mail: info.de@tharpa.com

Tharpa España (Spain)
Calle La Fábrica 8, 28221,
Majadahonda, MADRID, ES
Tel: +34 911 124 914
Web: tharpa.com/es
E-mail: info.es@tharpa.com

Tharpa France
Château de Segrais
72220 SAINT-MARS-
    D'OUTILLÉ, FR
Tel/Fax: +33 (0)2 43 87 71 02
Web: tharpa.com/fr
E-mail: info.fr@tharpa.com

Tharpa Japan
KMC TOKYO, Tokyo,
2F Vogue Daikanyama II,
13-4 Daikanyama-cho,
Shibuya-ku, TOKYO,
    150-0034, JP
Web: kadampa.jp
E-mail: info@kadampa.jp

Tharpa México
Enrique Rébsamen Nº 406,
Col. Narvate Poniente,
CUIDAD DE MÉXICO,
    CDMX, C.P. 03020, MX
Tel & Fax: +52 (55) 56 39 61 80;

Tel : +52 (55) 56 39 61 86
Web: tharpa.com/mx
E-mail: info.mx@tharpa.com

Tharpa New Zealand
2 Stokes Road, Mount Eden,
AUCKLAND 1024, NZ
Tel: +64 09 631 5400
DD Mobile +64 21 583351
Web: tharpa.com/nz
E-mail: info.nz@tharpa.com

Tharpa Portugal
Rua Moinho do Gato, 5
Várzea de Sintra,
SINTRA, 2710-661, PT
Tel: +351 219 231 064
Web: tharpa.pt
E-mail: info.pt@tharpa.com

Tharpa Schweiz (Switzerland)
Mirabellenstrasse 1
CH-8048 ZÜRICH, CH
Tel: +41 44 461 36 88
Web: tharpa.com/ch
E-mail: info.ch@tharpa.com

Tharpa South Africa
26 Menston Rd., Dawncliffe,
Westville, 3629, KZN,
REP. OF SOUTH AFRICA
Tel: +27 31 266 0096
Web: tharpa.com/za
E-mail: info.za@tharpa.com

Tharpa Sverige (Sweden)
c/o KMC Stockholm,
Upplandsgatan 18, 113 40
STOCKHOLM, SE
Tel: +46 72 251 4090
Email: info.se@tharpa.com

Index

The letter 'g' indicates an entry in the glossary

A

absorption of cessation 128, g
absorptions of the two
    concentrations 197–198
action mudra 60, 77, 84, 85,
    137, 197, 198, 199, 222
    qualifications of 81, 84
actions 232. *See also* karma
  non-virtuous 10, 78, 231, 235
  virtuous 10, 78, 231, 235
Action Tantra 27–49, 89
  concentrations of 29–44
  paths of 49–50
  root Tantras of 27
actor analogy 161
aggregates, five 165
Akanishta 52, 136, 228
Akshobya 51, 66–69, 176–177, g
  manifestations of 166
alcohol, drinking 78
Ambhidana Tantra 141
Amitabha 50, 70–72, 176, g
  manifestations of 166
Amitayus 50, g
Amoghasiddhi 71, 176, g
  manifestations of 166
analytical meditation 45, 111,
    113, g
anger 18, 74, 196, g

appearances 125, 164
Aryadeva 126
asceticism 75
aspects of Deities 127, 159,
    165–167
Atisha 71, 78, g
attachment 12, 22, 92–93, g
  path of 85
  transformed 13, 18, 131
Attachment Vehicle 12
attainments, common
  controlling 40, 47, 190, 225,
    227
  eight great 47–48, 225
  increasing 40, 47, 190, 225
  pacifying 40, 47, 190, 225
  wrathful 40, 47, 190, 225,
    227
attainments, uncommon 47
Avalokiteshvara 30–37, 50, g
  mantra 32
  self-generation 38

B

BAM 95, 100, 102, 147, 151,
    153, 154, 184
basis of imputation 33, g
Baso Chokyi Gyaltsen 140
bell 67, 77
  symbolism 67–68

Bhairawa 115
blessed self 206
blessings 69, 91, 162, 190, 225, 307, g
bliss 128–133, 164, 165, 306. *See also* spontaneous great bliss; union of bliss and emptiness
  and emptiness 164, 165
  five types 167–168
  non-conceptual 42, 45
  of the two stages 126
  two characteristics 129–130, 137
  types 128
bodhichitta 11, 75, 86, 136, 144, 161, 305. *See also* bodhichittas, red and white
  of Highest Yoga Tantra 57–59
  spontaneous 105
  Sutra 20, 57
  Tantric 20
  ultimate 137
bodhichittas, red and white 85, 102, 155, 222
Bodhisattva 129, 229
  grounds 12, 49, 60–63
  of Sutra 5, 57, 214
  Superior 12, 216
  tenth ground 6, 215–216, 219
Bodhisattva vows 7, 28, 74, 78, 83
bodies of a Buddha 45, 93, 192, 227, 230. *See also* Emanation Body; Enjoyment Body; Truth Body

body 75, 127
  gross 134, 135–136, 203, 207-209
  impure 136, 137
  subtle 208
  very subtle 134, 135, 208–209
branch commitments 77–79
  additional, of abandonment 79
  of abandonment 78–80
  of reliance 78
branch winds 177–179, 186–187
bringing death into the path 93, 94–98, 164, 308
  definition 93
  functions 94
  possesses four attributes 105
bringing rebirth into the path 93, 100–102, 310
  definition 94
bringing the intermediate state into the path 93, 99–100, 310
  definition 93
  functions 100
Buddha 165. *See also* bodies of a Buddha
  body, speech, and mind of 47
  good qualities 230–237
  Tantric 13
  ultimate intention 131
Buddhadharma. *See* Dharma
Buddha family 49–50, 53, g
  commitments of 276–277
  five 65, 67–68
Buddhahood. *See* enlightenment; Union of No More Learning

Buddha nature 134, g
Buddha's bodies. *See*
    Enjoyment Body;
    Emanation Body; Form
    Body; Truth Body
Buddha Shakyamuni. *See*
    Shakyamuni, Buddha
Buddhas, thousand 6

C

cause and effect 162, 231. *See*
    also karma
central channel 137–138,
    144–145, 151–153. *See*
    also yoga of the central
    channel
  heart 140–141, 143, 151
  ten doors 139–140
Chandrakirti 92, 123, 225, g
channel knots 145–146, 190
  at the heart 170, 173, 187,
    189, 193, 198
channel, left 145
channel, right 145
channels, drops and winds
    85, 144–148, 150–155. *See*
    also drops; winds
channel wheel 145
  of the heart 141
Chittamatra 76, 125, 165, g
cigarettes, smoking 78
clairvoyance and miracle
    powers 186–187, 190, g
clear appearance 68, 86, 109,
    113–115, 117
  on specific aspects 114–116
  on the general aspect
    113–114
Clear Lamp of the Five Stages
    225

clear light 58, 59, 126,
    212–219
clear light mind 6, 97, 135, 179,
    196. *See also* clear light
    of death; clear light of
    sleep; example clear
    light; meaning clear light
  actual 190
  definition 195
  dualistic appearances 212
  facsimile 190
  fourth empty 157, 170, 194
  realizing emptiness 6, 124
clear light of bliss 133
Clear Light of Bliss 60, 124,
    140, 157, 197, 206
  common tradition of 141
clear light of death 99, 125,
    171, 192–193, 199, 211
clear light of sleep 99, 223
close retreat 29
collection of merit 20, 159,
    192, g
collection of wisdom 20, 94,
    159, 192, 310, g
commitment being 37, g
commitments 53–54, 63–82,
    103
  individual five Buddha
    families 65–71
  of five Buddha families in
    common 73, 276–277
commitment substances 77
completion stage 62, 65, 76,
    121. *See also* five stages of
    completion stage
  definition 121
  divisions 125
  etymology 124

final results 225
five stages 59, 125
non-fabricated yoga 124
of the three isolations 223
of the two truths 117, 223
six stages 126
concentration 235–236, g.
See also tranquil abiding
pure 107, 116
concentration of abiding in
fire 41–42, 44, 47
purpose 42–43
concentration of abiding in
sound 43–45, 47
concentration of bestowing
liberation 44–47, 49
main function 45
concentration of the four-
limbed recitation 30–40
concentrations, four 29–44
concentrations without
recitation 41
concentrations with recitation
41
conceptual mind, g
levels of 196
Condensed six-session Yoga
277–278
contaminated aggregates 17,
33, 111, 116, g
continuously residing body
89, 134, 137, 147. *See also*
body, very subtle
continuously residing mind
134, 147. *See also* very
subtle mind
continuously residing speech
134. *See also* speech, very
subtle

conventional appearances 45,
106
conventional nature 163, g
correct imagination 87, 116
creative yoga 87

D

Dakini Land 111, 310–311
outer 114, 205
damaru 82, g
death 121, 125, 135, 210. *See
also* death process; signs of
dissolution
actual moment 172
clear light 98, 125, 192, 199,
211
ordinary 194, 200
deathless 134, 135, 142, 194, 199
death process 97, 171–172, 200
external signs 156
four empties 193
internal signs 94, 97, 105,
134, 156–157, 195
Deities, six 30–35, 41, 45, 47
Deity of emptiness 30–31,
35–36
Deity of form 33–34, 35
Deity of letters 33, 35
Deity of signs 35
Deity of sound 32–33, 35
Deity of the mudra 34–35
Deity 39, 118. *See also* Deities,
six
four types 29–30
personal 29, 67, 91, 209
Deity body, g
actual 89, 107
mentally generated 89–90,
106, 107

deluded pride 109, 111, g
delusions 17, 18, g
  innate 49, 133, 219, g
  intellectually-formed 49,
    133, 219, g
desire 232
desire realm 22, 228, g
Dharma 63, g
  giving 69
Dharmakaya. *See* Truth Body
Dharmakirti 92, g
Dharmavajra 140, 142, 207
distractions 38, 42, 123
divine body 87, 92, 107, 201, g.
    See also yoga of divine body
  gross 98, 100
divine pride 39, 68, 86,
    109–112, 117, 227
  basis 113
  of the Truth Body 93, 99, 309
  overcome ordinary
    conceptions 17, 68, 110
doors, nine 38
dream 125, 164–165
dream body 100, 203, 207, 209
drops 75, 85, 131, 144, 146. *See
    also* indestructible drop
  flowing 132–133, 157
drugs, taking 78
dualistic appearance 5–6, 61,
    129, 133, 212–214

E

EH letters 101
eighteen unshared qualities
    238–239
eighty-four Mahasiddhas 63
eighty indicative conceptions
    197

elements 155, 166–167, 176,
    232
  external 190
  of the body 97
  six 129
Emanation Body 93–94, 100,
    102, 229–230
  actual 106
  definition 229
  mentally generated 106
  two types 229
empowerment 7, g
  function 75
  of Action Tantra 28
  of Highest Yoga Tantra 53,
    57, 103
  of Performance Tantra 52
  of Yoga Tantra 53
  secret 86
empties 170, 193–194
emptiness 31, 85, 97, 98, 123,
    128, 159–160, 213–214,
    232, 307, 308. *See also*
    bliss, and emptiness;
    spontaneous great bliss
    and emptiness; ultimate
    nature
  correct view of 45, 86
  essential for Tantra 76, 161
  intellectual understanding
    123
  object 123
Enjoyment Body 93–94,
    99–100, 209, 216, 223, 230
  actual 106
  definitions 228–229
  mentally generated 106
  substantial cause 216
  three types 229

enlightenment 4, 20, 92, 200, 225, 235. *See also* Union of No More Learning
of Hearer 57, 236
of Highest Yoga Tantra 57
of Solitary Conqueror 57, 236
quick path to 98, 129
three types 236
Essence of Wisdom Sutra 159, 163, g
exalted awareness 11
example clear light 214–215. *See also* clear light
definition 214
divisions 214–215
of isolated mind 98
expressive sound 182, g
external method 85
of isolated mind 197, 218

F

faith 76, 162, g
families of Action Tantra Deities 49–50
families of Performance Tantra Deities 52–53
Father Tantra 55
fearlessness 70, 237
Fifty Verses on the Spiritual Guide 83
five certainties 228–229
five paths 49–50, 235
seeing 62
five paths of Highest Yoga Tantra 55–58
accumulation 57–58
meditation 59, 60, 220

No More Learning 59, 223
preparation 59
seeing 59–62, 133, 217, 219
five precepts 78
five stages of completion stage 59, 125. *See also* illusory body; isolated body; isolated mind; isolated speech; union
Five Stages of Completion Stage 125
Form Body 5, 49, 136, 137, 159. *See also* Emanation Body; Enjoyment Body
cause 19, 45
substantial cause 5, 137, 171, 191, 217
formless realm 32, g
form source 90
form that is a phenomena source 90, 107
four classes of Tantra 22–25
four correct, specific cognizers 237
four empties 170, 193–196. *See also* subtle minds
facsimiles 193
levels 193
of death 193
of isolated body 193
of isolated speech 169–171, 189, 193
of sleep 195
four fearlessnesses 237
four Mothers 166–167, g
four seals of Yoga Tantra 53–54
fourteen root downfalls 73–77

functioning thing 162, g
Fundamental Wisdom 123

G

generation stage 19, 58–59,
62, 63, 76, 86, 87–115, 225.
See also gross generation
stage meditation; subtle
generation stage
meditation; three
bringings
  benefits 91–92
  confusion about 90
  definition 87
  divisions 108–109
  four attributes 89–91,
  105–106
  four levels of practitioners
  118–119
  measurement of completion
  118
  realizations 58
  three characteristics 117–118
Ghantapa 84, 141
giving 69–70
Goddesses 23–25, 166–167
*Great Exposition of the Stages of
Secret Mantra* 21, 27, 51
Great Liberation of the Father
150, 155, 295–301, 305
Great Liberation of the Mother
150, 283–289
  explanation 305–312
*Great Mother Perfection of
Wisdom* 67
Green Tara 50
gross downfalls of the Secret
Mantra vows 79–81

gross generation stage
  meditation 109–113
  complete realization 115
  object 115
gross mind 6, 123, 196, 212,
216
  appearances to 125
  three levels 196–197
grounds
  of Highest Yoga
  Tantra 59–62
  Sutra Bodhisattva 60–62
ground of imaginary
  engagement 62
Guhyasamaja Tantra 55, 143
*Guide to the Bodhisattva's Way
of Life* 136, 161, g
Guide to the Middle Way 123,
163, g
Guru yoga 311, g
Gyalwa Ensapa 142, 207

H

Hearer 235, g
  enlightenment 10, 57, 236
hell 10, 92, g
Heruka 102, 150, 154, 180,
182, 306–307
  definitive 124, 125
  interpretive 124
Heruka Tantra 55
Hevajra 105
Hevajra Root Tantra 140
Hevajra Tantra 55
Highest Yoga Tantra 24,
55–80. *See also* completion
  stage; generation stage
  essence 25

Hinayana 6, 10, 12–13
  Foe Destroyer 216
  grounds 11
  Hearers' Vehicle 70
  paths 10, 235
  Solitary Conquerors' Vehicle
    70

I

I 31, 33, 35, 116.
  See also divine pride
ignorance 18, g. *See also*
  self-grasping
illusory body 5, 58, 59, 117,
  125, 201–209. *See also*
  illusory body, impure;
  illusory body, pure
  basis for 107, 135
  cause of gross divine body
    98, 100
  definition 201, 203–204
  etymology 201, 207
  of the fourth stage 224
  substantial cause 171, 191,
    201
illusory body, impure 99, 125,
  217
  definition 203
  fifteen characteristics
    203–206
  substantial cause 203
  two types 207
  when attained 207
illusory body, pure 99, 125,
  135, 216, 310
  contributory cause 137, 221
  definition 203
  substantial cause 203, 221

  when attained 60, 133, 207
imputation, mere 117, g
imputed object 33, g
indestructible drop 134,
  141, 146–147, 152–154, 193
indestructible wind 134
indestructible wind and mind
  134, 147–148, 153, 173, 184
intermediate state 171, 192, g.
  See also bringing the
  intermeditate state into the
  path
  being 102, 211
  body 99, 203, 209
internal method 85
  of isolated mind 197–198,
    218
Introduction to Buddhism 211
isolated body of completion
  stage 126–162, 141
  actual realization 154
  definition 126–127
  divisions 127
  during meditation 128–154,
    165
  during meditation break
    159–167
  four empties 193
  life exertion 149
isolated body of generation
  stage 126
isolated mind 58, 59, 77, 125,
  191–199. *See also* ultimate
  example clear light of
  isolated mind
  definition 191
  divisions 192
  example clear light 98
  external method 197, 218

four empties 193
internal method 197–198, 218
mere realization 198
ultimate 194
ultimate realization 198, 199
when attained 191–192
wisdom 192
isolated speech 58, 59, 126, 169–189
actual realizations 190
definition 169
four empties 169–171, 190, 193
life exertion 153

J

jealousy 18, g
Je Tsongkhapa 1, 14, 90, 103, 129, 131, 162, 163, 267, g
lineage Guru 140, 142
pure teachings 63
Joyful Path of Good Fortune 2, 66, 114

K

Kachen Yeshe Gyaltsen 51
Kadampa g
Kadampa Buddhism 335–336, g
Kadampa Tradition g
Kagyu 140
Kalarati 115
karma 10, g
contaminated 15
khatanga 82, g
Khedrubje 51, 310, g

L

Lamp for the Path to Enlightenment 43
Lamp of Condensed Deeds 126
Lamrim 1, 71, 86, 305, 335, g
root text 1
letter 181–183, g
Liberating Prayer 263–264
liberation 131, 133. *See also* nirvana
great 45
life exertion 143, 211
four types 143
of isolated body 149–158
of isolated speech 153
lineage g
lineage Gurus g
lineage of uncommon Vajrayana Mahamudra 140, 142
Little Sambara Tantra 171–172
Lojong 305, g
Longdol Lama 99, 144
Lotus family 49, 51
commitment mudra of 34
love 70, 74

M

Madhyamika-Prasangika 33, 76, 125, g
Sutra 165
Tantra 165, 216
magician analogy 109
Mahasiddha g
Mahayana 57
grounds 11
paths 10, 49–50, 235

Mairichi 50–51
Maitreya 6, 187, g
mandala 108, 113, 115
  body 34, 108, 115, 147, g
  of Heruka 67–68
  of Munivairochana 52
manifestations of bliss and
    emptiness 126, 159–165
manifestations of emptiness
  160–166
Manjushri 14, 50, 140, g
  self-generation 35
mantra 15, 39, 180–183
  four types 182
  mind protection 182
  root of 183
  ultimate 182
mantra recitation 39–41
  gross 39–40, 47
  mental 174, 181
  sound base 39, 41, 47
  subtle 39–40, 47
  types 39–40, 174
  ultimate 174
  verbal 174, 181
Marpa 211
meaning clear light 5, 19, 59,
    117, 125, 203, 212–219, 220
  definition 212
  divisions 217–218
  etymologies 213–214
  external pacification 218
  first ground 60
  indispensable 216
  internal pacification 218
  union of bliss and emptiness
    133, 135
  when attained 217
Meaningful to Behold 114, 161

mental awareness 179, 196, g
merit 162, 192, 225, g
method practices 19, 49, 54
  indivisible with wisdom 19
Milarepa 125, 140, 142–144
mind base 37–38, 41, 44, 47
mind of a Buddha 192
mind of enlightenment. *See*
    bodhichitta
mind protection 182
miracle powers. *See*
    clairvoyance and miracle
    powers
mistaken appearance 117
monk analogy 160
moral discipline 66
  of Highest Yoga Tantra 159
Mother Tantra 55, 83
motivation 105
mudra. *See* action mudra;
    Mahamudra; wisdom
    mudra
Munivairochana 52

N

Nagarjuna 63, 91, 123, 125,
    136, 207, g
new Kadampa Tradition 14
New Kadampa Tradition 336,
    g
nine mental abidings 114, g
nineteen commitments of
    five Buddha families
    276–277
nirvana 131
  non-abiding 45
non-fabricated yoga 124
non-faith 74

O

object
  appearing 89, g
  conceived 89, g
  incorrect 92
  mentally generated 92
  observed 89, g
  real 92
objects of desire 22–23, 25, 222
obstructions
  to liberation 17, 60, 220
  to omniscience 5, 17, 49,
    61–62, 216, 220, 223
Ocean of Nectar 161
offerings 71, 84. *See also* tsog
    offerings
  inner 181
  kusali tsog 69
  mandala 311
Offering to the Spiritual Guide
    140, 150, g
OM AH HUM 190
  recitation 184–188, 199–200
  source of 180
OM AH RA PA TSA NA DHI 37
OM MAIRICHI MAM SOHA 50
OM MANI PAME HUM 32,
    33, 39, 42, 43
OM PAMA UBHAWAYE SOHA
    34
only mind 165
ordinary appearances 15–17,
    38, 61, 98, 111, 165
  of body 126, 127
  overcoming 35, 68, 109, 159
ordinary conceptions 15–17,
    38, 111, 165, 221
  of body 127
  overcoming 35, 68, 109, 110,
    159

ordinary union 220. *See also*
    union of abandonment
Ornament of Clear Realizations
    187
other base 37, 41, 45

P

Paramitayana 12, 71, 214
path. *See also* five paths
  common 1
  external 9, 235
  Hinayana 10, 235
  internal 1, 9–11, 235
  Mahayana 10, 49–50, 235
  of attachment 85
  spiritual 10
  uncommon 1
  Vajrayana 1
penetrating
  another's body 137
  our own body 137, 141
Perfection of Wisdom Sutras 71
Performance Tantra 23,
    51–52, 89
  scriptures 51
phenomena source 90,
    101–103, 310
powers 233–235
Prasangika. *See*
    Madhyamika-Prasangika
Pratimoksha vows 74, 78, 83, g
Prayer of the Stages of the Path
    1, 2–4
preliminary practices
    149–150, 305–312
  common 150
  uncommon 141, 149
principal union. *See* union of
    realization

process of absorption 197–198
  holding the body entirely 197–198
  subsequent destruction 197
pure appearances 186
pure enjoyments 118, 205
Pure Land 91, 118, 129, 186, g
  See also Dakini Land
  of Akanishta 52, 228
pure view 82
purification 91, 118, 162, g

R

Ratnasambhava 69–70, 176, g
  manifestations of 165
rebirth 171
refuge 66, 305
Rinchen Sangpo 71
ritual objects 82
root winds 175–177, 186
  downward-voiding 132, 176, 189–190
  equally-abiding 176
  life-supporting 176–177, 179, 184, 189–190
  pervading 177, 198
  upward-moving 169, 176

S

samsara 32, 131, 171, g
  root of 15
Sanskrit vowels and consonants 181
Saraha 23, g
Sarvavid 53
scope, great 71
scope, intermediate 71
scriptures 183

Secret Mantra 1, 4, 14, 15, 67, 85
  benefits 21
  good qualities 14–21
seed-letter 39, 94, 155, g
self
  blessed 206
  gross 209–210
  subtle 206, 209–210
self base 30–31, 41
self-generation 47
  as Avalokiteshvara 30–35, 39
  as Manjushri 35
  as Vajrayogini 90–91, 108–109, 111–115, 135, 149, 308–311
self-generation of Highest Yoga Tantra 58, 68
self-grasping 32, 62, 116, 163, g
  antidote 32, 123
  mounted wind 131, 171, 172–173
seminal fluid 85
sense awareness 177, 196, g
sense powers 177, g
sensual pleasure 22
  transformed into the path 22–24
seven pre-eminent qualities of embrace 223, 228, 241
sexual activity 128, 131, 137
  transformed into the path 23–24
sexual misconduct 24, 78
Shakyamuni, Buddha 9, 12, 13, 52, 216, g
Shantideva 136–137, g
short-AH 140
signs of dissolution 95–96,

106, 134, 156–157, 189, 195
Six Session Yoga 65, 277–278
six stages of completion stage 126
summary 221
Six Yogas of Naropa 140
sleep 121, 195
clear light of 99, 223
snow lion 15
Solitary Conqueror 235, g
enlightenment of 10, 57, 236
Song of the Spring Queen 129
sound base 39–41, 47
speech 181
root of 169, 183, 190
very subtle 134, 147
spiritual ground. *See also* thirteen grounds of Highest Yoga Tantra
Bodhisattva 49, 60–62
definition 10
fourteen of Highest Yoga Tantra 62
Spiritual Guide 71, 74, 79, 142, g
spontaneous great bliss 120, 132, 222
and emptiness 13, 123, 190, 194
stages of the path. *See* Lamrim
Stream Enterer 105, g
subsequent attainment 118, 127, 170, 193, g
subtle generation stage meditation 115–116
complete realization 116
supreme object 115
subtle minds 123, 192, 195–197. *See also* clear light

mind; four empties
black near-attainment 5–6, 97, 155, 157, 194, 195–196, 212, 218, 220
black near-attainment in reverse order 195, 204, 221
contaminated 5, 212
mounted winds 179
red increase 5–6, 97, 155, 157, 195, 218
red increase in reverse order 195
white appearance 5–6, 97, 155, 157, 194, 218
white appearance in reverse order 195
suicide 76
Superior being 6, 219, g
meditation on emptiness 161
of Highest Yoga Tantra 59
Superior Bodhisattva 12, 216
Superior Mahayanist 62
superior seeing 45, g
suppleness 43, 128
of completion stage 133
Sutra 5–6, 70, 131, g
foundation for Tantra 9, 75, 131
meditation on emptiness 123
Sutra ground(s) 60
tenth 6, 214–215, 219
Sutra on the Four Noble Truths 71

T

Tantra 1, 4–5, 21–22
meditation on emptiness 123
pure 13

Tantric vows 7, 53, 74, 78, 86
Tarma Dode 211
Tathagata family 49
ten forces 230–236
thangka painter analogy 149, 307
The New Guide to Dakini Land 71, 84, 306, 310, 311
The New Heart of Wisdom 161
The New Meditation Handbook 2
The Three Principal Aspects of the Path 162
thirteen grounds of Highest Yoga Tantra 59–61
  first 60–61, 62
  second 60
three bringings 93
  completion stage 103, 120
  generation stage 103
  purpose 103
three-OM mantra 101–102, 180–181
three types of enjoyment 215, 222–223, 227, 229
Tibet 90
Togden Jampel Gyatso 140, 142
tranquil abiding 39, g
  object 42, 43
  of Sutra 133
  on generation stage 114
transference of consciousness 211, 310
Trijang Rinpoche, Vajradhara g
Truth Body 49, 93, 159, 229
  actual 106
  cause 5, 19, 45, 310
  definition 229
  indivisible bliss and
    emptiness 165, 309
  mentally generated 106
  Nature 230
  substantial cause 5, 136, 216
  Wisdom 230
tsog offering 77, 82, g
tummo 132, 144, g
turtle analogy 38
twelve dependent-related links 10, g
two purities of the emptiness of Buddha's mind 230
two truths 163, g
  of Highest Yoga Tantra 117, 223

U

ultimate clear light of isolated mind 199
  at death 200
ultimate example clear light of isolated mind 98, 125, 153, 203, 207, 213, 219
  at death 98
  contaminated 217
ultimate nature 31, 163, g
  of form 159–162
uncommon commitments of Mother Tantra 83–85
uninterrupted path 62
union 59, 126, 219–221
  definition 219
  divisions 220
union of abandonment 220. *See also* ordinary union
union of appearance and emptiness 54
union of bliss and emptiness 19, 124, 128, 136, 137, 306,

309–310
essence of Highest Yoga
Tantra 25, 67
meaning clear light 133, 135
union of meaning clear light
and pure illusory body 20,
60, 220, 224
Union of No More Learning
57, 62, 136, 142, 220, 223
union of realization 220, 222,
224
union of Sutra and Tantra 14
union of wind and mantra
174
union that needs learning 58,
220, 224, 227
union with a consort 81, 85

V

vacuole 146, 152
Vairochana 50, 65, 177, g
manifestations of 165
seven-point posture 184, g
vajra 19, 67, 77
symbolism 67–68
vajra body 50, 136, 137,
142–144, 180
pure illusory body 133, 135
vajra brothers and sisters 74,
78
Vajradhara 15, 55, 140, 171,
206, 311–312, g
Vajra family 49
vajra-like concentration 62,
215
vajra mind 180
Vajrapani 51, 52
vajra recitation 147, 173–189,
211

benefits 190
definition 174
divisions 174
etymology 174
loosen knots 170, 173, 187
mantra recitation 174
meditation 173, 183–190
on the pervading wind
198–199
purify winds 180
wind recitation 174
Vajra Rosary Tantra 171
vajra speech 50, 180
Vajrayana 1, 7, 11, 12, 19
Vajrayana Mahamudra 124,
147, g
of the unequalled Virtuous
Tradition 140
Vajrayana Spiritual Guide 15,
28, 53, 69, 129, g
Vajrayogini 19, 102, 149, 155,
180, 306
emanations 77
self-generation 89–90,
108–109, 111–115, 135, 149,
308–311
symbolism of skull garland
183
Vajrayogini Tantra 19
valid cognizer 90, 106, g
vase breathing 39, 210
Vehicle 57. *See also* Hinayana;
Mahayana; Vajrayana
attachment 13
Effect 18–19
Mantra 15–17
Method 20–21
of Sutra 70
Secret 14

Secret Mantra 7, 12
spiritual 10, 11
Tantric 21–22
very subtle mind 123, 134, 147, 196, 206
Vinaya 14
vows 71
Bodhisattva 7, 28, 74, 78, 83
of Highest Yoga Tantra 63
Pratimoksha 74, 78, 83
Sutra 86
Tantric 7, 53, 74, 78, 86

W

White Tara 50
wind, Akshobya 176
wind recitation 174
winds 38, 58, 144, 211. See also branch winds; root winds; signs of dissolution; wind, very subtle
definition 175
external 175, 190
gross 155
impure 170, 172
internal 38, 147, 175, 179, 181
pure 172, 186
subtle 155
subtle external 175
types 147
winds, entering, abiding, dissolving 58, 97, 120, 121, 132, 143, 180
signs of 155–158
wind, very subtle 171, 173, 206
continuously residing body 89, 137, 147, 209
root of speech 169, 183, 190

wisdom 11, 225, g
wisdom being 37, 111, 119, g
wisdom mudra 85, 223
wisdom practices 49, 54
indivisible with method 19
wisdom wind 173, 190
wishfulfilling cow 144
wrong awareness 106, g
wrong view g

Y

Yamantaka practitioner, story of 116
Yamantaka Tantra 55
Yidam. See Deity
yoga 87, g
yoga of divine body 87
four attributes 87–89, 105–106
yoga of the central channel 137, 144, 151–153
two characteristics 152–154
yoga of the drop 137, 144, 152–153
two characteristics 153
yoga of the second stage 124
yoga of wind 144, 153–154, 171, 173, 186
three characteristics 154
yogas, three 47
Yoga Tantra 23, 53–55
four seals 53–54
Tantras of 53
yoga without signs 21, 47–49, 48, 52, 54
yoga with signs 21, 48, 52, 54
yogic direct perceiver 92, 214, g

Further Reading

If you have enjoyed reading this book and would like to find out more about Buddhist thought and practice, here are some other books by Geshe Kelsang Gyatso that you might like to read, or listen to. They are all available from Tharpa Publications.

MODERN BUDDHISM
The Path of Compassion and Wisdom

By developing and maintaining compassion and wisdom in daily life, we can transform our lives, improve our relationships with others and look behind appearances to see the way things actually exist. In this way we can solve all our daily problems and accomplish the real meaning of our human life. With compassion and wisdom, like the two wings of a bird, we can quickly reach the enlightened world of a Buddha. Also available as an audiobook.

For a free eBook or PDF of *Modern Buddhism* please visit www.emodernbuddhism.com

THE ORAL INSTRUCTIONS OF MAHAMUDRA
The Very Essence of Buddha's Teachings of Sutra and Tantra

This book reveals the uncommon practice of Tantric Mahamudra of the Ganden Oral Lineage, which the author received directly from his Spiritual Guide. It explains clearly and concisely the entire spiritual path from the initial preliminary practices to the final completion stages of Highest Yoga Tantra that enable us to attain full enlightenment in this life. Also available as an audiobook and eBook.

MAHAMUDRA TANTRA
An Introduction to Meditation on Tantra

Tantra is very popular, but very few understand its real meaning. This book reveals how to practise Mahamudra, the essence of Buddhist Tantric meditation. Through uncovering the deepest level of our mind, and then using this very subtle mind to meditate on ultimate truth, we can purify our mind of all negativities at their root, and quickly accomplish the state of full enlightenment. Also available as an eBook.

THE NEW GUIDE TO DAKINI LAND
The Highest Yoga Tantra Practice of Buddha Vajrayogini

This comprehensive guide provides a detailed and practical explanation of the two stages of Vajrayogini practice. It shows how we can integrate these practices into our daily life, thereby transforming every moment of our life into the path to enlightenment. A unique guide to becoming a Tantric enlightened being in the modern world. Also available as an eBook.

ESSENCE OF VAJRAYANA
The Highest Yoga Tantra Practice of Buddha Heruka

A complete and detailed explanation of the generation and completion stage practices of Heruka body mandala. Buddha Heruka is a manifestation of all the Buddhas' enlightened compassion, and by relying upon him we can swiftly attain a pure, selfless joy and bring true happiness to others. This is a treasury of practical instructions for those seriously interested in following the Tantric path. Also available as an eBook.

CLEAR LIGHT OF BLISS
Tantric Meditation Manual

In a clear and precise way, the author explains how we can generate a blissful and concentrated mind, and with this joyful awareness uncover our true nature and destroy the root of all suffering and confusion. A highly acclaimed guide to Tantric Mahamudra, the profound and quick method for achieving the fully awakened state of a Buddha. Also available as an eBook.

To order any of our publications, or to request a catalogue, please visit www.tharpa.com or contact your nearest Tharpa Office listed on pages 340-341.

Finding Your Nearest Kadampa Meditation Centre

To deepen your understanding of this book, and other books published by Tharpa Publications, and its application to everyday life you can receive support and inspiration from qualified Teachers and practitioners.

Tharpa Publications is part of the wider spiritual community of the New Kadampa Tradition. This tradition has a growing number of centres and branches in over 40 countries around the world. Each centre offers special study programmes in modern Buddhism and meditation, taught by qualified Teachers. For more details, see *Study Programmes of Kadampa Buddhism* (see pages 335-339).

These programmes are based on the study of books by Venerable Geshe Kelsang Gyatso Rinpoche and are designed to fit comfortably with a modern way of life.

To find your local Kadampa Meditation Centre
visit: tharpa.com/centres